THE HORROCKSES

Frontispiece: 'Yellow Factory', by C.E. Shaw, from Hewitson's *History of Preston*, 1883.

The Horrockses:
Cotton Kings of Preston

MARGARET BURSCOUGH

Copyright © Margaret Burscough, 2004

First published in 2004
by Carnegie Publishing,
Carnegie House,
Chatsworth Road,
Lancaster LA1 4SL,
Telephone: 01524-840111
www.carnegiepublishing.com

British Library Cataloguing-in-Publication data
A catalogue record for this book is available from the British Library

ISBN 1-85936-104-8

Typeset by Carnegie Publishing
Printed and bound in the UK by Cromwell Press

Contents

Miss Clara Horrocks in the year of Our Lord 1869, her fifty-eighth year, sat at a table, prepared her pens, and began a monumental task. Inordinately proud of her grandfather and his achievements, she had determined that they should be recorded for posterity. Letters were dispatched to societies, friends and relatives requesting information about him and his family. Thus began the project which would occupy her for the rest of her long life.

Clara's research and writing, gathering up all the threads of her own and previous generations, were a godsend to the author of this book, who hopes that in using these valuable records she will fulfil Clara's wish of 1883 that somewhere in Preston would be a memorial to the life of her illustrious grandfather John Horrocks: 'He was a wonderful genius and his memory is dying away from his never having had a historian to properly write his life's labours'.

Horrocks family Coat of Arms and Crest of John Horrocks of Edgworth, granted 8 June 1804 by Heraldic Deed under Royal Charter. The spelling was fixed at Horrocks – earlier the version Horrox had also been used.

Preface

As a child in World War II I attended three schools which were all based within Samuel Horrocks's Lark Hill Estate in Frenchwood, Preston. The core of St Augustine's Infants and Primary Schools were originally his brick stable-block and yards, whilst the Convent Secondary School was built around his 1796 mansion home. Time passed and in 1978 Cardinal Newman Sixth Form College replaced the Convent School in the Lark Hill premises. Few, if any, of the pupils knew the history of their schools.

The late Mr Peter Newsome, Principal of Cardinal Newman, asked me to find out the origins of the Georgian part of the college, and it was this research which led me to publish *The History of Lark Hill, 1997–1989*. Further research, together with the discovery of the Horrocks archives in Australia and New Zealand, revealed to me the fascinating family story told in this book.

In my youth, Horrockses mills and tall chimneys dominated the town of Preston and a large proportion of the population worked in the cotton industry. Theirs was a way of life which has now disappeared, but it is still well remembered by the older generation. Eighty-eight-year-old Mrs Mary Agnes Hindle of Fulwood, a weaver in her working life, recalls what it was like in the mills:

> I liked my life in the mill. Weaving was the best end of the cotton industry and I was proud of my skills. I started when I left school aged 14 in 1929. That was the heyday of cotton when half of Preston worked in the mills. I was up at dawn wakened by the 'knocker-up' who tapped his stick on the bedroom windows. Over the years I worked in two or three mills weaving various fabrics, voiles, velvets and cottons. At Horrockses in the 1940s and 50s I went on 16 automatic looms, standing all day working them. The shuttles were held in the loom gate and if they came out or broke free then they would 'smash' all the threads. The tackler would come to straighten it out. He would be cross because he was paid piece work and didn't want the looms out of fettle. If we had a big smash the length of the shuttle we had to bring two men 'drawers in' who stopped the machinery and reset it

Barbara Castle MP (left) being shown the process of weaving cotton by Mrs Hindle.

all. There would be no money paid for the time wasted, although we were really supposed to be paid waiting time. The cotton was very fine woven and had to be perfect. If threads broke it was difficult piecing it all up and bringing them through the healds and reeds. I've often worked after hours to get straight for the next morning.

A picking stick knocked the shuttles backwards and forwards. If it caught your elbow it was very painful and you would be looking for your arm for the rest of the week! At dinner time I sat in my alley on a little stool to eat my food – at some mills you could take your dinner in a basin with your name on and they would heat it up in the engine room for you. They were long days. I worked 8 hours at Horrockses and was paid £5 a week. Really they were good employers: there were chiropodists, and a crèche for mother with infants. We didn't get any sick pay or holiday pay, just what we earned.

It was a happy mill on the whole; we made lots of friends and there was always a good camaraderie amongst the weavers. The noise of the machinery was deafening so we talked to each other with sign language, mouthing the words with our lips. It was called 'mee-mawing' and I still find myself doing it in noisy places.

The boss must have thought I was a good weaver because he picked me out for a special job once. In 1946 the new Labour MP Barbara Castle wanted to experience factory life and came to Horrockses. She was put on my looms and I had to explain my job to her and answer her questions. We got on very well together and I think she learned a lot that week about working conditions and mill life. Several years ago I met her again when she opened an exhibition in Preston. She remembered me and we laughed about her early efforts at weaving cotton. I always admired her for being true to the Old Labour ideals and speaking out for the working class.

In the 1960s I was very sorry to hear about the closing down of my shed at Horrockses. I felt a certain sadness because all my early days from leaving school had been spent in the mills. It is sad to think it's all gone now. I will always have an affection for it and for all the weavers I knew.

Samuel Horrocks Junior (1797–1846) was the last of the family to own and work in the family firm. After his death the business was sold to Thomas Miller, his partner. A succession of new owners ran the mills during the following 125 years, always keeping the slogan 'Horrockses, the greatest name in cotton'. In the middle of the twentieth century the whole of the British textiles industry suffered badly from foreign competition. The decline in trade continued and Horrockses never re-gained its place as leader in world markets. Workers were laid off as mill after mill closed down. The huge Yard Works complex in Stanley Street went in 1962, and was followed in 1980 by Centenary Mill in New Hall Lane, with the loss of 3000 jobs. In 1990 a small part of the business, employing 150 people, was transferred to Farnworth near Bolton, where it amalgamated with Vantona within the Coats-Viyella group. Thus two centuries of Horrockses presence in Preston finished.

This book tells the compelling story of one of Preston's most important and interesting families, and I hope it will stand as a fitting tribute both to the dynasty which put the town on the world map, and to all those mill workers whose toil helped the Horrockses to do so.

Margaret Burscough, September 2004

Acknowledgements

In compiling this book I have received help from a number of people, to whom I would now like to express sincere thanks and appreciation.

Joan (née Horrocks) and Rev. Joseph Gilbert of Edgworth for much genealogical and local history information of the early Horrockses and their birthplace, and for their unfailing kindness and hospitality.

Marion Roberts who has helped considerably with her extensive knowledge of Preston's old families and local history: and with John and Carola Beckett of Newton-in-Cartmel and Andrew and Sabine Gardiner of Arnside shared with me their research into the Miller family and 'Merlewood' (over many convivial lunches). See website http//mysite.freeserve.com/merlewood

Mary Boys-Adams (née Horrocks) of Devon who has supplied a large amount of original material, genealogy, wills, sketches, photographs, etc. I am also obliged to her and her friend Rosemary for discovering the Horrocks family at Penwortham Farm, New Zealand thus leading me to the valuable store of family archives from which Andrew and Fiona Horrocks of Wanganui, Chris of Masterton and John (Senior) of Remeura have kindly contributed information and photographs of their ancestors' portraits, etc.

John Horrocks (Junior) now of Wellington, NZ has been incredibly generous with his time in perusing family papers for relevant material and sending reams of photocopies, catalogues and illustrations. He and his wife Ginny took time out from a UK vacation to bring me a precious wallet of Clara's letters of the late 1800s. It was good also to meet their daughter Ingrid (who has made a special study of her ancestor Augusta 1815–99); and other relatives namely Berys (née Horrocks) and Dr Walter Jones of Boston USA and Jeremy, Alison and Jonathon Horrocks of Hawkes Bay NZ.

Pamela McTaggart (née Horrocks) of Mendinie, South Australia, introduced to me by Lynn Georgeson of Preston, kindly sent photocopies of the memoirs of both Arthur Horrocks (1819–72) of South Australia and his wife Ann Jacob, and other historical notes.

Nearer to home I am indebted to: Anne Dennison of the Harris Reference Library, Preston for her cheerful response to my queries; J. J. Francis of Edgworth Historical Society for allowing me to follow his guided tours of Horrocks' sites in Edgworth and to use material from his researches; North

British Housing Association for the co-operation of wardens at Penwortham Hall; Amanda Devonshire of Chertsey Museum and Bernard Pardoe for information about Beomond House, Chertsey; Elspeth Wills for locating Crossbaskets House in Scotland; Helen Southworth MP, my niece, for research in the House of Commons Library; Bernard Harrison, my brother, for research in London; Elspeth Hough, Melanie and Doreen of Cardinal Newman College Preston for their help in the IT department; everyone at Carnegie Publishing for a splendid production.

All my family have shown interest in this project, but I must particularly thank Rachel and Andrew for their input on the computer and both Rachel and Jim for reading the script and making useful suggestions; Fran for her artwork; Lucy for guidance on the Internet; and my grandson Joseph for his polite enquiries and comments.

It is with pleasure that I dedicate this book to my husband Frank (whose mother was a Horrocks) with special thanks for his constant support and encouragement.

Introduction

This is the story of John Horrocks, born 1768, a remarkable Lancashire man who founded a business empire at the time of the Industrial Revolution. It is centred in the town of Preston which for two hundred years was dominated by the factories bearing his name. Surprisingly his biography has not previously been published in detail. Research has led me to many parts of England and Scotland, and in correspondence abroad to Australia and New Zealand.

The present generation of the Horrocks family are proud of their successful ancestor, and have co-operated generously and enthusiastically in piecing together this story. They have willingly supplied material from family papers, and copied maps, photographs and portraits for illustrations. I am extremely grateful for their help. It has been interesting to find that they still use the old family names, John, Samuel, Gratwicke, Macintosh, and Eardley. In Australia and New Zealand they live in homes called Lark Hill, Penwortham, Dunchattan and Beomond, as did their ancestors in Georgian and Victorian Britain. Some of the original houses in England and Scotland survive, now put to different uses, but still standing proudly as they did so long ago.

In this book I aim to portray the lives of John Horrocks and his brother Samuel, and to show how their success in business affected the lives of their children and grandchildren. As far as can be ascertained the script is historically accurate and written mainly from original sources. I apologise now for any unintentional mistakes or omissions. *Mea culpa*!

CHAPTER I

John Horrocks (1768–1804)

In 1869 Clara Horrocks was living at the home of her brother, Major Edgworth Horrocks, a house called 'Mascalls' in Kent. Her family roots, however, were in Lancashire in the north of England, around the parishes of Turton and Bradshaw near Bolton. There had always been Horrockses living thereabouts, deriving the family name from the rocky nature of the local moorland.

Two hundred and fifty years earlier, in January 1615, William the son of Adam Horrocks was baptised and eventually became the progenitor of Clara's branch of the Horrocks family. Some generations later, in October 1745 a son John was born to Samuel and his wife Alice (née Harrison). He was to become Clara's great-grandfather.

John was their eighth child and the sixth son to be born at 'The Birches', an ancient hamlet, or fold, of four farmsteads built on a ridge above the village of Edgworth. His grandfather, another Adam, had leased one of the land holdings there from Thomas Belasyse (Viscount Fauconberg and Baron of Yarm). This information appears in the Papist Returns of 1717. Belasyse was a Catholic so had to pay double land-tax on his estates. He registered 'the Capital Messuage called Birches Farm, let to Adam Horrocks for the lives of James, John and Samuel [his three younger sons] at a rent of £2 6s. 8d. per year and 7s. 4d. (in lieu of) boons'.[1] (From 1730 the first Earl Fauconberg and his successors lived at No. 15 St George Street, off London's fashionable Hanover Square. By a strange coincidence in the late 1940s that same house was bought by Messrs Horrocks, Crewdson & Co. as their prestigious Head Office.)

In the year 1780 the Land Tax Returns showed that all four of the farm holdings were leased to the Horrockses at 12s. 2d. each. The family would continue to live at 'The Birches' for the next seventy years and farm the 210 acre estate.

On 3 June 1766 John, the middle son of Samuel and Alice Horrocks (who were Quakers) married a local girl, Jane Booth. They lived for a while in a rented house in Isherwood Fold and then at a tenement at Bradshaw Hall Farm. Eventually they moved back to The Birches, farming some of the fields and working a stone quarry on their land.

Birches Cottage, Edgworth, near Bolton, probably the oldest building in The Birches hamlet leased by the Horrocks family. The cruck-blade construction indicates a date before the mid-sixteenth century, and many of the original features have been preserved despite modernisation. Sections of the cruck-blades are exposed and ceiling beams, a stone screen and fireplace bressumer restored. (*Photographed by kind permission of the owner. Research by J.J. Francis of Edgworth Local History Society*)

We know little of the personal lives of John and Jane at this time, but William Ashworth who as a young boy lived in the next-door cottage remembered them well. He told their granddaughter Celia that 'they were known all over Edgworth and Bolton-le-Moors as the handsomest, cleverest and most energetic family all around there'. John obviously did not follow his father into Quakerism for their first children Samuel and John (1766 and 1768) were baptised at St Anne's C of E Church, Turton, within a month of their births. He was however interred in the Quaker burial ground in his parents' grave after his death in 1816.

In the years from 1769 to 1786 five more known children, all daughters, were born; Mary, Elizabeth, Margaret, Sally and Eliza.

Their stone quarry was on the southern part of The Birches land. John laboured there, excavating slabs of hard-grained stone as his father had done before him. He cut and polished the stone blocks in a small mill powered by water from Bradshaw Brook. They were formed into flat tables for printing figured patterns on calico cloth. A steady demand for these

Map of Turton Township *c.* 1844 showing The Birches land, Stone Mill and Vale House.

5

came from manufacturers all over Lancashire, the Peel family[2] being regular customers.

An interesting article which appeared in the *Preston Guardian* newspaper in 1895 told that an old account book dating back to 1746 revealed that workmen in Horrocks's quarry were often paid in kind. Entries detailed the amounts of cheese, bacon and other foodstuffs due to them in lieu of wages.

As John's two surviving sons grew up, Samuel worked with his father in the stone delph whilst young John was placed in Thomasson's Engine Mill in the village. Thomas Thomasson was a fustian (corduroy) manufacturer and dealer in cotton weft. His mill, on Bury Road, Edgworth on the bank of Walleach Brook, used Arkwright's water frame for spinning yarn which was then given out to handloom weavers. (Earlier, in 1780, a machine which he had installed was smashed in machine-breaking riots.)

Thomasson soon became aware of John's intelligence and natural ability

Gossypium hirsutum, the southern USA cotton plant from which yarn is spun.

so, at his own expense, sent him to the village school. Later he took the boy on the back of his horse to Manchester where he had a warehouse, and placed him as a boarder in a more advanced school in Shudehill. At the same time, John Taylor of Heywood, the boys' uncle, who did not wish to see Samuel left behind by his younger brother, took him into his own little school to educate him. A relative reported that Samuel was 'persevering and successful' there. These words could accurately have described him throughout the rest of his life.

When John was fourteen in 1782 Thomas Thomasson died unexpectedly of a fever, leaving debts of £600. This brought John's formal education to an end. He was obliged to return from the school in Manchester to work with his brother in their father's quarry, where they were paid wages of eighteen shillings per week.

John, however, would not waste the talents which his patron had recognised and nurtured. In Manchester and Bolton he had watched the growth of the new cotton manufacturing industry. Factories were opening all around those parts and John decided that he too would participate in some way.

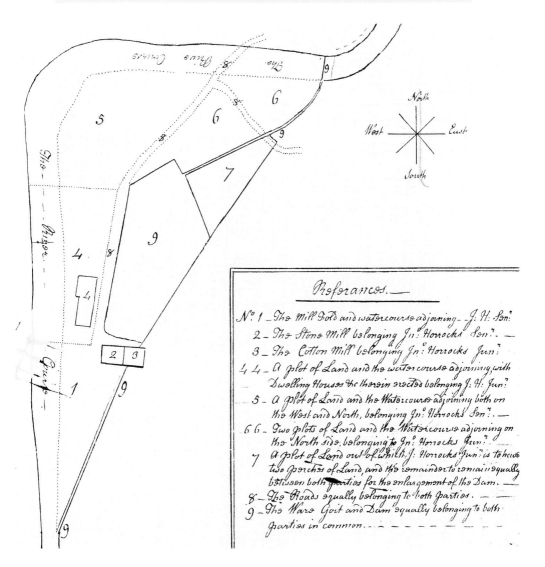

Map, c. 1795, showing the partition of land and premises of The Stone Mill, between John Horrocks (Senior) and his son John. (*Lancashire Record Office, ref. DDHS/76*)

Tentatively he erected a few spinning frames in a corner of his father's stone mill, and began experimenting in cotton-roving and carding.[3] John applied himself to his new venture with much vigour and enthusiasm, and was soon producing a saleable yarn. He was a good mechanic, and so thorough and painstaking in every respect that his yarn soon became known for its excellent quality.

7

Bradshaw Brook. Turton. Horrockses' 'Stone Mill' stood behind the mill-houses shown here, in the eighteenth and early nineteenth centuries. This photograph was taken before a housing estate was built on this site.

There was no need to look far beyond his own village for outworkers. A long-established network of spinners in the local farming community had traditionally worked at the wheel to supplement their meagre incomes. The work was often done by the unmarried women in a household, hence the term 'spinster'. John travelled around to their farms and cottages, on foot or with a pack-horse, delivering the raw materials and collecting the finished yarns.

As his small enterprise grew, he began to look further afield for customers. Manchester and Bolton were already well supplied so, after some enquiries, he decided that Preston might be a suitable market. Although the town had for centuries been a centre for the manufacture of quality linen and woollen cloth, there was at that time only one cotton-spinning mill, built in 1777 by William Collinson.

John began taking his yarn over to Collinson's Mill to sell, often walking the eighteen miles over the moors with the heavy pack on his back. He had to deal with Collinson's partner John Watson, who proved to be a hard bargainer; but for a while John accepted his terms and traded with him.

Inevitably, however, he became frustrated with the low prices, and a dispute led to a serious row between the two men. In anger young Horrocks stormed out of the mill and vowed that he would trade there no longer, but would take his business elsewhere. In fact, he threatened, he would come to Preston, set up in business himself, and 'become a thorn in Watson's side'.[4] Still smarting from the confrontation he returned home to Edgworth to reconsider his situation.

The cotton-spinning venture in his father's mill was thriving and could be developed, but needed more space. So father and son decided to reorganise their premises and land. A plan was drawn up by which both businesses – the stone-polishing and the cotton-spinning – could run side by side. The mill building was divided into two equal parts, and the land and watercourses reallocated between both. The dam serving the waterwheel was strengthened and enlarged to provide the extra power needed. There were two stone-built houses on the bank of Bradshaw Brook next to the mill. It is likely that

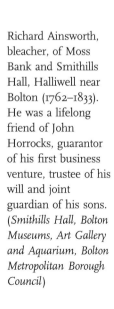

Richard Ainsworth, bleacher, of Moss Bank and Smithills Hall, Halliwell near Bolton (1762–1833). He was a lifelong friend of John Horrocks, guarantor of his first business venture, trustee of his will and joint guardian of his sons. (*Smithills Hall, Bolton Museums, Art Gallery and Aquarium, Bolton Metropolitan Borough Council*)

John Horrocks (1768–1804). This is the first known portrait of John, as a young man, probably in the early 1790s after he had founded Horrocks & Co. in Preston.

John moved into one of them, with relatives – perhaps his parents or brother Samuel – in the other.

John needed money to back his business propositions and talked this over with his friend Richard Ainsworth. Richard's position in his family's bleaching business at Halliwell meant that he was financially secure. He was happy to help and promised John £20,000 as security at this crucial time in his career.

With his business plans completed to his satisfaction, John decided that the time had come for him to leave bachelorhood behind and settle down. On 22 April 1790, he married Mary, daughter of Richard Lomax of Ainsworth, at Bolton Parish Church. They were a very handsome couple, each strong in character and similar in looks, with dark hair and good features. The bride, at twenty-one, was a year younger than her husband. It was written of her 'she was of a respectable family near Bolton, her father renting a farm of 60 Cheshire acres, which in that situation . . . is considerable'. Unfortunately little else was ever recorded about Mary Horrocks, so she becomes an enigmatic

'The South Prospect of Preston in 1728', showing the town before the Industrial Revolution. (*Lancashire Record Office, ref. DP189*)

figure in the family chronicles; always there as wife and mother, but an unknown presence in the background.

After some serious consideration the young bridegroom decided that Preston would be the place for his next venture into business. Towards the end of 1790 he returned there, leaving his brother Samuel in charge of the mill at Edgworth. It was an insignificant entry, on foot, with his belongings loaded on a pack-horse.

Preston was then a small, select, aristocratic market town not more than one and a half miles across, well set out with three broad, straight streets and a good market square. It had grown in importance due to the large numbers of resident lawyers, clergy and gentry. Almost all the public offices for the administration of law in the County and Duchy of Lancaster were there, so that it served, in all but name, as the County town. There were some fine houses, the grandest of which, Patten House on Church Street, was owned by the Earls of Derby, acquired in a 1688 marriage settlement.

The Earls and entourage would come to Preston for the Season, entertaining with open house, especially in Race Week. Their presence in the town was a great social asset, drawing other gentry and minor adherents to follow them. In 1709 Dr Calamy had described his visit to 'a very pretty town with an abundance of gentry' and Daniel Defoe wrote 'this is a fine town full of attorneys, proctors and notaries'.[5] The population had averaged about three thousand for generations and the people were described as 'living their lives in refined stagnation'. The Devis family of Preston, Arthur and Anthony and their sons Arthur and Thomas – all accomplished artists

– have left portraits and paintings showing the typically genteel but apparently staid families of this period.

This was the town, then, which John Horrocks had chosen for his new life. What would lie ahead for him there?

In January 1791 John moved into a rented workshop – not more than a small outbuilding – in Turk's Head Court, off Church Street in Preston, a dingy passageway that led down to the Syke Brook at Avenham. There he erected two carding engines and with his first employee, young Joseph Dearden, started work. They were soon producing best quality yarn, and began to give it out to handloom-weavers in the neighbourhood.

Word spread that a new yarn was available, and the local people came to him for work in increasing numbers. This led to a cash-flow problem with his suppliers, as he lacked a financial backer to discount the bills. He asked a local linen merchant, Samuel Crane, to oblige him thus. Before committing himself Mr Crane needed to know more about John's enterprise so he walked down Turk's Head Yard to see for himself. There he found the young man lying full length on the floor oiling his machinery. This was enough to satisfy Crane as to John's application and character: he needed no further security and, from then on, happily discounted[6] Horrocks's bills.

Business was increasing daily and a larger workshop was soon required, so John rented another building, at Syke Hill, for a warehouse. He really needed much bigger premises but, at that time, lacked the capital to expand. He decided to seek a loan from a local banker, and approached Mr George Bolton of Messrs. Shuttleworth, Bolton, Clayton and Moore. Mr Bolton was persuaded that expansion was financially viable, and agreed to put up the money for a new factory.

John drew the plans himself and builders soon began work on the site. One day Mr Bolton thought that he would have a look at the new structure, but when he saw it was so alarmed at its size that he withdrew his backing.

John Horrocks, however, soon found two other bankers who had no qualms about the venture. Richard Newsham and Thomas Greaves became his new partners. In May 1792 the three men started an interim spinning business in Bolton's Court. At first they rented a building there for £16 17s. 4d. per annum, and each advanced £200 for the purchase of spinning machines.

John would run the business, supplying the partnership with prepared cotton and buying back the finished twist. He was still trading as a cotton-roving merchant and for this would have the exclusive use of the bottom floor of the factory. Very soon, however, he felt the need to be freed from this partnership; so he withdrew and gave away his third share, half to his

Money order dated 20th May 1795 and signed by J and S Horrocks, 3 Bow Churchyard, London. (*Lancashire Record Office, DDHS*)

brother Samuel and half to a cousin, Isaac Horrocks, who moved from Edgworth to manage the business.

The Bolton's Court factory remained in the family until 1835, always run very profitably, but quite separately from the main business, by a succession of relatives: Isaac, George, and later a nephew, another John Horrocks. An early apprentice, George Jacson, bought a share in the partnership which then traded under the name Horrocks, Jacson & Co.

John had been living in Woodcock's Court, a yard with no thoroughfare, off Fishergate in Preston. He was still returning to Edgworth regularly collecting yarn, but in place of the 'ambling nag' of former days he now indulged in the luxury of a gig, and began to acquire status in the quiet neighbourhood of his birth. His three sisters, who worked hard for him winding yarn, felt that they should now have some share in his success; so they issued an ultimatum. Their work would be put down undone until their demands were considered. They wanted their wages to be doubled and, as a gesture of goodwill, their brother must buy each of them a new silk dress! After a night's consideration John agreed to their terms and work was resumed. Thus his first 'industrial dispute' was settled amicably, and recorded.

At about this time he and his father closed down the old millstone manufacturing business and turned all the premises at Stone Mill over to cotton production under the name of Samuel Horrocks. A nephew, Henry Horrocks, was made mill manager, and James Booth was the spinning master.[7]

The open fields around Stone Mill were gradually being built upon, and the building of the new Bradshaw Turnpike Road transformed their ancient layout, opening the district for industrialisation. The new road somewhat isolated the Horrocks' family homes up at Birches Green, so that they remained, as they are to this day, in a quiet little oasis virtually cut off from the bustle of Edgworth village life.

Changes were affecting John Horrocks's life too. His wife, Mary, was expecting their first child, a son, who was born on 17 March 1791 at Edgworth, and christened Peter. Encouraged by his new paternal status John returned to Preston to oversee the completion of his first factory in Dale Street, now fitted out and ready to start production. It was an enormous building for those days, five storeys high and seven windows in length, and so well built that it would be in constant use for the next hundred and fifty years, the nucleus of Horrockses' 'Yard Works'. At some stage the exterior brickwork was colour-washed and from then it acquired its name 'The Yellow Factory'. There were no suitable fast-running streams to provide power, as in Edgworth, so the driving shaft for the spinning machinery was worked by a horse in the cellar below. This would be John's only ever one-horse-power factory.

He continued to be surprised at the huge number of people who flocked to him looking for work. Not all of them were townsfolk: many were unemployed farm labourers and others from the countryside thrown out of work following the recent Land Enclosure Acts, and introduction of agricultural machinery. As it was clear that there would be a sufficient workforce available to staff more factories he set to and built them, this time with his own money.

In 1793 came 'The Yard Factory', the second and bigger one to be built in Dale Street. A year later he bought some land adjoining Magdalen Lane, round the end of Friargate. These were narrow plots in an ancient part of the town known as Magdalen (Maudland) Fields, and also included the Corporation's old Pinfold at the edge of Spittal Moss. On this site in 1794 was erected 'Spittal Moss Factory'. In the following year, due to ever in-creasing demand for cotton, Frenchwood Factory was built on land off Swillbrook Lane called 'Gate Meadows' and 'The Bottoms' (now Arno Street and Tiber Street, off Manchester Road).

All four of these mills were brick-built with wooden fittings, and were insured for £16,350. Soon, however, claims would have to be made for the rebuilding of 'Yard' and 'Frenchwood' when both accidentally burned down shortly after erection. In 1796 the last of this group was 'Canal Mill', six storeys high and sixteen windows long, built on the site of Joseph Bray's house and garden on Spittal Moss. This was the first of Horrockses' mills to be powered by steam.

After the disastrous fire, the spinning mill at Frenchwood was rebuilt, bigger than the original and with a cupola and weather-vane on the roof. Its large steam engine of eighteen horse-power was housed in its own

The Yellow Factory, Dale Street, off Church Street, Preston. John Horrocks's first cotton mill, erected 1791, demolished 1942.

Spittal Moss Factory built in 1794 by John Horrocks and still standing, now a public house, in Fylde Road.

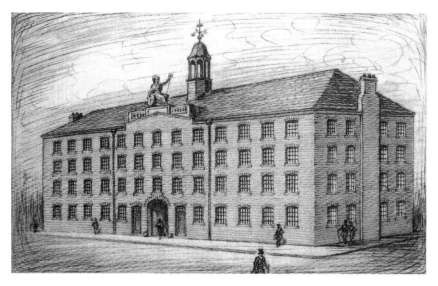

Britannia Mill, built 1805. (*Published in The Story of Horrockses*)

engine block, and water was provided in a huge reservoir built below the steep drop of land behind Dickson Street. To reduce the problem of fire hazards, all new mills were brick built on iron frames with the use of wood reduced to a minimum. Horrockses[8] then introduced the first public fire-engine to the town. Although intended to protect their own factories the machine was used to put out fires all over Preston.

As the huge number of workers employed to operate John Horrocks' mills needed homes, he built rows of terraced houses, small and for cheap rent, next to each mill. Many were three-storeyed with a cellar workshop to house a handloom for home-weaving. (Most of them stood until they were demolished in the 1960s.)

At the edge of the town in a narrow field along New Hall Lane he erected a number of large sheds for handloom weaving, with a few short streets of cottages nearby (now the site of the 1891 'Centenary Mill'). This district known as New Preston later became densely populated by mill workers.

John's huge and rapid development was not the slapdash 'jerry-building' that happened in later years in the town, but a carefully considered plan. The mills were sited in different parts of Preston with access to roads and the canal. New housing areas developed in the streets around them. Many of the workers who came from rural areas, however, found difficulty in adjusting to the enclosed confines of huge, noisy factories. Handloom weavers, on the other hand, had the advantage of working in their own homes weaving mechanically-spun yarns. The booming market for cotton goods guaranteed them full employment; so that the years at the end of the eighteenth century became their heyday. Workers flooded into Preston from all the surrounding countryside hoping to benefit from the employment bonanza.

One questions how Horrocks was able to expand so rapidly. The answer is that he was in the right place at the right time: a man blessed with the shrewdness and vision to realise and seize the opportunity; a man whose integrity was unquestioned. He was also an accomplished mechanic who understood the workings of machinery.

There was no doubt that the town of Preston was the ideal place for his venture. Centrally situated close to the sea, river and proposed canals, its crossroads position gave access to all the surrounding country. The trading cities and ports of Liverpool and Manchester were easily accessible. The Preston to Lancaster canal was under construction, and opened in 1798, later to be extended to Kendal. In 1802 the canal to Wigan was built, and connected to the heart of Preston by a tramway system for carrying in coal.

During the following years, the main roads to the south and north were vastly improved. The ancient, narrow winding lanes were replaced by straight, wide roads: London Road southwards to the new bridge at Walton; Garstang Road northwards up to the Withy Trees Inn and beyond; Fishergate Hill was levelled to an easier gradient and widened to cope with the increasing volume of traffic; Friargate Brow too was levelled and the 'hump' removed.

An important element in cotton-spinning was the climate which, in this part of Lancashire, was ideal. The suitably damp atmosphere prevented the yarn from splitting and causing unevenness in the cloth.

The timing, too, of John's entry into the business of cotton manufacturing was perfect. The inventive genius of a whole band of men, Hargreaves, Kay, Arkwright, Crompton and Watt had already revolutionised production methods in the textiles industry. In this last decade of the eighteenth century, he would make use of their new machinery in Horrockses' factories.

Problems did occasionally arise, as in 1796, when the design of one of their spinning engines led to legal proceedings being taken against John and Samuel Horrocks. At that time, Messrs. Boulton and Watts were building single-cylinder, double-acting beam engines which achieved the regularity of motion needed in mule spinning. Their main competitors, Messrs. Bateman and Sherratt of Manchester infringed James Watts' patent by using his separate condensers and air pumps on their inferior engines in a bid to obtain this regularity. So Watts set about to prove their piracy. He sent spies into Preston factories who reported back that a few such Bateman and Sherratt engines were indeed being used there, including three supplied to John and Samuel Horrocks' mills. One had been working 'some years' whilst of the other two, which were 'still erecting', one pirated Watts' parallel motion invention. The outcome of the legal proceedings is not noted. But four years later Watts' son visited Horrocks & Co. 'to see the 6 or 7 engines operating there'.

John Horrocks was fortunate that there was then a vast open market waiting for cotton goods. For centuries past, working people had worn clothes made generally of linsey-woolsey, a heavy, coarse material, a mixture of linen and wool. This dark, drab cloth was difficult to keep clean, and garments were often worn until they dropped to pieces. The new cotton fabrics came as a revelation: they were lightweight, reasonably priced, and easily washed and ironed. For the first time in their lives poor people could wear clean, hygienic clothes, and have decent bedding and towelling. They had been given the priceless gift of self-respect. Their demand for inexpensive cotton goods became almost insatiable.

Nevertheless, he always knew that the market was very competitive and to win a worthwhile share his product would have to be the best. He was one of the first factory-spinners to use cotton grown in the Southern States of America, buying "above average quality" grade from a number of Liverpool and Manchester merchants. Others were still using coarser quality cotton from the West Indies.[9] His emphatic insistence that all cloth leaving his mills must be the most excellent of its kind was rigidly adhered to. Consequently the trade name 'Horrockses' soon became synonymous with quality, and remained so for the next two centuries.[10]

Having won his share of the market he was loath to lose it during the adverse trading conditions of the Napoleonic War years. The blockade of continental ports against British vessels meant the end of his busy trade through Hamburg. Farington, the diarist, noted that John 'was left with a great quantity of goods remaining unsold. Instead of adopting half-measures which might have affected his credit he sold them at a loss of possibly £40,000. By that means he obtained sufficient [money] to settle his bills and was also able to offer to discount bills drawn on him'.

'At about this time', as James Horrocks of Heywood told his grandson John James, 'it was reported that there was a chance of him being bankrupt.' Apparently he heard of the rumour, 'called his creditors round him and paid them every farthing. Then he hired a faithful man, James Hamer of Holcombe Brook, to wheel all his remaining gold through the streets of Preston in a wheelbarrow'.

An enormous boost restored his fortunes in the following year when, on merit, he won the most lucrative customer abroad. The Government's East India Company set up a competition to select a supplier of cotton goods to the Indian market. Horrockses were judged to be the finest quality cottons entered in the open contest, and won the contract. Already supplying a large share of British sales there was now the certainty of guaranteed foreign trade. A London office was opened, first at 3 Bow Churchyard, and later at 5 Bucklesbury, but existing Lancashire export agents were used to supply the Indian market. Adjustments had to be made to the mill machinery for the much finer muslin fabrics needed in hot climates.

This was the beginning of Horrockses' export trade to the Far East which would, over the following century, expand to cover most of its countries. John Horrocks had become one of the fathers of the Industrial Revolution, joining the band of historically important entrepreneurs who changed the towns of England and set the pattern for an industrial way of life all over the world. Through their enterprise, Britain's fortunes were restored after the lean years of the French wars. Their trading led to the development of the British Empire, in every corner of which John Horrocks's cotton would be found. He came to embody the nineteenth century like the hero of a Thomas Hardy novel.

John's financial future was secure. The days of living in Turk's Head Court and Woodcock's Yard, where he had often slept on a sack of straw, were behind him. He had been living in rented accommodation at the top of Woodcock's Court in Fishergate. Now he was ready to move up in the world, and took a lease on a house next to his Yard Works (later the King's Arms Hotel in Stanley Street). It was a smart detached house owned by the Derby Estate, and he moved there with his wife and their two young sons Peter and John.

Changes were also made in Edgworth at this time. Cousin Henry Horrocks was put in charge of the Stone Mill, thereby relieving John's brother Samuel, who moved over to Preston, and in 1794 was made a partner in the main company with one-third share in profits. The two brothers seem to have been accepted fairly well in Preston; John was made a burgess of the borough, a coveted ancient standing granted only to the sons of burgesses or to 'worthy newcomers'.

In June 1794 the Rev. T. Wilson wrote in his diary that he 'was in Preston spending a few days with Dr St Clare. The King's birthday was celebrated in great style. I found the town in great political commotion, "the King and John Horrocks" sung and said and vociferated in every street'.

Not surprisingly, however, there were some who were not well-pleased with the changes taking place. What had been a pleasant market town was being transformed before their eyes. Where there had been green fields and

The Old Market Place, Preston: illustration in C. Hardwick's *History of the Borough of Preston c.* 1857.

gardens were now huge factories, and the population was increasing at a remarkable rate. Whereas there had been only 5,500 townspeople in 1760, there would by 1801 be an incredible increase to 11,887, and by 1816 Horrockses were employing 7,000 'hands'. Some of the male handloom weavers in the New Town area were described as 'an exceedingly rough lot ... they would swagger about in top boots, and often extract what, to their minds, was enjoyment from badger-baiting, dog-worrying, cock-fighting, poaching and drinking'.

One prominent resident, attorney Thomas Winckley, was insulted and took umbrage when a fishmarket trader served John Horrocks before him. His daughter, Lady Frances Shelley, wrote in her diary that the young newcomer had bought the rather fine turbot which her father had wanted. This was the last straw to Winckley, who pronounced that Preston was no longer a fitting place for a gentleman to live, and left the town for Walton-on-the-Hill near Liverpool, where he died in 1794.

Politics

During these years Prestonians generally showed a keen interest in local politics, a subject regularly discussed and debated. With their unique voting rights the men of the town enjoyed the most democratic franchise in the whole country. All males over the age of twenty-one who had resided in the borough for the six months immediately preceding a General Election could vote; provided that they were not criminals, paupers or Roman Catholics.

In the previous decade the Corporation had been in serious dispute with the townsfolk over who should nominate Parliamentary candidates and who could vote. Elections became scenes of great lawlessness and rioting, with both sides battling to retain their rights. In one episode candidates accused of standing illegally were fined and imprisoned, and the election of other successful candidates was annulled as 'unlawful'. In 1784 an appeal that 'persons who were not freemen had voted illegally' was rejected by Parliament who then confirmed the right of 'all Preston men without demur' to cast their votes.

During these years the bitter quarrelling caused great rivalry and even hatred between the townsmen and some of the Corporation. Behind the scenes was the influence of the 12th Earl of Derby, whose animosity towards the Corporation caused a rift in the town. His Whig followers and the old Tory groups gradually divided into two camps.[11] Neither would support the other's concerns, but set up in opposition in their daily lives. For instance, each had its own racecourse on Preston and Fulwood Moors, its own pack of hunting-hounds in party colours, double sets of sedan chairs for their ladies, and the men sported suits with appropriately coloured collars. They even had separate private armies recruited to defend against a possible French invasion, the Corporation's Royal Volunteers, and Lord Derby's 'Loyal' Volunteers.

By 1796 the rivalry had become ridiculous and reached an impasse. The Corporation was desperate to gain control over Lord Derby and reunite the town. A solution would be to oppose him at the next General Election with their own candidate. Would John Horrocks, now the Town Bailiff, be the man who could make the breakthrough?

He was approached and agreed to take up the challenge. Behind him he could count on the support of the Corporation of Preston, the Lancashire Cotton-Masters, his own workforce, and the powerful 'Church and King' Political Club of Manchester 'which exercised a very potent power in the politics of the County'. But he was fighting powerful, experienced opponents.

The Derby family's position and influence had been paramount in Preston since the first Earl was given land there in 1498. They controlled the town from their mansion 'Patten House' on Church Street, and on the whole were popular with its people. Their two seats in Parliament were valuable assets which they would not give up without a fight. In 1796 they put forward their two Whig candidates as usual, Lord Stanley aged twenty-one, the 12th Earl's only son, and Sir Henry Philip Hoghton, Baronet.

Horrocks threw down the gauntlet and stood as Tory candidate. On 26 May his election placards were displayed informing the voters,

> Friends and townsmen, consider your interest in the present contest ...
> the Man who has on every occasion supported the town ... asks you
> to come forward and give your vote, and, with a free voice, say JOHN
> HORROCKS for ever.

The campaign was keenly fought over eleven days, and the final result very close: for Lord Stanley 772 votes; for Sir Henry Hoghton 756; and for John Horrocks 742. John was greatly encouraged that he had almost snatched victory from the great landowners. Lord Derby saw that most of Horrocks's supporters were his colleagues and workers in the cotton industry. In a bid to gain access to that group of voters, he himself built a cotton mill off Church Street (which was sold shortly after the next election).

He also tried to thwart his young opponent in another way. The Derby family owned Horrocks's Church Street house, and promptly gave him notice to quit. Undeterred, John built a new 'double' house on his land in Golden Square and moved there, biding his time until the next election.

The second half of the house was intended for Samuel, but this unfortunately led to a rift between the two brothers. Samuel, now thirty years old and the father of a growing family, was different in character from John; less well-educated and apparently of a dour, stubborn personality. John had been very generous towards him, giving him a partnership in his business and teaching him the cotton trade. Now, however, he discovered that Samuel had been negotiating to buy himself a huge new house with grounds, next to their mill in Frenchwood. John considered this to be a rash and premature venture at this stage in the company's growth, and told him so in no uncertain terms.

The disagreement grew into an estrangement between them. Samuel was determined to have his mansion but John continued to oppose the move. It appears that Samuel may have left Preston for, over the next two years, we find him working at a mill at Spring Hill in Blackburn, which had been opened earlier by a Mr Anderton, as the town's first cotton-spinning factory. Then he returned to Preston and was reconciled with his brother.

In January 1797 he finally moved into his Frenchwood mansion which he called 'Lark Hill'. He would live there until his death forty-six years later.

During the years of the French Wars there was serious concern in England about the possibility of invasion by the enemy. A friend of the Horrocks brothers, Nicholas Grimshaw, founded the Royal Preston Volunteer Force, two corps of local men sworn to the defence of their town and its populace. When he needed to form a third corps, Samuel and John volunteered their services. Both were accepted, Samuel as 2nd Lieutenant of the Riflemen and John commissioned as captain on 23 February 1798. They had to vow 'to serve the town and up to five miles around it', and were allowed to carry arms and ammunition.

In the event of foreign invasion the Force of about 360 men would assemble to march into the county and repel the enemy. They were well trained and drilled at home and at weekend camps at Fleetwood. Fortunately never called to take up arms, the brothers continued their connection with the Royal Preston Volunteers for some years subscribing £250 annually to its funds. John also made a handsome donation of £1,000 to the corps.

He was now, decidedly, a committed Prestonian, an Alderman of the Borough and ready to put down roots in his adopted town. As the eighteenth century came to a close, he had a bell cast for his company inscribed 'John and Samuel Horrocks 1800', and hung in time to ring in the new century 'which would bring the firm an almost unclouded era of prosperity and expansion'. There would also, no doubt, be celebrations at the news of trading figures for the year to 31 December 1799. With capital of £105,000 the profit yield was £55,000, shared by John and Samuel in the ratio four to one. Now a very wealthy man, John was ready to invest some of his money in a permanent home more suitable to his status.

Negotiations began for a site south of the river at Middleforth, Penwortham. There were twenty-one acres for sale, seven each of meadow, pasture and open land, in two lots. On New Year's day 1800 he bought the plot, paying £1,435 for the main portion. This was land known by the old names, 'Buckfields', 'Critchleys', and 'Half Acres'. The Charnley family had lived and farmed there for generations, except for a short period from 1687 when William Heaton bought it and changed the name of the farmhouse from 'Charnleys' to 'Heaton House'.[12]

A smaller plot of about an acre, called 'the Rood Land' was bought from Edmund Lodge for £100. The land lay mainly on the western side of the road from the old Penwortham bridge (now Leyland Road) and included other closes of land, some gardens and a barn and shippons (cow sheds).

Golden Square House, Yard Works built by John Horrocks *c.* 1797. Given to Thomas
Miller (Senior) when he became a partner in 1803. It was here in 1823 that Andrew
Ryding attempted to murder Samuel Horrocks MP.
(*Harris Reference Library*)

It was an ideal site for a home, on a hill overlooking the river and pleasant
countryside, well-placed away from Horrockses' mills. John began building
immediately. It is not known who were the architect and builders of his
new mansion but it could be that he employed the same men who had
recently built his brother's house. Messrs Timothy Wren, William Corry
and Seth German were known by him; and Penwortham Lodge and Lark
Hill House (1796) shared some similar features.

John wanted his house to be perfect. There was, however, one thing
which displeased him. Part of an old mill lane ran directly across the land,
threatening his privacy and spoiling the view. It was of little use there, as
the windmill it served had long since been demolished, so he applied to
have the road closed. On 10 February 1800 an Inquisition was held at the
nearby Horse Inn to consider and discuss the matter. A jury of ten local
gentlemen was brought before the Sheriff of Lancashire. They were required
to swear an oath that 'to inclose and stop up a certain part of the Mill Lane
highway would not be to the damage or prejudice of their Lord King, or
any other person', and that another replacement road to be built at the
petitioner's expense would still allow 'His Majesty and all his liege subjects

to pass and repass with horses, carts and other carriages'. The Sheriff and jury considered this to be a fair solution so permission was granted for the old Mill Lane to be closed and demolished.

John Horrocks' replacement highway, called New Lane, ran east to south of his land. Two paths led to the house, one from New Lane and the other from the old causeway (called Marshall's Brow by William Marshall, a later owner of the estate). His original 1800 house was extended, certainly within the next twenty years, to form the impressive mansion which still stands today.

Mr Harry Spencer, a builder, whose family owned the estate from the 1950s to 1980s wrote in 1967 'I have an idea that the house … was a three storey brick building which John Horrocks called Penwortham Lodge; subsequently to this house was added a stone building, two storeys high but under the same roof, the ceilings in the rooms of this portion being much

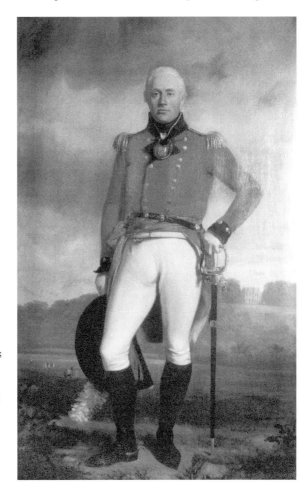

Portrait of Nicholas Grimshaw (1758–1838) as Colonel of the Royal Preston Volunteer Force in 1822. He was a friend of John Horrocks, executor of his will and joint guardian of his sons. (*Harris Museum and Art Gallery*)

higher ... It was an easy matter to separate the dividing wall between the two portions of the building; so that one is three storeys and one is two'. The brick-built side was renamed Penwortham Lodge and the stone main house Penwortham Hall.

When the property was offered for sale in 1930, Messrs. Cunliffe, Greg & Co. of Manchester published a sales brochure for the property, which provides an insight into the home life of its earlier occupants. Penwortham Hall is described as 'a noble stone and brick-built mansion of attractive elevation, on a wooded eminence in parkland, with gravelled drives leading up to a stone-pillared entrance. Within is a large hall with a staircase lighted by a glass-domed roof. The large and beautiful drawing room connected through fine mahogany double doors to the equally spacious dining room making a splendid apartment for parties and dancing. There is a handsome billiard room 30 foot by 20 foot, and a 17 foot square library fitted with mahogany glass-fronted bookcases. The back hall leads to

John Horrocks (1768–1804). A portrait of *c.* 1800 by an unknown artist which was used on presentation certificates to employees of Horrocks & Co. (*Courtesy of Brian Swarbrick*)

the domestic offices, 2 kitchens, a butler's pantry, scullery and large cool larders. There are also wine cellars and a range of storage rooms in the basement.

'On the first floor are 5 main bedrooms, 4 with dressing rooms, the principal bathroom and 2 wcs: servants' accommodation of 5 bedrooms, 3 on the second floor and 2 in a separate wing with its own bathroom and back stairs.

'The house is fitted with carved marble fireplaces in the downstairs rooms, with gilt-framed mirrors over mahogany mantels'.

By the time of the auction in 1930 the grounds had reached maturity and were impressively timbered with specimen flowering trees and cedars. There were shrubberies, plantations, an orchard, a large pond and rich pastures. At the back of the house was a large conservatory with peach and tomato houses and a vinery. At the front was the extensive stable block enclosed by a brick wall in a large yard.

This, then, was largely the house which 130 years earlier John Horrocks had built for his family.

They moved into Penwortham Lodge in 1801 and one can imagine the delight of the whole family in their new home. The boys Peter and John, now ten and seven years old, would be thrilled by the extensive grounds with ponies in the stables. Their previous playground had been the millyards in Stanley Street. Their mother, too, must have had great pleasure in her beautiful new home with all the latest furnishings and equipment, although we know nothing of her feelings on this change in her life.

In buying his mansion John was giving out the message that he wanted to be seen to be a gentleman. Yet he always remained a 'man of the people', a Lancashire man with a strong northern accent. His coat of arms displays two shuttles, a hank of cotton and a bee, symbolic of hard work. The choice of his motto 'Industria et Spe' (Work and Hope) announced to the world that he was proud of his success in business. Nevertheless he was conscious of his incomplete schooling. To remedy this somewhat he began a collection of books for his new library, and took the opportunity to have Latin lessons from his sons' tutors.

His next step was to buy a London home, separate from the Gunnersby premises. He chose a place in Blackfriars, then a fashionable area, near to the Thames. In November of 1801 he wrote to his friend Richard Ainsworth, 'I have bought a good house in Bridge Street. I hope it will be ready to accommodate you when you come to town.'

This was just ten years after his first venture into business in 1791 and he was obviously making the move from 'working' to 'middle' class without difficulty.

The nineteenth-century Preston historian William Dobson described him as 'a tall, handsome, well-built man with a ruddy countenance, a prepossessing expression and a quick observant eye. Although his manner was somewhat hasty he was liberal and generous to all with whom he had dealings. He was especially anxious to advance the interests of those connected with him ... and totally devoid of jealousy of the prosperity of others. His conversation was tinged with the dialect of the district in which he was brought up, and he retained much of the rustic in his bearings'.

A glance at his portrait shows this to be an accurate observation, and the comments of contemporaries bear out his characteristics of honesty, generosity and intelligence. The word 'rustic' however could be applied fairly only to the manner of speech and country ways learned in his youth. His letters are well-written in good English in a clear and firm hand. Although he was one of the early 'nouveau-riche' industrialists, he was obviously not the type of millowner portrayed later in Victorian novels – Bounderby in Dickens' *Hard Times*, for example, which was reputed to be based on Preston's 'Great Lockout' of 1853. In their book *Ten per cent and No Surrender*, the authors Dutton and King stated that in the early nineteenth century John Horrocks **was** in fact the cotton industry in Preston. Corry in his *History of Lancashire* thought him 'an adventurer in commerce whose genius surmounting the difficulties of indigence and obscurity soared into public notice with a buoyancy and lustre which left every competitor far behind', and a man

Above and opposite Photographs of Penwortham Hall in 2000.
(*By kind permission of North Bristish Housing Association*)

Penwortham Hall (formerly Lodge). It was built in 1800–1801 by John Horrocks and occupied between 1817 and 1829 by Peter his eldest son. This lithograph by G. J. Greenwood, one of a series entitled 'Country Seats of Lancashire', was published after William Marshall bought the estate *c.* 1830. He changed the name when Rawsthorne's earlier Penwortham Hall was demolished in 1832.
(*Harris Reference Library*)

with whom he transacted business, Baron Alexis Doxah of Switzerland considered him 'one of the clearest, shrewdest and most handsome of the men he ever met or knew'.

One quality learned in his youth, that of thrift, he apparently never lost. When he heard of a fund to buy a new organ for the Parish Church he generously gave all of the £500 needed. But he could not resist asking that he should be given the wooden packing-case in which the new organ would be delivered.

There is no doubt that John was quick to help others up the ladder. He never forgot that his first employer had educated him at his own expense. Taking a leaf from Thomas Thomasson's book, he in turn helped the young people around him. On one occasion a piece of timely advice was all that was needed. Young Richard Palmer, an aspiring lawyer, was appointed clerk to the Trustees of Penwortham Toll Bridge, but apparently he arrived half an hour late for a meeting of the Committee. Horrocks later took him to one side and in a kindly way impressed upon him the importance of punctuality: 'Young man, miss your meals if you will, miss your rest and

John Horrocks (1768–1804). A portrait of *c.* 1803, used as frontispiece in *The Story of Horrockses*, published by the company in presentation copies after his death. (*By courtesy of Marion Roberts*)

miss your pleasure, but never miss fulfilling an engagement. Be ready at the fixed time'. Palmer took these words to heart, and it was noted after his death that in his long lifetime he never missed a session of the Lancaster Assizes. He owed his appointment in 1799, as Coroner for the County, to John Horrocks who persuaded the Committee that he was the best candidate and must be given the job. Moreover to save the three impecunious young applicants the expense of contesting and canvassing for the post he insisted that the decision should be made known to them before any money was spent unnecessarily.

Successive Horrockses' employees were encouraged to go out and set up their own businesses. Notable among them were Richard Riley and John Paley who had been foreman mechanic and joiner at Yard Works. In 1798 John Horrocks took another 'adventure in commerce' by allowing them to open a machine shop at Spittal Moss Factory and a second one at Canal Mill. Soon they were making all his machinery and set up a foundry and mill in Heatley Street. Horrocks' money enabled them to join William Leighton in a successful cotton-manufactory at Bank Top Mill, Salmon Street, and later a second one in Queen Street. Horrockses remained partners

John Horrocks' London home at 31 Bridge Street, Blackfriars, where he died, aged 36, in 1804, stood along the block from the Blackfriars Inn near the Thames (house now demolished).

in this company until 1815, and Riley lived for a time at Albyn Bank House on the Lark Hill Estate.

John Bairstow was another employee who benefited from Horrocks' sponsorship. He was made manager and soon partner in a large new warehouse at Bolton. Eventually he was taken in as partner in the main company.

Another 'hand' at the Yard Works was William Shakeshaft, a labourer who was promoted to surveyor of the mill buildings. Horrocks, realising his aptitude for measuring and cartography, encouraged him to study the subjects. His success in that field can be seen in the accurately detailed map of the town of Preston made by Shakeshaft in 1809. He went on to become Land Steward at the Rufford Hall estate of the Hesketh family.

The sons of some better-off local families were placed in Horrocks & Co. as apprentices. That they learned well was evident in the successful lives of men such as Thomas German and George Jacson and the eminence to which they rose within the town.

The parish church of St John in Preston has stained glass windows presented as memorials by the families of Jacson, German and Bairstow. A marble bust of Thomas German, twice Mayor of Preston, survived the Town Hall fire of 1941 and now stands in the rotunda of the Harris Art Gallery.

A letter of recommendation dated 4 November 1801 sent by John Horrocks to his friend Richard Ainsworth, of Halliwell, illustrates the personal interest he took in his protégés. It concerns Mr

Spencer a young salesman for the company. He wrote, 'I think him a very deserving young man and I have no doubt that he will do our business to our entire satisfaction. I wish to render him every assistance in my power to procure him consignments and will take it as a favour done to myself if you can recommend any people to make trial of him as a salesman ... I am quite satisfied with respect to his stability ... and our House at Preston will discount his acceptances on the same terms as bankers provided they take bills as well as cash'.

The most outstanding example, however, of John's benevolence was undoubtedly his treatment of warehouseman Thomas Miller, whose story follows.

Thomas Miller

The management of Horrocks & Co. had, since its foundation, been undertaken by the two brothers alone. As a much stronger team was now needed to share the workload, in 1801 John began to look for new partners. An obvious candidate was his brother-in-law John Whitehead, husband of Mary Horrocks. He was brought over from Edgworth to manage the two mills at Spittal Moss, and a house was built there for him and his family. He would be given one-twentieth share of the profits.

The next appointment was to have significant consequences affecting the future both of the Horrocks family and of their cotton business.

A warehouseman at Yard Works named Thomas Miller[13] had impressed John Horrocks since their first chance meeting many years earlier. He was, however, a poor man and lacked the capital to buy into the company. Nevertheless John followed his instinct about the man's ability and invited him to join the Board. He also would take one-twentieth share of the profits and was appointed Manager as an incentive to continue the firm's profitable position.

The two new partners entered Horrocks & Co. at a time when profits were fluctuating. In 1801 they amounted to £20,769; in 1802, £45,109; and in 1803, £13,291; of which John Horrocks took six tenths and Samuel three. Miller and Whitehead would share the remaining tenth but were not expected to carry any losses which might occur in future years. Each was provided with a home and the prospect of a good income for life. Thomas Miller proved to be a loyal and competent partner, and a true friend to both Horrocks brothers throughout his life.

The circumstances of that first meeting as related by granddaughter Clara make interesting reading. She wrote that as her grandfather was walking along Fishergate one day, 'a labouring young man approached him and asked to be directed to Mr Horrocks' mill. He said he had walked from Cumberland looking for work, and at Garstang was told that he would surely find a job at Mr Horrocks in Preston'. There and then John Horrocks did indeed offer him work as warehouseman and he soon proved to be a good employee.

As the years passed Miller took on more responsible jobs and was obviously a capable and intelligent man. In 1798 at St John's Church he married Catherine May of Preston who took in washing and sold eggs for a living. She was given a job as laundress to John Horrocks' family in their home at Golden Square. One day she was there in the kitchen ironing shirts when the mill-owner came in, sat down, and made a startling announcement which left her dumbstruck:

'Mrs Miller, I have this day given your husband sufficient capital wherewith to become a partner in my firm, and I have also given him this house. As I am going to live in Penwortham the house is now yours and you are its mistress. You need no longer do the work that you are now doing.'

Mrs Miller said afterwards that on hearing this she was made speechless and could not answer but just sat and stared at her master.

Clara wrote, 'From that day until the day on which she died the Horrocks children and their families had no more true friend than Catherine Miller. She was grateful to her heart's core for all that had been done for her, for her husband and for her children.'

This was the beginning of the long and remarkable association between the Miller and Horrocks families which would bring great wealth and status to both, but also some heartache and troubles along the way.

Preston, 1802

The year 1802 was to be a momentous one in the Horrocks' family chronicles. John's political ambitions had not abated and, having reorganised his business affairs, he felt free to stand as candidate in the next Parliamentary elections. In fact he did not have to contest the seat. The Derby and de Hoghton families were aware that since the last election he had so consolidated his popularity among the electorate that he would now be unbeatable. A compromise was reached that the Corporation of Preston would nominate him as their Tory candidate and he should stand with the Whig, the young Lord Stanley (son of Lord Derby). Sir Henry Hoghton withdrew from the contest.

This solution was brought about through the intervention of Thomas Butterworth Bayley of Hope, Manchester, and the decision was ratified by the signatures of eleven gentlemen of Preston and the leaders of the parties.

Both men were returned unopposed and agreed to go to Westminster together as a coalition. Although this arrangement seems to have been undemocratic it proved successful and would continue through the next six elections.

In the town of Preston, a peaceful co-existence between the two political parties was restored, and everyone was satisfied. The manufacturing sector at last had their own man in Parliament and the Corporation had succeeded in undermining the power of the Derby interest. From this time John's rivalry with the Derby family ceased, to such an extent that his granddaughter Celia could write 'the good Lord Derby never thought his receptions complete unless attended by John Horrocks'. In the next generation the sons of these men also had a close bond of friendship.

In that same year of 1802, Samuel Horrocks held the office of Mayor of the borough, having served Fishwick ward as Councillor and later Alderman. He was thirty-six years old and completely indebted to his brother for the incredible change in his fortunes over the past decade. The historian William Dobson described him as being 'a diamond in the rough without the slightest pretence to be a scholar'. Nevertheless, when Prince William Frederick came to Preston to review the volunteer corps it was Samuel, as Mayor, who received His Royal Highness and presented him with the freedom of the borough.

Thus it came about that Mrs Jane Horrocks of the village of Edgworth could, in that new century, sit with her husband in Preston's parish church and watch her two sons walk down the aisle in procession; her elder son Samuel in the livery of Mayor of the town, and her younger son John its Member of Parliament. She was overcome with pride at the sight. All her family had benefited by their success for John had not been slow to include his relatives in his enterprise. This was noted by a contemporary, Richard Hodgkinson, in his 'Letters and Journals'.[14] Replying in 1816 to a query from his friend Rev. James Blundell who was curious about Horrocks, Hodgkinson wrote, 'His character was that of kindness and benevolence. His dutiful attention to his parents was exemplary, and to his poor relations he was charitable in an eminent degree'.

This was quite true. Cousins George and Isaac had been given the thriving mill in Bolton's Court; cousin Samuel of Sidcup in Kent was established in Horrockses' London office; one brother-in-law, John Whitehead, was a partner at Preston, and a second, John Rostron, had been backed in his business at Bury. Their mother could justifiably be proud of her sons' achievements.

Those were halcyon days for John. The business venture was a phenomenal success, he was the popular MP of his adopted town and living in a fashionable new home with his beautiful wife and two sons.

As if to crown everything, 1802 was also the year of Preston's Guild Merchant, a unique event celebrated every twenty years to commemorate the granting of the town's Royal Charter in 1179. Their friend Nicholas Grimshaw was Guild Mayor and the Horrocks family took a leading role in ten days of festivities, enjoying them to the full.[15]

As a consequence of their commercial success, the Trades Procession through the town was the longest ever known. This was the first time that the new cotton-manufacturing industry was officially represented, and the Masters put on a splendid display. The Company of Weavers and Spinners walked proudly under their new banner in the middle of the town's ancient trading companies. Before them went the Tanners, Skinners, Glovers, Wool-combers, Cabinet Makers, Carpenters, Coopers, Chairmakers, Millwrights, and Tailors. Following them were the Smiths, Plumbers, Painters, Glaziers, Watchmakers, Cordwainers (Shoemakers), and Vintners. The textile workers' contingent was the largest in the procession. The crowds watching were duly impressed and gave them a great reception.

William Abram wrote that 'the most striking feature of the procession was the novel one of a Spinning Mule (from Horrockses Mill) drawn upon a stage, and worked as it went along by a young boy and a ten year old girl'. Later in the day the Guild Mayor gave the delighted lad a tip of £1 (but took care to be reimbursed later from Guild funds).

Following the float walked '24 of the prettiest girls then engaged in the factories, attired in dresses of their finest cotton fabrics, decorated with fringes and blue ribbons. Each of them carried a small artificial cotton tree in full bloom, ingeniously made by Mrs Horrocks and her female relatives ... Mr Horrocks and John Watson [his business rival], their differences settled for the present, followed arm-in-arm carrying white wands'.

Behind them walked upwards of one hundred workmen from the different manufactories in the town; then came the Masters and their sons, and over two hundred more workmen. A board carried aloft bore the inscription 'May the ingenuity and industry of the cotton manufacturers ever find protection and support in this United Kingdom'.

It is interesting that William Abram in his history *Memorials of the Preston Guilds* also wrote that 'in 1802 John Horrocks was the man of most con-sequence of the citizens of the borough'.

John and his young sons, with his brother and cousins from Kent, were among the 3,000 men admitted and registered as In-Burgesses of the town, a prestigious honour accorded only to sons of existing burgesses, and to a chosen number of worthy men who were not born Prestonians.

An intriguing entry in the official list of Guild expenses is a payment of £1 for 'removing the pianoforte to and from Penwortham Lodge'. Where was the Horrocks' piano taken? Maybe to the Town Hall for the entertainment of the ladies at the Mayoress's breakfast; or perhaps to the Guild Mayor's home for one of his evening parties. Fishergate Hill was steep and stony in those days, so no doubt the instrument sustained a few knocks and bumps on its way to and from Penwortham.

John Horrocks took up his parliamentary seat in 1802. He travelled to London taking with him young Peter who at eleven years old was to begin formal education. His first year was at Rev. J. Ruddock's school in Fulham, before starting at Rev. Dr Locke's school in Farnham, Surrey, where he arrived armed with a family treasure, the copy of Robert Ainsworth's Latin Dictionary given to his father by Richard Ainsworth, the compiler's cousin. (In later years Peter's daughter, Clara, recalled that the volume had arrived back from Dr Locke's in considerable disrepair and had to be rebound).

An MP's duties were not onerous in those days, and John would have had time enough to run his business affairs. He soon became known in Parliament for his common-sense and business acumen. A particular friendship developed with William Pitt the Younger, during the two years of precarious peace from 1802–1804. Pitt had resigned as Prime Minister in February 1801 and was returned to power in May 1804. It was said that if he needed advice on industrial matters he would 'send for John Horrocks, whose answers were always plain, graphic, short and clear'.

William Dobson writes of an occasion when the young MP had to visit Woolwich, and was surprised to see workmen in the ordnance factory boring cannon by hand. He told the manager he would advise Pitt that machinery should be used for such a job. Soon afterwards a boring-machine was introduced into the department.

In 1803 Pitt presented John at court to King George III and the Prince Regent. Eighty years later, his grand-daughter Clara still treasured items of his court dress uniform: shirt ruffles of finest Brussels lace, silver shoe buckles, and his ceremonial sword. She wrote that following the presentation he was offered a knighthood which he declined as 'trumpery'.

It would appear to the onlooker that young John Horrocks had led a charmed life, at least in his twenties and early thirties. Nothing written about him gives a hint of how things first began to go wrong. But, at the peak of his public success, the foundations of his private life began to crack. At some time late in 1802, when he was away from home for long periods, came a bolt from the blue: the revelation that 'he suspected his wife of infidelity'. No further details emerge either at that time or later.

John must have been deeply affected, for his reaction was swift and severe. He could not forgive her. Whatever her sins she would be shown no mercy and would pay for them dearly. There would be no cooling-off period or reconciliation. Before the year was out, Mary was obliged to leave Penwortham Lodge and was set up in a house in Leyland. The long, happier years when she had lived in sometimes unpleasant accommodation while her workaholic husband was building up his business; the loneliness when he was absent on town affairs or away at Westminster; and her dutiful attention to her two sons seem to have counted for nothing.

Legal proceedings were started and the separation became official, final and somewhat acrimonious. Documents record that 'as unhappy differences have arisen between them' the marriage was ended on 15 January 1803 when both of them were thirty-four years old. They had been married for a twelve-year period which could only be described as momentous. There were no divorce laws as such, but from the date of their separation Mary would live as a *femme-sole* (now termed a divorcee), supported financially by John. He would pay her £500 per annum through her solicitor and her brother Richard Lomax. To guarantee this payment a mortgage was arranged with the deeds of Penwortham Lodge as security.

John was to have custody of their two sons, 'the sole and exclusive care, tuition, and control of Peter and John, and provide for their maintenance and education and bringing up at his own expense. But nevertheless the said Mary Horrocks shall and may at any reasonable and convenient time have free access at any school or seminary of education etc. or other place where they may reside for their instruction … provided that such residence be not then in any of the dwelling houses, warehouses or other place of business or abode of John Horrocks … Mary Horrocks shall not in any degree … be at liberty to take them from such school or other place on any account whatsoever without consent first of John Horrocks obtained in writing under his own hand'.

Her solicitors stipulated that she should be allowed to keep all the jewels, belongings and money already in her possession and that her estranged husband should leave her free to live her own life, wherever she wished and with whom, without interference.

This sad episode was never publicised, but was kept secret within the family, to such an extent that even close relations and descendants appear not to have known of the separation. Such a revelation would no doubt have caused a scandal and brought disrepute on the ambitious young Member of Parliament. Events of the following year would also contribute to the family's closing of ranks on the subject.

Mary did not stay long in the Preston district and went first to her father's home at Planetree Hall. Later she settled into a house, No. 12 The Crescent, Salford, where she lived alone with her maid until her death in 1829, nearly thirty years later.

John and Mary's paths crossed again on only one occasion when they passed each other by chance on a street pavement in London. Neither acknowledged the other. But Mary asked her maid to turn round and look. John Horrocks stood still, watching his ex-wife until she went out of view.

During the first three months of 1803, the young MP had been approached to try to obtain some financial reward for a distant relative who had been unjustly treated by the Lancashire Cotton-Masters. Over twenty years earlier, Samuel Crompton, living in a tenement at Hall-i-th-Wood, had invented the 'Mule',[16] an ingenious machine which transformed the production of very fine yarns, and made fortunes for the mill-owners. He was too poor to afford a patent and had received no benefit from his invention.

John Horrocks asked Parliament, on 14 March and again on 20 April, to give him access to figures and accounts relating to the export of cotton wool and cotton twist. With the backing of the cotton merchants and bleachers he proposed to petition the House for a private Bill to consider remunerating Samuel Crompton. The Mule machine had brought increased wealth and tax revenue to the country at a time when its coffers had been emptied in the war years. It was only right and just that the inventor should be rewarded.

On 21 April he wrote to his friend master-bleacher Richard Ainsworth, 'The fact is I give the Deligates [sic] the advice of a prudent father to his children. I have just time to say that every day's experience confirms my opinion that I am right, and the Minister is convinced that I am so, and will take care that my ideas are properly considered. Yesterday I wrote Mr Crompton on the subject which must either bring them forward or let the matter drop. No time must be lost and it would be well to follow their steps and for you to know their proceedings. This business will be well managed provided that the Country backs my opinion with petitions. I told the Minister that "the Bleachers" was a strong body and would petition. The remarks upon the Cotton trade shall be sent in a few days, much improved.'

Unfortunately, the time limit set by the House for receiving petitions for private Bills elapsed before the petitioner obtained leave to present his plea. John Horrocks' work in rallying the merchants and preparing the case had been in vain and it would fall upon another Horrocks' shoulders to take up the plea again in the future.

Events continued to be less than happy for John. In the spring he made heavy purchases of raw cotton amounting to nearly £25,000 at about three shillings per pound. The price in the market devalued soon afterwards by one third. At the same time an unexpected drop in the price of manufactured goods left him with stock-in-hand much reduced in value. After three years of very profitable trading he was faced with a loss, in 1804, of over £8,000.

Such business worries and parliamentary duties, together with the stressful problems in his domestic life, began to weigh heavily on John. For the first time in his life he became unwell, suffering painful and recurring symptoms of indigestion. In trying to obtain relief he visited several spa-towns for the medicinal spring-water treatment. In April, after a worrying attack of his ailment in London he wrote to his good friend Richard Ainsworth.

The letter is interesting in that it reveals his religious belief. We know that he attended Preston Parish Church and donated new bells for the church tower and so on; but this is the first indication, in his own hand, of his faith and trust in God: 'I am much better than when in town on Saturday. But the very strong sleeping draughts I have had seem to have unhinged my bowels, that it is with the greatest difficulty that I can get anything to pass through me. I perspire very much which prevents me gaining strength so fast as I otherwise should. But thank God I am wonderfully recovered. I hope and trust in the Almighty that he will favour me with what is best for me. His goodness is unbounded to those who mean well to all humankind. The physician thought it better that I did stay in the neighbourhood of London for three weeks or a month in order that they could see and watch the state of my health. I purpose at present to stay a few days or a week in Matlock [spa] on my way home to Lancashire when I should be very glad if you could meet me there'.

In September he was at Cheltenham Spa staying in the same inn as Joseph Farington, the artist, who wrote in his diary, 'Mr Horrocks was the only person that I remarked there. He has the appearance of being an active man and his look is vigilant ... He sat opposite to us at dinner and I was pleased on observing his plain and simple manner. He does not appear to be above 40 years of age' (in fact he was 35). The diarist continued, 'By over application to business he has brought on indigestion. He seems to be very temperate ... and possesses Decission (sic) that characteristic feature of a strong mind ... A bed may be had here for 2 shillings a night ... the food is good but the wine in Cheltenham much complained of'.

Unfortunately John's health did not improve; in the week of Christmas 1803 he prudently drew up his will.

After the recess he returned to Westminster but was now suffering some alarming symptoms which Clara described as 'como vigil attacks brought on by overwork and anxiety', probably what are now called blackouts.

In March, during a sitting of Parliament, he was taken ill, 'seized with a sort of sudden brainfever from which he could not rally'. An urgent message was sent for his brother Samuel to come from Preston. His young sister Ann-Eliza was in town and she nursed him in his home, but the doctors were unable to find a cure. One week later, on Saturday 1 March 1804, John Horrocks died, in the month of his thirty-sixth birthday. On the following day Samuel arrived, too late to find his brother alive.

The elder brother was stricken with grief, and with difficulty wrote to Nicholas Grimshaw, John's friend and solicitor:

31 Bridge St
Sunday 2 o'clock

My dear Grimshaw,

Yesterday would bring you the melancholy news of my dear brother's fate, and the only consolation we have is that he departed this frail life properly reconciled and resigned. No arrangement whatever is made for the funeral, but we shall certainly bring his remains to Preston.

This distressing circumstance, together with the state of my own family, is naturally very afflicting, and I think no man ever had so unpleasant a journey to London as this has been to me. I only got here three hours ago. I am so distressed that I can scarce write at all ... This conveys all that I can say at present.

I remain etc.
S Horrocks

John's death was a shattering blow to everyone; to Samuel, to his young sons, his parents and family, and to all his friends and workpeople. He was the anchor in their lives and, for many, the source of their incomes. What would happen to them now?

His elderly parents were living at Penwortham Lodge when the news first reached Preston. They were so distraught that they could not bear to stay in their son's house, but went straight home to The Birches at Edgworth taking Jack, the boys' pony, with them.

Young Peter was away at school in Surrey and one can only imagine his shock and dismay at hearing of his father's death. His aunt Elizabeth informed him 'in a most touching letter, lamenting over the loss which he and his younger brother were not old enough to understand in all its bearings'.

His father's body was brought back to Preston and buried near the porch of the old church of St Mary, just a short distance from Penwortham Lodge.

John Horrocks' tomb in St Mary's Churchyard, Penwortham.

John Horrocks had made his will on 19 December 1803. After his death on 1 March 1804 the will was proved at Chester; and on 17 September, at London, administration was granted to the executors, Samuel Horrocks, Richard Ainsworth and Nicholas Grimshaw. The estate was duly administered according to his directions.

John's younger son John, aged ten, was to inherit at his majority the business 'Horrocks & Co.' and the Penwortham Lodge house and lands. His older son Peter, now twelve, would receive a bequest of £50,000 outright, without interest. The three executors were appointed trustees of the estate and guardians to the boys, whose maintenance and educational costs in the years until they came of age would be paid from estate funds.

To his youngest sister Ann-Eliza Horrocks, John bequeathed £5,000 at twenty-one. The spurned wife Mary was cut out completely with the unforgiving words 'the testator's wife Mary shall have no part of it'. (Samuel and Peter Horrocks, however, continued to pay her the £500 annuity secured on a new bond on the Penwortham Lodge property as previously.)

The running of the company would fall on Samuel Horrocks' shoulders, as both the other trustees were busy men in their own professions. Richard Ainsworth[17] was a very successful businessman, and Nicholas Grimshaw, a practising solicitor, was also Town Clerk of Preston and Acting Cursitor (Chancery court clerk) for the County of Lancashire.

The contents of the will were surprising in one respect. The elder son, Peter, was not left any share in his father's business, nor his house Penwortham Lodge. The wording stipulated clearly that the younger son John would inherit both; and in the event of his having no heirs, they would then pass on to his uncle Samuel Horrocks of Lark Hill, and his heirs. Peter's share of the Estate was limited to the bequest of £50,000 at the age of twenty-one.

One can only speculate on the reason for this. Perhaps young Peter was too close to his ostracised mother who had been cut off from ever benefiting from Horrocks & Co. Or perhaps he was already showing signs of the restless personality which he developed in later years. His father was a shrewd man who evidently wished to ensure that the business would be in competent hands after his death. Peter's children in later life bitterly resented their father's exclusion from Horrocks & Co.

Clara wrote in her records, 'My grandfather's early death was, and has been, the undoing of his sons and descendants.' She regretted all her life

St Mary's Church, Penwortham, Preston in 2000. Photo by John Horrocks of NZ. t

hat John Horrocks had not received the honours due to him declaring that 'after his death it appeared that William Pitt had his name down for a baronetcy which he would have offered him in a few weeks time.' Later chapters of this family chronicle will reveal the extent of the their 'undoing'.

After John Horrocks' funeral, the stables at Penwortham Lodge were emptied and the coach-horses sold to Sir Charles Hoghton. Relatives stayed in the house until it was boarded up and closed while the boys were away at school. Peter was still at Dr Locke's and John at Rev. Hadfield's private school at Smithills. The grandparents had returned to The Birches at Edgworth, Mrs Mary Horrocks was at The Crescent in Salford and Uncle Samuel and family were at Lark Hill. It was to these three homes that the boys would return to spend their school vacations, under the supervision of their guardians.

Samuel Horrocks was the most personally involved executor of John Horrocks' will. Until his brother's untimely death, Samuel had been the subservient one, following where John led, while sharing financially and socially in his success. Now he would have to come centre-stage and play the leading role. There is no doubt that he was devastated at the loss of his mentor, and would happily have continued the status quo. But fate decreed otherwise and Samuel found himself suddenly faced with unexpected challenges.

Following his charismatic brother would be a difficult proposition; they were quite unalike in character. Where John had been quick and extrovert with unbounding energy, Samuel was slow and thorough with a reserved personality which at times could be dour. He lacked John's natural generosity of spirit and benevolence. Nevertheless, John must have had sufficient confidence in Samuel to leave him responsible for both his business and his children. How would this confidence be repaid?

CHAPTER 2

Ann-Eliza Horrocks (1786–1825)

Ann-Eliza Horrocks, born at Edgworth in November 1786, was the beautiful, much-beloved youngest sister of John Horrocks the cotton-master. He was twenty years older than her, and having achieved financial success was able to pay for her education and to introduce her into society at his London home. All this was brought to a sudden sad end by his untimely death in February 1804 when she was eighteen years old. His bequest of £5,000 to her, an appreciable sum, was put aside for a marriage dowry.

John's home in Preston, Penwortham Lodge, was left empty as his parents, in great distress at his death, returned to their family in Edgworth. Ann-Eliza went to live at Penwortham Lodge for a few months to help the Executors sort out her brother's affairs. Family pets, livestock and horses had to go to new homes. The pony was already at Edgworth, and the coach-horses sold to Sir Charles Hoghton. John's two sons Peter and John were still minors and away at school, Peter at Rev. Dr Locke's in Farnham, Surrey and John at Rev. S Pearson's in Parsons Green, London. Penwortham Lodge Estate would be inherited by John when he came of age; meanwhile the house must be closed down and its contents stored.

In the midst of all the upheaval the families received another tragic blow. They were all concerned about the health of their Aunt Alice of Lark Hill, wife of Samuel Horrocks. She had not been well since before John's death and had gone to Lytham for the sea air. On 16 July 1804 Ann-Eliza wrote to young Peter 'I believe she is much better now'. But she was wrong. Only a week later Alice died, leaving her eight young children motherless and Samuel a widower. Ann-Eliza must have felt that her family was disintegrating around her as Penwortham Lodge was boarded up and she moved over to Lark Hill to console her nieces and young Sam. Lark Hill remained her home for the next three years during which a close friendship developed between her and Samuel's children. She was very concerned about her brother John's sons too and corresponded with them regularly. Peter treasured her letters and kept them until he died. In the 1880s his daughter Clara copied some and sent them with family pedigrees to her nephew Leonard Brownlow in New Zealand. They give an interesting picture of the Horrocks family in the early years of that century and reveal the caring character of Ann-Eliza. She wrote to Peter in an affectionate manner, sympathising over the loss of his father and assuring him of her family's love for both brothers. She tried to amuse with snippets of local gossip and kept him up to date with all the news. Each letter included a mention of his pets, the dog Julie and Jack the pony which had been put in the care of his cousin John Rostron at Edgworth. 'Poor Jack is growing quite fat, your grand-father rides him down to the factory in this hot weather', and 'Do you remember what fun you had with the Wilkins at Penwortham when you all three rode Jack, poor thing'. In 1806 she told him 'Jack is now almost blind in both eyes. They want him to be sold this horsefair, but I would not let him be. He has lived with us so long he shall pay the last debt to nature with us.' As time passed her letters became more newsy and amusing: 'Miss Mortimer [the governess] and I have been spending two or three days at Croston Hall with the Masters. We were such a party there. In the evening they dressed me up in the Robes that Lady Coventry wore at the Coronation, a very droll figure I was and caused no little fun for them. I almost fancied afterwards that I had lost an inch of my height for I was weighed down with gold tassels etc'. In 1807 she reported 'Preston is quite gay, nothing but Routs. I was at a very gay one at Dr Law's where we were quite dazzled with the Red coats, I did not return before 12 this morning – staid the night.'

At Race Week she was disappointed that they had very little company, but hoped perhaps John Leigh and his brother might come over from Liverpool 'as he is a man who likes every sort of amusement'. Lord Derby had a horse running and Her Ladyship was expected in town soon.

Ann-Eliza was constantly on the move visiting relatives and friends all over Lancashire and relaying messages from them to young Peter. She had the idea on one occasion to enclose a gold half sovereign securely under the sealing-wax of her letter to him, but unfortunately did not have the right coin. Soon however one arrived at his school sent in that manner by his Uncle John Whitehead. Her letters show that during these years she was escorted on her outings by female friends or male relatives. But in June 1807 we hear that she has become engaged to a young London barrister, Robert Robbins, and would be married in September. The family, with their grandparents from Edgworth, gathered at Lark Hill for the occasion, and Eliza wrote to Peter 'I am very busy preparing my mind for the eventful day'.

She told him that after the wedding they were to stay at the home of Robbins' particular friends Mr and Mrs Pitt at East Court House, Cirencester. She expected that they would stay about a month and 'as they are such a charming family I assure you we shall regret leaving them'. (Later events would change Ann-Eliza's opinion of one of these 'particular friends'.)

After her wedding a trust fund was set up to invest the £5,000 dowry from her late brother John. Joseph Pitt was one of the trustees.

The young couple left Robert's house after their honeymoon and set up home at 23 Lincolns Inn Fields, London. There they lived a happy life surrounded by friends, and relatives visiting from the north. Their house became a second home to the Horrocks family and a constant stream of letters passed between Lincolns Inn Fields and Lancashire. Whenever Samuel Horrocks travelled to Westminster he would take one or two of his older daughters for a visit to the Robbins, and her letters show that Ann-Eliza looked forward to seeing them. She was an excellent hostess, amusing, fashionable and generous in her hospitality. There was much to interest her guests in London in this heyday of the Georgian era, when the city was being redesigned. Old properties were replaced by fine squares and streets of elegant stone houses. The Preston girls eagerly viewed the new fashions in interior design. Upholstered furniture, draperies for the tall sash windows, oriental rugs and carpets were replacing the old less comfortable styles. Their father was spending a fortune furnishing Lark Hill and landscaping the grounds. Earlier Ann-Eliza had told Peter 'you will scarcely know this place when you come back, your Uncle has made such improvements'.

In the first six years of their marriage the Robbins had four children born to them, three sons, William, George and Perceval, and a daughter, Caroline. But sadly their happy married life was to be shortlived, and once again the Horrockses were destined to lose a treasured and well-loved member of their family. Robert began to feel unwell in the summer of 1813 complaining of weakness and pain in his side. In the hope of restoring his health the family spent the summer months at Sandgate on the Kent coast with their friends the Bowyers. Letters describe how they found Sandgate 'an agreeable little place'. The children enjoyed the freedom of the beach all day long and in the evenings their parents played whist with the Bowyers. At Dover they were surprised at 'how near the French coast appeared to the naked eye', and that 'with the aid of a glass we could see very plainly the wind-mills going round'. Ann-Eliza discovered that many of the local people were smugglers and 'busied myself in buying smuggled French gloves and tarsnet'(dress material). During the following winter her husband's health gradually deteriorated and she, always optimistic of a cure, tried hard to keep up his spirits; 'We invite one or two to dinner every day which is a little variety and has the means of rousing him more than if he were left alone. In the evenings we play Bagatelle with our friends'.

Her family in Lancashire remembered them with kindness. A letter to her niece Eliza Whittaker thanked 'her and her good man for their liberal present ... The beef was thought excellent and went off famously at breakfast and luncheon, the pork was quite a treat, and the hares and pheasants were in excellent order'. In a Christmas letter we hear how 'the cook made some mincemeat the week before last. On Saturday she made some pies of it, but your Uncle thought them so bad he begged we might never have any mincemeat of her making again. So they eat it made into pies for the kitchen'. She added, 'Tell Mr Whittaker he might make a fortune by sending salmon to London if he were a little nearer, for it is nine shillings and sixpence a pound this morning.'

Robert Robbins' illness was caused by an enlarged heart, which eventually led to heart failure. He died quite suddenly aged about thirty-five in February 1814. Ann-Eliza was nearing the end of her fifth pregnancy and shortly after his death her second daughter, Elizabeth, was born. Fortunately the birth was straightforward and the baby healthy and contented, so the young widow found strength to cope with her distressing situation. Eliza Whittaker came down from Clitheroe to be with her Aunt and care for the children, and the Bowyers and other friends supported her. Soon she had to face the upheaval of moving from the house in Lincolns Inn Fields and finding a new home for herself and the children. Her husband's family and friends pressed her to leave London and move nearer to them in Gloucestershire; so Cornelius Pitt, the son of Joseph, her husband's friend, took it upon himself to find them a house.

In the months before she left London her home was filled with relatives from the north. One sister, Mary Whitehead, made a prolonged visit and was then joined by Sarah and her husband John Rostron. Ostensibly they were to help with the move to Gloucestershire. But their visit came at a crucial time in the history of England, coinciding with the Declaration of Peace following victory in the French Wars. They could not have chosen a more momentous time to be in London. The capital was ablaze with triumphant rejoicing and the people went wild with excitement. No one could blame the Horrockses for forgetting their mourning and leaving the widow at home. Joined by brother Samuel, and Thomas Miller his partner, they followed the excited throngs. As Ann-Eliza commented, 'certainly such times can never happen again.' They declared the magnificent procession of the monarchs' state coaches in full regalia to the Guildhall to be 'the grandest sight ever seen in this country', and were delighted with the Review in Hyde Park. They were out from early morning to evening, and then went to parties or to join the revellers in Vauxhall Gardens. The official Declaration of Peace 'pleased them more than anything'. The climax came with the visit of 'The Allied Sovereigns' in June. The Czar Alexander of Russia, the King of Prussia, ruling European princes, statesmen and army generals adjourned from the Congress of Vienna to London to pay homage to the country which had finally defeated Napoleon. Ann-Eliza ruefully wrote to their families at home warning them not to expect any letters, and adding 'it is only astonishing that she [her sister Mary Whitehead] is well, considering the fatigue, loss of sleep, and seldom getting any dinner'. Mary and her relatives were witnessing the most momentous events of their lives.

The Robbins family's move from Lincolns Inn Fields to Gloucestershire 'was affected with many painful and agonising regrets'. Cornelius Pitt proved a good and reliable friend and found them a house in the beautiful Cotswold village of Chedworth near Cirencester, not far from his own and the Robbins' grandparents' homes. Ann-Eliza was a true Horrocks and her strong, matter-of-fact character carried her through this distressing period in her life. She was determined that her children should not fall behind in their lessons, and undertook teaching them herself. Percy would soon be going to school and needed to be coached to reach the required standard. She wrote to her niece Eliza 'you will be glad to know the schooling goes on very well. Percy and the children begin to reward me for the pains I take with them by improving quite as fast as I would expect. I never thought I was calculated for a schoolmistress, but it is by patience and perseverance that I have performed better than expected. Percy has now learned his Latin Grammar, writing accounts, Geography, spelling and so on ... he is a dear affectionate boy the image of his father whose memory seems more dear to me than ever'.

In the background, supporting her during these years was young Cornelius Pitt, son of her husband's friend Joseph Pitt. Cornelius, who had been an Oxford friend of her nephew Peter Horrocks, was devoted to the young family, and had always been a welcome guest in their homes. His father, a very wealthy lawyer, was an executor of Robert Robbins' will, so would be aware of Ann-Eliza's reduced financial situation. As MP for Cricklade he would no doubt also have known her brothers, Samuel who sat in Parliament as member for the town of Preston, and John who had held the seat until his death. When Cornelius informed him that he had fallen in love with Ann-Eliza and intended to marry her he reacted angrily and forbade him to continue the courtship. Mrs Robbins, five years older than his younger son and with five young children, although accomplished and still beautiful, was not at all the bride he had visualised for him. Cornelius would not be swayed, despite his father's threats, and in May 1818 married Ann-Eliza. Immediately his father cut him off financially and refused ever to speak to him again. He would now have to make his own way in the world. To earn a living he was induced to enter the church, and was taken

The Norman Church of St Andrew, Chedworth, Gloucestershire where Rev.
Cornelius Pitt was curate from *c.* 1818 to 1830. His wife Ann-Eliza (Horrocks) died in
1825 and is probably buried in the churchyard.

on as curate by the local vicar at Chedworth. The stipend was a mere
pittance but Cornelius became friendly with Lord Stowell whose brother
gave him a second position as rector of nearby Hazelton Church. During
the early years of their marriage the couple experienced poverty for the first
time in their lives, and the demands on their meagre income were increased
by the birth of two more children, Joseph in 1818 and Henrietta Sarah in
1820.

Their grandfather was a man of great wealth and yet he did not know
his new grandchildren. He did nothing to help them, though his landhold-
ings included about a dozen Church of England 'livings', any of which
could have provided a good income for his son. Joseph Pitt's own childhood
had been lived in poor circumstances in Little Whitcombe village. He would
go from there into Cirencester to hold gentlemen's horses for a penny, and
was noticed by a solicitor who rescued him and educated him in the legal
profession (in the same manner that John Horrocks had been educated by
the mill-master, in Edgworth). Rev. Thomas Witt, a contemporary of his
son Cornelius at Oxford, wrote: 'his enterprise as attorney, banker, speculator
in land and many other ways of gaining or losing fortunes have been
eminently successful and have elevated him to a very prosperous situation

in life.' One of these enterprises was the proposed scheme to build at Cheltenham a magnificent estate of over 500 houses in beautiful parkland and gardens, to be called Pittville. The centrepiece was to be a magnificent, palatial 'Pump Room' overlooking an ornamental lake, and a church would be built for the residents and visitors to the Spa. Joseph Pitt, after rejecting his son, lived to reap his just rewards. In later years the development of Pittville foundered. He fell deeply in debt and died in 1860 owing over £150,000.

In 1824 when the youngest of her seven children was about four years old Ann-Eliza was taken ill. Her doctor did not seem able to diagnose the problem which incapacitated her and was gradually worsening. Cornelius was distraught as she became wracked by pain which weakened her and confined her to bed. At the same time he received the news that their niece Jane Monkhouse's husband, Thomas had died of pulmonary consumption. In a letter of condolence to John Monkhouse on 2 March 1825 he wrote, 'I have not been able to mention this to my dear wife who is in a sad and dreadful state of pain. We are looking forward in the hopes that her extreme suffering may be a prelude to the disorder yielding, so says our medical adviser, but God only knows the result.' Sadly there was to be no 'yielding of the disorder' and Ann-Eliza lived only for another four months. She died on 6 July 1825. Once again one of the brightest lights of the Horrocks family was prematurely extinguished. Cornelius Pitt was left alone to rear his large family. Five years later in 1830 Rev. Thomas Witt again referred to him in his diary describing him as 'a shrewd and intelligent man', 'a good man and a worthy magistrate'. By then Pitt was also serving a third parish as Curate of Notgrove. His three churches were all ancient foundations situated in the beautiful Cotswold uplands near Cirencester. (A bell ringer's notice signed by him in 1831 still hangs in St Andrews' Church, Chedworth).

At some time in the 1830s the years of estrangement between Joseph Pitt MP and his son ended. The two were reconciled and Cornelius accepted the living of St Peter's parish Rendcomb, which was in his father's gift. The parishioners, however, were unhappy at his appointment and objected strongly to having a vicar imposed upon them by this 'wealthy upstart'. When Cornelius and his seven children arrived at Rendcomb they found the church and vicarage gates securely locked against them, and had to bring a locksmith to remove the padlocks. It did not take long however for the parishioners to realise their mistake, for Cornelius was a good man and became an exemplary vicar.

In the year 1834 after his five Robbins stepchildren had reached the age of twenty-one they were each paid out £1500 from their natural father's estate. This was money which had accrued from the marriage dowry left to their mother by her older brother John Horrocks MP of Preston at his death in 1804. Cornelius Pitt served Rendcomb parish well until his sudden death when on his parish rounds in 1840. It had been his hope that young Joseph would succeed him as vicar at Rendcomb, but at his death his son had not finished his studies; so the post was left unfilled until he was ordained two or three years later. In 1846 Joseph married a vicar's daughter, Barbara Strange. Their only child died in infancy. His fourty-four years of service to St Peter's parish proved to be golden years in the development of the church. He built a parish school, installed a church organ and replaced the roof of the chancel with the present carved one. At the age of sixty-nine, Joseph Pitt retired as vicar of Rendcomb and lived for six more years at Torquay. He died in Buxton in May 1893 and is commemorated by a brass plaque in the church at Rendcomb which is now part of a public school.

None of the sons born to Ann-Eliza and Robert Robbins had children. William became a General in the Indian Army. Percy had an adventurous career in the Foreign Office as a Queen's Messenger delivering 'bags' to embassies all over the world. George lived all his adult life in Gloucestershire, first at Chedworth and later at Clay Hill. He married a widow, Josephine Stewart of Tenby in Wales. Their sisters Caroline (Robbins) and Henrietta (Pitt) very wisely kept in touch with the Preston relatives. How pleased would their mother and her brother John have been, could they have known this. For in 1844 and 1845 the sisters married the two Miller brothers, Thomas (junior) and Henry, both partners in the Preston business. Their first cousin Sam Horrocks had earlier married the Millers' eldest daughter Eliza, and was now the head of Horrocks, Miller & Co. When he died the following year aged forty-nine, Thomas Miller stepped into his shoes as sole proprietor of the company, with the founder's niece as his wife.

Elizabeth, the other daughter of Anne-Eliza Horrocks and her first husband Robert Robbins, who was born after her father's death, followed her sisters to Preston. She married her first cousin Walter Whitehead, ship's captain of the East India Co. He was the son of her mother's sister Mary and John Whitehead, partner in Horrockses. They produced several children and grandchildren who lived in the town of Preston.

CHAPTER 3

Samuel Horrocks MP
of Lark Hill (1766–1842)

When John Horrocks died unexpectedly in 1804 he left his older brother
Samuel in charge of his business empire 'Horrocks & Co.' (always known
and referred to as 'Horrockses'), and also one of the legal guardians of his
two sons. At this crucial turning point in his life thirty-eight year old Samuel
was living in his beautiful home in Frenchwood with his wife Alice and
their eight children. Unlike John, who had moved out of Preston over the
River Ribble to Penwortham, his brother chose to build his house very close
to the location of their factories. When Frenchwood Mill was being erected
in 1795 he had begun to purchase land on the same south-facing hillside,
known for centuries past as 'Albyn Hey' on the eastern side of Swillbrook
Lane. (This lane, now Manchester Road, is thought to follow the route of
the Roman road north from Walton-le-Dale). The Swillbrook, which formed
the boundary between Preston and Fishwick Township, ran diagonally
through the valley site on its way to the Ribble. At that time there was no
habitation south of Church Street in Preston, much of the area around
Grimshaw Street was common land consisting of water-willow fields.
Frenchwood House, built by the Starkie family of Huntroyde, Padiham,
stood alone on the southernmost ridge overlooking the Ribble, and Walton
Flats. Around 1794 Thomas Starkie, who had bought the land from the
Dunkenhalgh Estate, Burnley, sold part of the Albyn Hey plot to three
builders, Timothy Wren and William Corry, joiners, and a plumber and
glazier named Seth German. They built two houses there, Albyn Bank
House on the eastern side, and a mansion at the top of Swillbrook Brow
for Samuel Horrocks.

For a description of this house, which he called 'Lark Hill', we must
move forward to the year 1859 when the Horrocks family sold Lark Hill
and the sales papers described the property: 'A substantial brick building
elegantly proportioned, the entrance through a handsome gateway flanked
by a pair of postern lodges'. A sweeping drive led to the entrance through
a Doric portico enclosed and fitted as a conservatory. Its windows were of
stained glass in brilliant hues with heraldic designs. The mahogany front

Samuel Horrocks MP
(1766–1842) of Lark
Hill, Preston, brother of
John Horrocks MP.
Portrait by Lonsdale.
(*Harris Museum and Art
Gallery*)

Below Preston in 1774
before John Horrocks
built his cotton mills on
Town End Croft.
Samuel Horrocks
purchased the shaded
area, Albyn Hey, for his
Lark Hill home.
Opposite in the meadow
across Swillbrook Lane
was built Frenchwood
Mill. (*Redrawn from
George Lang's map*)

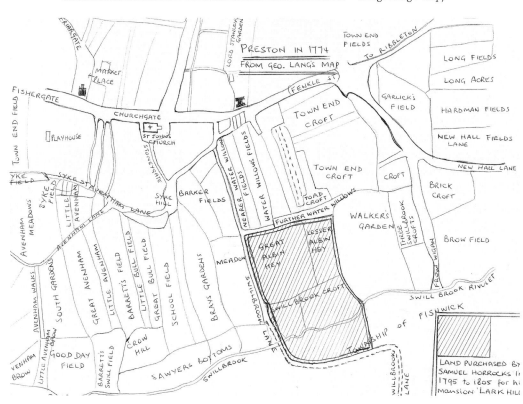

Lark Hill House from the south, drawn by James Foreman for the
Lonsdale Magazine 1821.

door opened on to a large vestibule decorated in classical style with fluted columns and ornamental friezes. This entrance was dismantled in 1893 and rebuilt on the south-facing wall. A suite of elegant apartments on the ground floor faced south overlooking the distant country scene. The principal dining room was the largest with a semi-circular bay and mullioned windows. Its walls were finished with stucco cornices, paper hanging, gilt mouldings and a marble fireplace. Next door was the library and audience room in similar style and on the far side a smaller dining room and private door to the garden. Opposite across the hall was a side entrance to the house through a gateway and a flight of stone steps into a vestibule. Domestic rooms were beyond to the left and then the back stairs and servants' hall. A 25-foot square kitchen completed the ground floor rooms. Back stairs led to a spacious basement containing a bakery with brick-built ovens, ale and beer cellars, bottling rooms, four large wine vaults and a coal cellar with air-heating apparatus for the whole house.

On the first floor a handsome landing was lighted from the roof by a stained glass skylight. Off this was the most splendid room in the house – the drawing room with its treble mullioned windows opening on to a wrought-iron balcony (this is now the office of the Principal of Cardinal Newman College). The view to the south from this room was beautiful – open countryside to the distant vista of Hoghton Tower, Rivington Pike,

55

Cuerdale and the hills beyond. On this floor were four principal bedrooms, four dressing rooms and bathrooms each with plunge and shower, and three small bedrooms. Off the rear landing was the chambermaid's room and a water-closet. A narrow staircase went up to the servants' quarters in the attics, nine bedrooms off a well-lighted corridor. An outlet to the roof led to a small fitted observatory.

Behind the house were extensive outbuildings containing a brew-house, dairy, fitted washhouse with copper boilers, laundry and drying rooms; also a well-built heated conservatory 30-feet long with a mushroom house, peach house and fitted toolrooms. On the north side of the house was the stableyard with stalls for eleven horses and two substantial brick-built buildings with slate roofs. One was the coach house big enough to take eight carriages, the other contained the harness room and a high loft for hay and straw. All the buildings[18] in the cobbled stableyard were built of the best available materials. There was a wooded copse to the south west of the house which screened the grounds from Frenchwood Mill opposite, and fell steeply from the lane down to the brook. In May 1803 Samuel bought this one acre plot for £325 from Joseph Myers of Brockhole.

Lark Hill was a palatial home indeed befitting the new head of Horrocks & Co. as he took over at the Counting House. Before him lay the daunting task of managing the ten mills and numerous warehouses, weaving sheds

The site of Horrockses Head Office at 9 Bread Street London for over fifty years from 1805. Now occupied by the Bank of England.

and depots scattered throughout Lancashire, where 3,000 'hands'[19] earned their livelihood. Within weeks the surprising invitation was extended to him by Preston Corporation that he should replace his brother in Parliament. There was no hesitation in his response, and leaving his wife and children behind, off he went to London, as John had done so optimistically only two years earlier. He would open a new head office there, leaving John Whitehead and Thomas Miller in charge in the North. The arrangement proved successful. With Samuel away in London, establishing the new head office at 9 Bread Street Cheapside (with living quarters above) the two men became very competent managers. In the years until Whitehead's death in 1810 they produced an average 6 per cent return on capital. Profits were divided 9/20th each to Samuel and his young nephew John Horrocks Junior, and 2/20th between Whitehead and Miller.

These men lived 'on the job' in good houses at Moss Mill and the Yard factory. In 1810 John Bairstow, one of John Horrocks's first apprentices, was brought from the Bolton warehouse to replace Whitehead in the partnership. He became active and prominent in the company, and in the town of Preston.

Parliamentary records show that Samuel Horrocks became a Member of Parliament on 17 March 1804 and represented Preston for twenty-two years during which time he never lost an election and the unique Horrocks/Derby coalition survived. It was written of him, however, that 'he proved to be little more than a cypher in Parliament and gained the reputation of being a "silent member"'. His opponents at elections seized upon this as a subject for jibes and doggerel against him. He was nicknamed Sam O'Horrocks as 'he said nothing' and a long-standing joke told how a street hawker in Preston peddled 'copies of his speech' which proved to be a blank piece of paper, given away with the comment 'Wha, he said Nowt'. More seriously charges were levelled against him that he paid his weavers insufficient wages – seven shillings a week in 1807 – which he ascribed to 'the dislocation of the cotton trade by commercial warfare'. An independent candidate denounced him as 'a supine supporter of three successive administrations, an ill-educated man with no skill in parliamentary affairs'. In the 1812 election he boasted 'I can act as independent a part as any man in Parliament' and certainly did not always toe the party line. This could have been due to the influence of the Stanley coalition or that he did not have a strong leaning towards any party's policies. But that sentence seems to have been his only recorded public utterance in his constituency. We are left with scant records of a long parliamentary career.

Details of his voting are brief:

1805 8 April: Against the Censure of Melville, but;
1805 12 June: For his criminal prosecution.
1806 30 April: For the repeal of the Additional Force Act.
Numbered by Ministers among the staunch friends of slave trade abolition.
1809 15 & 17 March voted against the Government on the Duke of York scandal.
1809 25 April: Against on Castlereagh's alleged Electoral Corruption
1810 For in the Walcheren Inquiry.
1811 21 January: Against on a clause of the Regency Bill.
1813 24 May: Opposed Catholic Relief.
1815 10 March: Against the Corn Bill.
1817 17 February: For the salary of the Secretary of the Admiralty.

The General Election of 1807 brought an independent candidate forward in the hope of breaking the Preston coalition, which had existed since 1802. Colonel Joseph Hanson, the son of a Manchester merchant, was politically active and popular with the textile workers. His presence at the hustings led to riotous confrontations in which a man was killed. He had failed to be elected in two previous attempts at Chester and Stafford; nor was he to succeed at Preston, although the poll was kept open for twelve days. He retired on the eleventh day after receiving 1,001 votes, and this number was taken up as a slogan by the political groups of the Independent party. '1001' was painted on the walls in Preston and used as a 'toast' for years afterwards. One of Hanson's supporters wrote a 'Squib' in the local newspapers likening the hustings to a horse race.

Samuel Horrocks was described as 'the Corporation's strong built horse Sam. Being in very good condition it is still supposed he will make a good start. He was got by that well known sleek horse, Alderman out of Bribery and Corruption. He is brother to Peculation who rode so hard in 1802 against the town and trade of Preston (i.e. his brother John Horrocks). Riders colour blue'. Hanson, defeated, returned home to Manchester where in the following year he was imprisoned and fined £100 for allegedly inciting weavers to riot.

Before the next election in 1812 Joseph Hanson died, but his brother Edward came to Preston to stand as Independent candidate. The campaign was turbulent and lasted for eight days. Much of the canvassing was done around the town's alehouses where barrels of beer were provided by the candidates. When the opposing factions met, tempers ran high and violence erupted. On the evening of the seventh night of the poll, Hanson's supporters gathered in London Road and advanced along Queen Street to Lark Hill.

Windows were broken in the Horrocks house and windows of the Lodge, but no one was hurt. Samuel and his family were given a bad fright and took care not to put themselves at risk until the election was won. A family friend, Mrs Bishop of Rugby wrote to young Eliza 'I think Mr Horrocks' resolution of remaining at home these dark evenings is a wise one and I hope he will adhere to it. I saw in the paper that your house had been beset by the mob; you must all have been greatly alarmed.'

On the eighth day of voting the Coalition emerged the winners, taking four-fifths of the votes. Benjamin Shaw, a Preston weaver wrote in his journal that it was 'traditional for the winning candidates to ride through the town from barr to barr, all the while being fêted by the populace and distributing largesse in the form of celebratory drink'. After this they retired in the evening with their supporters to the Bull Hotel and the Red Lion Inn opposite for a victory dinner. But as the company left they were pelted with stones and mud by inebriated followers of the opposition. The poll cost the enormous sum of £5,670 for meeting rooms, bands, music, ribbons, orange and blue colours and a great quantity of alcohol. In December young Samuel wrote to his aunt, 'Thank goodness we are now delivered of our guard and my father's fears somewhat abated.'

There were obviously some debates during his parliamentary career which inspired contributions from Samuel Horrocks. In 1812 he was involved with a committee formed to consider a new Petition by the hapless Samuel Crompton who was still attempting to obtain remuneration for his invention of 'The Mule' spinning-machine (see John Horrocks' efforts in March 1803). At last a decision was made that the Government would pay Crompton a grant of £20,000. On 11 May 1812 the Prime Minister, Spencer Percival, saw him in conversation with Robert Peel outside the House of Commons and imparted the good news privately to them. By an incredible stroke of misfortune as he left them and went to enter the House the assassin Bellingham struck, and the Prime Minister was shot dead. The papers authorising Crompton's grant lay unheeded in his briefcase. Parliament was dissolved and, in the general confusion following, no action could be taken. Once again Crompton received nothing. Years later in 1826 a grant of £5,000 was paid to him, most of which had been used up in the expense of yet another appeal. He died an embittered and poor man in the following year.

Life at Lark Hill, 1804–1814

Shortly after Samuel Horrocks went to Parliament in 1804 fate struck him a cruel blow. He had left his family behind at Lark Hill where there was concern about his wife's health. As the months passed her condition did not improve so she was taken to Lytham to benefit from the clean sea air. Her home in Preston was in the centre of a group of cotton-mills where the atmosphere was heavily polluted by chimney emissions. In the summer her children and their governess joined her, and on 16 July her sister-in-law wrote optimistically. 'I believe she is much better now'. But she was dying, and lived for only another five days. Her body was brought back to Preston and laid to rest in St George's churchyard. The nature of her illness is not known but no doubt Samuel had been referring to his wife's indisposition when he wrote in a letter, from his brother John's deathbed four months earlier, 'This distressing circumstance together with the state of my own family is naturally very afflicting.' It is possible that Alice died after giving birth to a son who did not survive. There was only one boy in the family – seven year-old Sam; but when he died in 1846 a memorial plate described him as 'the only surviving son of Samuel Horrocks'. The Horrockses were a close family and rallied round to help with the motherless children. Samuel's sister Ann-Eliza, who was only four years older that her brother's oldest daughter, went to live at Lark Hill. An older lady Miss Bullock was engaged as housekeeper. With their father absent in London for long periods the children would in effect feel they had lost both parents. Ironically their cousins Peter and John were in the same sad situation following their father's sudden death and their mother's enforced isolation from them. Despite their great wealth the families of the two Horrocks brothers were shattered, within a matter of months, by divorce and double bereavement. They would be affected for generations to come by these tragedies.

During the momentous early years of nineteenth-century England, Samuel Horrocks led a busy, fulfilled life. As Member of Parliament he was fêted regularly in Preston. Victories at sea and on land, the King's 50th Jubilee and birthdays, election successes, and other events were all celebrated in style. Sumptuous dinners became a feature of his life. Preston's winter 'season' following the January Horse Fairs saw him at all the social functions. A grand Masqued Ball in the Assembly Rooms was particularly enjoyed by his daughters, and remembered as a very jolly affair. In 1809 a dinner was given at the Bull Inn for the two MPs when '150 men sat down at table' This was arranged 'in appreciation of their conduct on the late enquiry respecting the Duke of York and Mrs Clarke'. (Both men had voted against a charge that Prince Frederick had connived with his mistress in accepting bribes for War Office posts and army commissions. He was cleared of the charge, but sanctioned by demotion from his army post.) Most of these gatherings were for men only, which suited Samuel well. He was never a 'ladies' man', but when a partner was needed, his beautiful young sister,

Section of Baines's survey map of Preston 1824. Lark Hill House with Frenchwood
Mill next to it can be seen to the south and Horrockses Yard Works off Stanley Street.

Ann-Eliza, was pleased to accompany him. She lived *en-famille* at Lark Hill until her marriage in 1807, after which her young nieces were regular visitors to her home in Lincoln's Inn Fields. They also travelled about the country visiting relatives and friends. Their father and his late brother, however, unlike most successful Georgian gentlemen, seem never to have taken holidays, and certainly never did the popular Grand Tour of the Continent. Occasionally, but rarely, Samuel visited the Lake District, particularly following the marriage of his daughter Jane to Thomas Monkhouse of Penrith. But most of his life was spent between London and Preston. His younger children were growing up under the care of a new housekeeper Mrs Mortimer, who came to Lark Hill from Canon Masters' family at Croston Rectory. Sam was sent to Eton College where he studied with the same tutor as the young Lord Stanley and his cousin Mr Hornby. They were good friends and became known as 'the three Lancashire boys'. This Christmas poem written out for his father in Latin, and a copperplate letter were kept by his sister Eliza:

'The Advent of Christ

Behold! Christ, who existed from the beginning, now visits earth;
Behold! He is here as a mortal, who hereto was God:
The minds of men now see clearly the words of the prophet,
"The virgin shall conceive, and will soon give birth."
Lo! The world's Saviour comes! The Son stands by
His mother, who never knew husband or companion,
Infant and Lord, this man from heaven come to intercede.
At once both feeble and mighty,
Surrenders to death, but we shall live in Him:
For he washes clean the penalty of our guilt, in his own blood'.

His sisters were well taught by governesses and music masters. The older girls probably went away to a school in the Bristol area of Gloucestershire, for their letters reveal that they had many friends thereabouts. Two separate descriptions by cousins tell us that they were all 'intelligent and talented', but also 'gay, restless and impulsive' (true 'Horrocks' characteristics as we find again and again in these chronicles). At home they lived under a disciplined routine. But when school terms ended the arrival of Sam from Eton and their cousins Peter and John transformed everything. The house was filled with noise and laughter as the boys organised rough and tumble games of blind-man's-buff, battledore and shuttlecock, hunt-the–slipper, and hide and seek. Provided that their father was away from home the seven girls gleefully joined in their lively adventures and pranks. The housekeeper

Miss Mortimer was 'a very prim stately old lady', methodical, keeping all in strict obedience. But she was quite unable to manage the teenage boys, who wilfully led her a dance. Sometimes their jokes were carried too far as niece Celia tells us: 'One evening it was getting late and time to dress for dinner, when their father would be returning from his counting house. After a game of hide and seek Peter was nowhere to be found. Miss Mortimer gave the order "Young ladies, retire to your rooms." The stately old lady went to hers, shut the door and was taking off her dress, when a figure suddenly sat bolt upright in her bed with her large frilled nightcap on its head calling out "Here I am!" She gave out a loud scream and rushed into the passage. Hearing it, her charges ran to her. The angry lady telling them of the unpardonable affront she had suffered, vowed she would inform their father. This formidable threat (they were all in awe of their father) so frightened them they went down on their knees begging her forgiveness. At length she relented, knowing how highly he disapproved of frivolity in anyone.'

The absence of frivolity in his family would make life easier for Samuel Horrocks, who instilled such awe in the youngsters. Celia remembered him as 'a thick-set strong man of middle height with large square head and face, solid looking. All this in unison with his slow, measured, calculating step and stern countenance; one mass of common sense without a spark of imagination, but industrious, persevering and courageous'. No doubt they all kept out of his way when he was displeased, as in May 1807 when during a dreadful storm huge hailstones shattered the glass in his greenhouses. Or as on the occasion an important letter containing £175 in banknotes went missing. It had been posted to him at the General Post Office in London but was lost or stolen in transit. Offers of a substantial reward failed to discover its whereabouts. Nor was he very amused at an episode which took place at the Counting-house; one of his apprentices discovered a pipe of fine port which the Master kept there ostensibly for visiting customers. He gathered some of his young workmates to come and taste the contents. In boring a hole in the cask they were disturbed and had to beat a hasty retreat. Fortunately a passing workman saw the red wine trickling down the wall and plugged the leak. Surprisingly they were not chastised by Samuel, once he satisfied himself that they had not diluted or otherwise harmed his precious port. Perhaps there was a 'spark of imagination' lurking somewhere behind that 'stern countenance', after all. There was an occasion when the Lark Hill household must have been sadly affected. One of their maids had a dreadful accident as she attempted to take down a large glass lamp to clean it. Unfortunately the suspending chain broke and the counterpoise, which weighed nearly thirty-five pounds, fell on her head. Her skull was fractured severely, and although every attention was given the poor girl died shortly afterwards.

Lark Hill House was always very special to Samuel Horrocks and much of his time was spent in extending its gardens and 'pleasure grounds'. At the end of 1804 he began negotiations to buy some land to the south-east of the house which would even up his estate into a roughly rectangular shape. The two-acre field called 'The Further Bridewell' stretched down the hillside, bounded at the bottom by the Swillbrook rivulet, and had been bequeathed by its owner, William Walton, to the Free Grammar School at Penwortham (now Hutton Grammar School). The trustees sold him the plot on 2 February 1805 subject to a ground rent of £20 per annum payable half-yearly on the feasts of St Martin the Bishop and Pentecost. The estate was now complete. Samuel, well pleased, set about landscaping the grounds and enclosing them by a stout brick wall around the perimeter. The hill south of the house was terraced, the slopes turfed and footpaths laid. The Swillbrook was reconstructed to form two decorative fishponds joined by a cascade waterfall and a metal bridge. Specialist trees and shrubberies were planted and a lawn and pleasure gardens around the house completed the transformation. (Most of this landscaping has survived for 200 years. One of the fishponds was filled in in the early 1900s to provide sports grounds, and the brook was culverted). Aunt Ann-Eliza wrote in 1805 to young Peter, 'You will scarcely know this place when you come home, your Uncle has made such improvements. But what do you think old Mr Starkie is going to do – to build a street from the bottom of the grounds to Walton – a great nuisance as it will hide the beautiful prospect from us'. Mr Starkie owned the Frenchwood House estate to the south of Lark Hill. The only through road until then had been a narrow pathway called Swillbrook Lane which wound its way past Lark Hill, and alongside the course of the brook, before turning right and descending the steep gorge through Mrs Walmsley's strawberry fields down to the river (now Manchester Road, Selbourne Street East, Bence Road, Strawberry Gardens and Swillbrook Lane).

There were other changes on the horizon, as the Horrocks children grew up and began to fly the nest. The first to leave, in 1812, was Eliza, the eldest daughter, who married Charles Whittaker of Simonstone Hall near Padiham. Her father, delighted by her choice of husband, made her a marriage settlement of £3,000. His first son-in-law, a charming man from a very old Lancashire family, was a graduate of Brasenose College Oxford and a captain in the Blackburn regiment of Local Militia. The bride was twenty-one years old when the wedding took place at St John's Parish Church Preston on 20 January, witnessed by her cousin Peter, Dr William St Clare (the bridegroom's guardian) and Nicholas Grimshaw the Mayor. The young

Preston Parish Church of St John, 1796, an engraving from an original drawing by
W. Orme. This tower was pulled down in 1814. The church was rebuilt in 1853.
(*Published in 'Records of Preston Parish Church', Harris Reference Library*)

couple moved into their new home 'Roefield', a grey stone house owned
by the Whittaker family on the river bank at Edisford Bridge Clitheroe.
The house became a haven for Eliza's family who were introduced to
many of the gentry of the Ribble valley and East Lancashire by their brother-
in-law.

Eliza was a prolific correspondent and some of her letters and replies
still exist. From them we discover a little about life at Lark Hill in those
years. The only son Sam[20] had been taken to London by his father as a
young boy, and after two years at Mr Pearson's preparatory school in Parson's
Green was educated at Eton College. He then started work with his father
at the Bread St Office and would meet his sisters at their Aunt Ann-Eliza's
house in Lincoln's Inn Fields. He became the family's 'errand boy' in
London and was kept busy collecting their purchases and sending 'the Box'
back to Preston on the Post Coach. In August 1814 he wrote: 'The tea is

at last packed off … the late arrivals from India will probably make some alterations in the price. I could not have sent you but a small quantity. The next you have will I expect be cheaper. Kerfoot has transmitted to Preston a copy of what has been advanced for you in London:

16 May 1814	Cash	£5 0s. 0d.
	A pair of hats	£0 13s. 6d.
29 June	A hat	£1 10s. 0d.
	2 Fans	£1 14s. 6d.
August	Tea	£5 12s. 0d.

Miss Ridley, their London dressmaker, was employed to make outfits in the latest fashions as were Soames the shoemaker and André the hatter in Bond Street. After the girls had returned home the arrival of the London coach carrying the box of purchases was awaited with eager anticipation. No doubt their appearance at St John's Parish Church, Preston wearing the latest creations would cause quite a stir in the congregation. Their new dresses were of the lightest and flimsiest lawns and muslins, high waisted and worn with straw bonnets and velvet pelisses (capes). But such fashions did not come cheap.

'I expected my bill from Miss Ridley to be about £20 and it amounted to £49 18s. 6d., literally for nothing but making-up things – except for my white satin and primrose slip. I think Sarah and Jane's bills will be trimmer'.

From their letters and other writings we know that the Lark Hill kitchen larders were well stocked and the family kept a good table. Preston market was one of the best in the country. Local market gardeners, farmers from the Fylde and Ormskirk, and fishermen's wives from Fleetwood and Lytham sold their top quality produce from its stalls. Sugar and other imports were bought wholesale at Liverpool Docks. Tea from London, an expensive luxury, was stored with care in locked, lead-lined boxes. Salmon was plentiful, fished from young Eliza's husband's stretch of the river at Edisford Bridge. When guests were entertained more exotic dishes were served in the beautiful dining room. Aunt Eliza wrote, 'I believe you have been dining on turtle, and much grouse is being directed to you. Such rich foods are not good for you!' No doubt there was plenty of home-brewed ale and beer too.

In later years Samuel bought his own farm which would supply all their meats, dairy products and vegetables. After the laying-out of Moor Park c. 1834 superfluous land on Preston and Fulwood Moors was offered for sale. He acquired an established farm of 45 acres just outside the town's northern boundary and put in a tenant farmer, Robert Robinson. (Horrockses Farm after 1850 became the site of the Freehold Land Development's

Albyn Bank House, adjoining Lark Hill House. Built *c.* 1800 by Messrs Wren, Corry and German, and purchased from Preston surgeon Edward Tomlinson in 1833 by Samuel Horrocks. Now the St James' Arts Centre of Cardinal Newman College (so named to commemorate the years when it was the Vicarage of St James' Church, Avenham Lane).

'Fulwood Park'. Its old barn still stands on Victoria Road, now part of Christ Church buildings. An inscription 'Cadley and Fulwood school' recalls the years when it was used as a school).

Among Eliza's letters is a rare one from her grandmother Jane Horrocks, well-written in her own hand. In it she refers to the premature death of Robert Robbins her son-in-law:

Edgworth, 2 March 1814

Dear Eliza

In obedience to your request we hand you these few lines to let you know how we are both going on, and are thankful in saying we are as well as can be expected, considering the severe weather which has been experienced here. Your Grandfather has not been quite so well this last fortnight, and for some days he has not ventured to go out of doors. But if the weather will be a little warmer, he is in hopes he can go out again. We hope both you and Mr Whitaker are well. We

Vale House, Bradshaw, built by John Horrocks (Senior) in 1805, and occupied after his death by Henry Horrocks, manager of nearby Stone Mill.
(*Published by kind permisssion of the owner*)

received on Monday last a letter from Sam Horrocks announcing to us the melancholy account of Mr Robbins' death, which we can assure you has given us a great deal of trouble and concern, as the loss of a husband is almost irreparable, but we must all submit to the will of the Almighty, give our best love to all friends and accept the same yourselves,

who are, yours very affectionately,

J. & J. Horrocks.

P. S. Your grandmother Duckworth is very well.

The grandparents, John and Jane Horrocks lived at 'Vale House' in Edgworth, a fine stone house they built in 1805. John helped James Booth, manager of the cotton spinning at 'Stone Mill' owned by his son Samuel. After his death in March 1816 a cousin, Henry Horrocks, took over as mill manager and moved into Vale House with his wife Mary-Ann. Grandmother Jane lived with them until her death in 1822. Stone Mill, the birthplace of Horrockses' textile business, was extended over the years and remained in the family's ownership until 1869 when it was bought and demolished by

Messrs. Barlow and Jones. On the site they built New Vale Mill. In 1823 a report on Stone Mill, made after the First Factories Act, said that the building was very clean and well-ventilated, much more healthy than other mills inspected, and that the 100 employees worked 11½ hours per day (about normal at that date).

The two decades between 1810 and 1830 saw a vital period of expansion by Horrockses, when foundations were laid for the vast overseas trade which would make theirs the greatest name in cotton in the world. The first foreign agency was opened in Portugal in 1823, followed by India in 1830, and by the end of their first century of trading Horrockses products would be exported to every country worldwide. The London agent William Bowman who developed the Far East trade was rewarded for his phenomenal success by a partnership in 1845.

To accommodate the huge numbers of workers needed to produce cotton goods, thousands of houses were built around the mills for cheap rental. Horrockses houses were generally well built although small, but other mills were springing up all over Preston. There were no building or public health

Yard Factory, Horrocks Miller & Co. published by Rock & Co., London, in 1855.
(*From Hardwick's History of Preston*)

Interior of Yellow Mill 1864 (*Story of Horrockses*)

controls, and the houses were soon being shoddily produced of poor quality materials. They were usually in long terraced rows following the lines of the narrow field sites. Some of the houses with two rooms upstairs and two rooms downstairs were built back-to-back with the only entrance through the front door. Others had small unhygienic yards behind the houses, containing an earth closet and ashpit. Very few had drains or a water supply and there was no sewerage system.

These primitive, unhealthy conditions inevitably brought great problems. Water had to be carried in pails from the town's wells, or bought from travelling water-carts. Many of the new families were country people who kept a pig or some poultry in their back yards and fed them on scraps of food and rubbish. The cellars in some of the older houses, which had been built for handloom weavers, were soon housing whole families. In the streets near to Samuel Horrocks' Lark Hill home (Duke Street, Leeming Street, King Street, Vauxhall Road, Paradise Street) 1835 records give details of such cellar-dwelling families. Wages were low and hours of work very long. To bring in a little more money children as young as six or seven were expected to work a full day at the mill with their parents. These appalling conditions continued unaltered for most of the century. In 1842, the year of Samuel Horrocks' death, the Rev. John Clay made a 'Report on the sanitary conditions of Preston' which revealed that the life expectancy

Illustration from Horrockses' booklet 'The Test of Time' from the nineteenth century.

HORROCKSES'
LONG CLOTHS & SHEETINGS

of the poorest class of Prestonians, due to their squalid living conditions, had fallen to a mere eighteen years (against the forty-nine years of the wealthier residents). Evidence of this could not be seen more touchingly than in the family journal kept by Benjamin Shaw, a poor working man whose adult life revolved round Horrockses mills at the beginning of the nineteenth century. When the journal was published in 1991 as Vol. CXXX of the Record Society of Lancs and Cheshire, the editor Dr Alan G. Crosby wrote, 'Benjamin Shaw is one of the few genuinely working-class autobiographers before the age of universal elementary education ... his learning acquired by his own efforts.'

In this extract Benjamin refers to his second son, William (punctuation has been added for clarity). William Shaw, son of Benjamin and Betty Shaw was born 29 July 1791 at No. 1 Dale Street near to John Horrockses' new Yard Factory. 'He was sent to the factory young and wrought in the Yard at Horrocks in the Card room.' When he was fourteen his father 'would gladly have got him a trade ... but trade was bad and we could not ... so we agreed with Edward Salisbury [at No 10 Dale Street] to learn him to weave ... Soon after, he went to New Preston to learn his Bisiness out etc. [i.e. to Horrockses weaving sheds]. He continued at this place many years. In July 1826, 'weaving has gone very Bad of late years and is now so Bad a man cannon get scarse a living, without a family etc, William is now in Horrockses factory, overlooking the drawing frames ... this is a little better wages. He has now 5 children and the wife is near her time of another'. The entry for 1830 records 'this year our William Shaw died, rather suddenly; he had been ill long but not so but he went to work. [i.e. not too bad to work] He was ill the last winter and in this spring was in the Dispensary long but got no better, he coughed much and was hoarse and short of breath and weak but was much better when warm than cold, and his room where he wrought was warm. He continued to go to work until the last

Photograph of 1913 model of Horrockses factories at Yard Works, Stanley Street, Preston (now the site of Homebase). In the centre is the house and garden which John Horrocks gave to Thomas Miller Senior when he made him a partner in the Company in 1801. (*Harris Museum and Art Gallery*)

Workers leaving Horrockses Yard Works in 1913. Notice the large number of young employees, and the typical Lancashire clogs and shawls worn by the older women.

week of his life for he had 7 children most of them small and was poor and afraid of loosing his work. He continued as long as he could, for on the last day he was obliged to be carried home, he died at 2 o'clock on 17 October and was Buried the 19th at St Pauls church near his mother ... William Shaw was about 5 foot high and had he been in good circumstances might have been a stout man, but he was poor and had to live upon a little. He was dark complexioned, rather crock-kneed, was a plain man, simple and honest, well meaning man, he enjoyed but little of this world's good, wrought hard; lived poor and died without much attention from doctors or others. He has left 7 children, he was 35 years and 3 months old' (and at the time of his death was living in Thomas Street Preston).

In contrast, Samuel Horrocks lived to the ripe old age of seventy-six due to his healthy and better living standards but also thanks to a certain amount of good luck, for in 1823 he survived an attempted murderous attack. He was described about that time as 'a worthy man of charitable and humane disposition and much respected by all who knew him'. This respect was evidently not shared by a poor young Prestonian called Andrew Ryding who in April 1823 wrote to him, anonymously from Manchester, 'Sir, If you do not advance the wages of the cotton spinners at least 20 per cent you may expect your life to be taken by a cotton-spinner from Manchester. You was the cause of the falling of wages, in Preston spinners are working more than 20 per cent under Manchester and I understand the spinners at Bolton and their Masters are at difference about dropping the wages there. The Masters offer them more than you give but I hope they will be obliged to give them the same as they had before. There are many cotton masters deserve to lose their lives, but you are it is said, and I believe it to be true, the worst of them all, therefore your life must go first and the rest in rotation'.

Ryding attempted to carry out this threat on Sunday 27 July. Samuel Horrocks had attended morning service at Preston parish church, and afterwards strolled along Church Street to pay a call on his friend and partner, Thomas Miller. The house was in Golden Square, near Stanley Street, and in front of it was a gravelled coach road closed off by a gate. He had entered this area when he felt a blow to the top of his head, and thought something had fallen off the house. But he then received another tremendous blow on the back of his head. When he turned he saw a man about to strike him again with an iron cleaver. A struggle followed in which he was struck several more blows about the arms, before he managed to knock the cleaver from the man's hands and bystanders detained him. Dr St Clare attended to Samuel's injuries and found a severe wound on the back of his head which had cut through to the outer plate of his skull. His arms and hands were also cut and bruised. Fortunately his top hat had prevented the head-blow from being fatal. Dr St Clare recognised the assailant as Andrew Ryding, a young man who had attended the Dispensary on the previous Thursday complaining of headaches and deafness and showing symptoms of venereal disease. Ryding was arrested by the constable and confined in the House of Correction. On the following day, Nicholas Grimshaw, Horrocks' solicitor, took the prisoner to Lark Hill to see the injuries he had inflicted. He was taken into the bedchamber, where Samuel lay on his bed with a white sheet, and covered by a white quilt. He said later, at his trial, that he thought the man was dead, for he had only ever seen a white sheet and bedcover used when a corpse was 'laid out'.

Samuel made a good recovery from his injuries, and was present at Lancaster on Monday 18 August when Ryding was tried, before Mr Justice

Bayley, for attempted murder. His counsel told the court that the prisoner, who was twenty-two years old, lived with his parents in a very poor home in Mount Pleasant, near Marsh Lane, Preston. The prisoner's mother told the court that her son had been a wanderer, moving from job to job and from town to town. He suffered badly from headaches and deafness, and had been trying unsuccessfully to get into the 'House of Recovery' for treatment. He had been behaving irrationally before the murder attempt, and had not been able to sleep. Ryding spoke in his own defence and appeared 'articulate beyond his station in life', although his evidence was rambling and at times irrelevent. He said he had planned for two years to harm Mr Horrocks or Mr Miller. He thought that 'they were the instigators at the recent "Lock-out" in conspiring with the other mill owners to lay-off and sack the workers and reduce their pay-rates'.

The jury returned a verdict of 'Not guilty on the grounds of insanity', and the judge ordered the prisoner to be detained in custody at Lancaster

Mount Pleasant Street, Preston. Built by Horrockses with cellars for handloom weavers *c.* 1796 (now demolished). Andrew Ryding, imprisoned for the attempted murder of Samuel Horrocks in 1823, lived here. (*Harris Reference Library*)

prison, at the pleasure of His Majesty, to prevent him doing any further mischief. Family letters from that time include two from Robert Peel, the Home Secretary, reassuring Samuel that his assailant would be securely imprisoned at Lancaster with no possibility of escape. Another, from Sam Horrocks (junior) tells how he often visited Ryding in prison before the trial. He found him 'anxious to converse on all aspects of the melancholy event' but showing no remorse for his actions. He insisted that he had planned the attack alone without accomplices, and had never been employed at Horrockses Mills. A sad postscript to this unhappy episode is an entry in the Preston parish church register recording that Andrew Ryding died and was buried on 19 June 1825, just two years after the attack.

The Horrockses were soon able to turn their attentions to happier events, for there was a succession of weddings at Lark Hill in the years 1824–25. Two of the sisters were already married, Eliza, the eldest to Charles Whittaker of 'Roefield' near Clitheroe in 1812. Jane, the third in age, married in 1820 Thomas Monkhouse a close relative and friend of William and Mary Wordsworth. Following this marriage William Wordsworth took to visiting Lark Hill when he was passing through Preston en route to the south of England (e.g. January 1824: 'We are going to Coleorton [in Leicestershire] ... on Wednesday we take the coach for Preston and shall halt one day at Mr Horrocks' wrote Dorothy Wordsworth).

In one year, four of the five remaining daughters all left home. First in November 1824 Susannah aged twenty-four married the Rev. Thomas Raven, curate of St John's Parish Church Preston where the following weddings took place:

Also in November 1824: Mary to Rev. William Birkett of Clitheroe, curate at S. Tawton, Devon;

May 1825: Alice (aged twenty-five) to Rev. James Streynsham Masters of Croston, Vicar of Chorley;

December 1825: Sarah (aged thirty-two) to the family's doctor William St Clare (Junior), a well-known Prestonian living at No 3 Fishergate Hill.

In marrying, Dr St Clare won for his friend Alderman Miller a wager which had been made lightheartedly amongst a group of men probably at a meeting of the 'Parched Pea and Oyster Club' on 25 November of that year. The prize was a 'rump and dozen' to be provided by Mr George Sidgreaves (probably a joint of beef and twelve bottles of ale). The bet was that Sidgreaves would 'enter into the Holy state of Matrimony before Dr St Clare'. Witnesses to the wager were the Mayor Alderman Newsham, Mr Marshall, Rev. Robert Harris, Lt. Col. Hulton, Messrs Bairstow, Lodge, Edmund Grimshaw and Dr Robinson.

The youngest daughter, Ann, aged twenty-three in 1825 and not in good health, lived at home with her father for the rest of his life. It is interesting to see that all but one of the daughters chose husbands with traditional professions. A dozen years earlier when the eldest daughter had pleased her father by marrying one of the 'landed gentry' Samuel Horrocks had provided a marriage settlement of £3,000. There were to be no (known) dowries for her sisters. Their niece Clara who knew them all well wrote on the subject, 'He was a hard man towards his married daughters, as well as to his son, in his money transactions towards them; their husbands at the time of their marriages being very poor. He gave each of his daughters the smallest of annual incomes.' Was he perhaps disappointed that none of them brought a man from the textile manufacturing world into his family to be useful in the business?

It is obvious that he was not enthusiastic about his son Sam's business ability. Poor Sam wrote in confidence to his friend John Monkhouse, 'You seem to attach considerable importance to my having at length seriously turned my attentions towards business. I trust it may prove so, but I will have to contend against so many obstacles both real and imaginary that discourage me no little. I am very far from wishing to throw blame upon my own father but I cannot help feeling, and also expressing to you, that my firm conviction is, were I the son of Mr Miller or any other partner I should be placed in a position of responsibility and have a position of confidence reposed in me which is at present denied ... I will endeavour however to prevent them finding fault with me. They expect me to obtain a knowledge of business by intuition as to any information I may pick up. I must not look to those I see daily at the counting house for it.' Referring to the influence of the Miller family he wrote, 'I am forcibly reminded of Mr Fox's East India Bill that the power of the Crown is increasing, has increased and ought to be diminished'.

John Monkhouse's family had an estate in Sebergham, Cumbria. Sam had purchased a small property at Kirkby Lonsdale and as such was a free-holder of Westmorland and permitted by Lord Lonsdale to shoot on his moors, with John Monkhouse and his brother Thomas. The three had been friends since 1816 when Tom took an apprenticeship in Preston.

On first impressions his father's reluctance to give him a proper job is surprising. Perhaps he thought him destined to become a gentleman having been educated at Eton and raised in a mansion by seven doting sisters. In contrast the Miller boys (although later 'finished' in Manchester and Paris) had lived in the mill manager's house in the tough environment of Horrockses Yard Works, and attended the Rev. Robert Cree's little school across the road in Church Street and Preston Grammar School, so they grew up well prepared for mill life. Nevertheless his father's attitude troubled Sam and caused his earlier envy of the Miller boys. (An advertisement in the *Preston Chronicle* of the time shows that Rev. Cree taught English, French, Greek and Latin Grammar, with Arithmetic, Geography, History, Natural Philosophy, and, 'other branches of useful and polite learning'. Fees for day scholars were six guineas, and £40 a year for the four boarders.)

Although much of Sam's life so far had been spent with the 'hunting, shooting and fishing' set of the Ribble valley at Browsholme, Downham, Hoghton, and at Inskip etc. he now began to be involved in more serious affairs. He followed his father into local politics and represented Fishwick ward on the town council. He became a Justice of the Peace, and in 1820 served as Bailiff to Thomas Miller during his Mayorship. In later years he was chosen to be Common-Council-man of the Borough and a Deputy Lieutenant of Lancashire.

He was very popular with his sisters and cousins, prompting Clara to recall, 'We loved our cousin Sam, he was very handsome. Like his father he had a fresh complexion, ruddy cheeks and large blue eyes'. Her sister Celia thought that 'totally unlike his father he was impetuous like the general race' [of Horrockses]. He was still a bachelor having made no progress in the pursuit of 'the amiable Miss Leighton' whom he greatly admired.

In January 1825 there was a surprising event in Sam's life which was revealed in his will after his death. At the age of twenty-eight he became the father of a daughter born out of wedlock. The mother of the child was a weaver who lived in the desparately poor and squalid Turk's Head Yard. Her home was a tiny terraced cottage in George's Court built next to a slaughter-house and old warehousing. The christening register at Preston Parish Church shows that the mother was Mary Standing and the baby was named Alice (the same name as Sam's deceased mother). He acknowledged the child to be his and probably supported her. In his will he left her £500, to be used 'towards her advancement in the world'.

No doubt Sam would be given a stern 'talking-to' by his father, and perhaps urged to settle down with a legitimate spouse. If so he took the advice to heart, for in September 1827 he married. Knowing his earlier opinions of the Miller family one is prompted to consider whether this was just a marriage of convenience uniting the two business families, for his bride was Eliza the daughter of Thomas Miller. While there is no evidence to confirm this view neither was there any previous suggestion of affection between the couple.

All that we know of Eliza at this time is a comment in a letter from William Wordsworth to his sister Dorothy in 1825. 'Reached Preston first and slept at S. Horrockses. Mrs St Clare was luckily away from home as also was the old gentleman. S's wife is a very pleasing woman and plays upon the harp power-fully. Her father, Miller, is a native of Whitehaven but of vulgar manners'.

Samuel Horrocks obviously approved the marriage and made a settlement of a £5,000 marriage bond on his son. Certain valuable properties in East Greenwich, London were also transferred to his ownership. They had been bought by his father in 1817 for £9,500 and were situate from Church Street to Brooks March and consisted of 'Messuages, tenaments, wharfs, lands, hereditaments and premises' (By 1846 they were bringing income of £707 15s. 9d. p.a.)

Nothing more is known of little Alice; but years later in 1861, when Sam's childless widow was living for a while at her brother-in-law's house, Pen-wortham Hall, the census records that one of the housemaids was named Mary Standing. Was this a coincidence or was Eliza Horrocks employing the mother of her husband's child? There were few other families in the Preston Index with the surname Standing.

The pattern of Horrocks/Miller marriages would continue nearly twenty years later, when two of the beautiful daughters of Samuel and John Hor-rocks' sister, Ann-Eliza, came from Gloucestershire to Preston to marry the Miller brothers Thomas and Henry.

Whereas the marriage of Sam and Eliza was childless Caroline and Henrietta produced ten children for the Miller family whose line continued down to the present day.

A third sister, another Eliza, also came to Preston and married Walter Whitehead, son of her mother's sister Mary, and John Whitehead partner in Horrocks & Co.

At the General Election of 1826 when he was sixty years old Samuel Horrocks decided not to seek re-election. He retired from Parliament and gave up his seat in the Commons. Preston Corporation appreciated his twenty-two years' service as MP for the town and invited his son Sam to replace him as candidate. Although honoured by the proposal Sam declined the offer, a wise decision for the election was hard fought and at times riotous. Again, as in the previous election of 1820, when the anti-coalitionists stirred up by the radical Henry Hunt had battled to break the status-quo, the military had to quell the anger of the mob. The Radicals, this time led by William Cobbett, entered the contest. Four of the eight candidates were soon eliminated. Large amounts of free alcohol were distributed to bribe the voters, and Cobbett, who came last in the poll, bragged that at least he had forced Stanley to part with a fortune to win his seat. The Whig, Hon. E. G. Stanley and Liberal John Wood were elected, bringing to an end the twenty-four years old Horrocks/Derby coalition.

This was the last election before the passing of the Catholic Emancipation Act. One of the candidates, Captain Barrie R. N. insisted that the Oath of Supremacy should still be taken by all voters. So the Catholic men of the town, as they had done for over 200 years, abstained from voting. It is not clear what Samuel Horrocks' stand was on this subject. Whilst he voted in Parliament against the Catholic Relief Bill of 1813, in Catholic Preston he was wise enough to keep out of church affairs.

He knew the value of education however and always supported the institution of new day and Sunday schools. In 1823 Horrocks & Co. paid for a school to be built at New Preston for 200 children and gave cottages for St Peter's and St Paul's parishes to use as Sunday schools. They also

Winckley Square, Preston, where Samuel Horrocks and Thomas Miller lived.

subscribed to the cost of three other schools, the National in Avenham Lane, St Wilfrid's (R.C.) and St Thomas's (C of E). In later years Horrocks & Co. gave land next to their mills for the site of St Saviour's parish school, off Queen Street. Many of the children in these schools would be his 'half-timers', who attended classes for half the day and worked in the factories for the remaining hours. In 1870 St Augustine's school log book recorded the entry of '70 new children, short-timers from Horrockses & Miller's factories and the following day more factory children came who had heard that they were [now] allowed to go to their own schools'.[21]

Child labour in factories was widespread in the Lancashire cotton industry. At Horrockses, 75 per cent of the workers were under eighteen years of age. In 1816 Robert Peel chaired a Parliamentary committee to investigate the conditions of child employment.

Samuel Horrocks wrote to his daughter Eliza, 'It is impossible to say when I may return into the country. Sir Robert Peel gives us much trouble, but I feel confident we can oppose him successfully.' Peel's new Bill was meant to control the use of labour in mills. Successive Factories Acts were passed over the years to regulate the ages of children in employment and their hours of work. But, as there was no provision for supervision of the system, few mill owners implemented the new rules. Families depended on the extra money their children brought in, so they continued to work long hours throughout the nineteenth century.

When he was sixty-seven years old in 1833 Samuel decided that the time had come for him to retire from active business and install his son his successor as proprietor of Horrockses. At the time of the handover, their factories had over 1,700 employees: spinning operatives 1300, weaving 400, dressing 22. These figures do not appear to include labourers, warehousemen, office staff and so on. There then only 30 firms in Lancashire employing over 500. Records of the company show that they were exporting textiles to Canton, Bombay, Calcutta, Ceylon, Manila, Mauritius, Singapore, Bolivia, Lima, Valparaiso, Havana and Lisbon. Capital was valued at £482,788.

On 3 June 1833 Samuel also resigned his seat on the Corporation of Preston. The members presented him with a fine silver box and scroll 'in appreciation of his public character and service to the town' (it is now in the Preston Exhibition in the city's Harris Museum). He continued to sit with his son as a magistrate on the town bench and on that of Amounderness Hundred. He was also a Guardian of the Preston Union of the Poor which supervised the local workhouses, and was a trustee of both Dr Shepherd's Library in Cross Street and of the Literary and Philosophical Society which met regularly in the Corn Exchange.

Moves had at last been made to provide essential public services to the town and Samuel invested money in two of the new companies involved. Years earlier Preston had been the first provincial town to be lit by gas following scientific experiments done by Professor Rev. Joseph Postlethwaite, a Jesuit priest at Stonyhurst College. When he gave a lecture on the subject at the Bull Inn in 1812 Father ('Daddy') Dunn of St Wilfrid's parish and Mr Isaac Wilcockson were stirred to introduce the new gas lighting in Preston's town centre. In February 1816 Messrs. Horrocks and Jacson's cotton mill was probably the first industrial building ever to be lit by a public gas supply and the Frenchwood and Church Street factories soon followed. Moons Mill in Walton-le-Dale had its own private supply in January 1816. William Taylor and a Mr Elsworth, engineers at Horrocks & Co., were actively involved in the installation and maintenance of gas pipes for many years in Preston town centre.

Lark Hill had some of the best greenhouses and conservatories in the district, and now that Samuel had some free leisure time he became Steward of the local Horticultural Society.

He was able to spend more time with his large family, but shortly after his retirement they were all shocked by the death of Jane who died of typhus fever in Clifton, Bristol. Samuel still had the company of his youngest, but ailing daughter Ann-Eliza, at home. Next door renting Albyn Bank House were Susannah and Rev. Thomas Raven with their young family. In 1833 Samuel bought this property, which stood within the perimeter of his Lark Hill Estate, from Edward Tomlinson, (a surgeon who founded the First Botanical Society of Preston). Sam and Eliza were in Winckley Square, not far from Sarah and Dr William St Clare at 4 Fishergate Hill. Eliza and Charles Whittaker had moved from 'Roefield' to the family seat, Simonstone Hall near Padiham. Further afield were Mary and Rev. William Birkett at Great Haseley Rectory near Oxford. Alice and Rev. James Master were at Chorley. Two of the family, Sam and Sarah were childless and Ann-Eliza was not married. Samuel always loved his mansion home and kept a full staff of servants and gardeners to maintain the house and grounds in good order. In his later years he and Ann-Eliza were cared for by ten resident staff. There were two manservants, William Lewis and James Livesey and three young female servants, Martha Lightfoot, Esther Artley and Nancy Lewis. The gardener, Henry Crossthwaite lived in the lodge with his young wife Eliza. In 1842 the Corporation elected Sam to the prestigious office of Guild Mayor. But sadly his father did not live to see the Guild Year. On 2 March 1842 Samuel Horrocks' long and active life came to an end. He died at Lark Hill at the age of seventy-six.

As the only son and heir much responsibility fell upon Sam's shoulders.

St Peter's Church, Great Haseley, where Rev. William Birkett, husband of Mary (née Horrocks) was vicar in the mid-nineteenth century.

He arranged the funeral and burial of his father at St George's Church, Preston where Samuel was laid to rest in the churchyard with his wife Alice.[22] There were no surprises in his father's will. The Lark Hill estate was bequeathed to Sam, on trust, for his lifetime. He also inherited all his father's other properties and assets outright and the residue of his estate. The surviving sisters were all well provided for, Sarah, Mary, Alice and Susannah each receiving a personal gratuity of £200 for the next four years: then with their husbands an equal share of £40,000 put into a trust to be paid out over ten years. Ann-Eliza the youngest and unmarried daughter, who did not long survive her father received £10,000 outright and an annuity of £200 for the next four years.

There had been changes in the management of Horrocks & Co. during Samuel's last years. In 1838 the founder's son, Peter Horrocks, was forced to withdraw from the partnership and paid out on his shares. In January 1840 Thomas Miller (Senior) died aged seventy-three years. For nearly forty years he had been Samuel Horrocks's business partner, right-hand man and good friend.

The Horrocks/Miller relationship had become very close. During the years when Samuel was away at Westminster Thomas Miller virtually ran the Lancashire mills. He also served Preston well as Magistrate and Alderman, and was three times elected Mayor of the town. He had well repaid John

The Rectory of St Peter's Church, Great Haseley. When Samuel Horrocks died in 1846 his sister Mary used some of her Horrocks inheritance to rebuild parts of the house. Her family crest crossed with that of the Birkett family was placed over the rear entrance. (*Published with the kind permission of the owner*)

Horrocks' early confidence in him, and become a wealthy man in the process. Since 1828 (following young Sam Horrocks' marriage to his daughter), Thomas Miller was the major shareholder, for Samuel Horrocks had then split his 9/20th share of the profits with his son, whereas Miller continued to draw his full 6/20th share until his death in 1840.

Samuel Horrocks Junior, 1842–1846

The year 1842 was an eventful one for forty-five year-old Sam Horrocks, as he and his wife left their Winckley Square home and took up residence at Lark Hill. There were no children of the marriage, so he thought it prudent to draw up his will, giving precise instructions as to the future of his father's mansion.

He was soon faced with problems in the town, the outcome of which affected him personally and caused him great distress. There had been a serious depression in the cotton industry for the past five years which badly hit the Preston mills, including Horrockses. Wages were cut, causing resentment among cotton workers across the whole of Lancashire. In August

St.George's Church pre-1850 with Samuel Horrocks' grave in the foreground
(*C. Hardwick*)

1842 the threat of further wage cuts brought the Manchester workers out on strike. Within a week the strike spread to all the north-west mill towns. In Preston there was already widespread discontentment. Handloom weavers' wages had been cut by 25 per cent and spinners by 10 per cent. Joseph Livesey, the moral reformer, wrote 'weavers are wandering about and willing to take work at any price. Everybody's spirits are down'. The local 'chartists' organised a meeting on the open ground called the Orchard on Friday 12 August and the decision was taken that Preston operatives would join the strike and withdraw their labour immediately.

On the following Saturday morning, 13 August 1842, there was a great disturbance in the town centre. Trouble had started at 6 a.m. when a militant group persuaded those arriving for the early shift at Catterall's mill to 'turn out' and join them in Fishergate. The militia had been forewarned and were waiting at the Bull Inn, Church Street whilst the Mayor, Samuel Horrocks, discussed the situation with the police and magistrates. Men of the 72nd Division of Highlanders armed with long muskets spread themselves in a line across Fishergate near to the Shelley Arms Inn (now

Thomas Miller Junior
(1811–1865). Partner and
later sole proprietor of
Messrs Horrocks Miller &
Co., he married Henrietta
Pitt, niece of the founder
John Horrocks.
(*Harris Musem and Art
Gallery*)

Woolworths site) with the police lined up in front of them. They met the angry crowd near to Chapel Walks. Some of the women had carried stones in their aprons from the canal in Wharf Street and piled them up at the roadside.

Sam Horrocks took up a position on his horse and in an attempt to prevent further trouble read out the Riot Act to the crowd: 'Our Sovereign Lord the King chargeth and commands all persons being assembled immediately to disperse themselves and peaceably to repair to their habitations or to their lawful business'. Stones thrown at him knocked the paper from his hand and wounded him in the leg. The Chief Constable and a Police Superintendent then tried to persuade the mob to retire, without success. The Constable was knocked to the ground by a stone. When his men charged forward they were stopped by missiles.

The crowd moved down into Lune Street Again they stoned a Captain of the Sappers and Miners (cartographers working in the town) who had left his office in Fishergate to warn them that they would surely be fired on if they did not disperse. They would not be stopped, however, and when the soldiers were ordered to advance they surged before them down Lune Street. At the bottom near to the Corn Exchange their numbers were strengthened by another group who had run down Fox Street and climbed up scaffolding on the building.

The order to fire was given, and the first volley was aimed by the soldiers over the people's heads. When the next order was given the musket balls were fired into the crowd, killing three people and injuring others, one of whom later died. Within minutes the streets were emptied as the terrified strikers, defeated, fled to their homes. The strike in Preston had lasted less than two days. The soldiers of the 72nd Division of Highlanders left the town the following day and were replaced by the Bolton Yeomanry. On the following Wednesday a large group of Chorley workers intent on closing down the Preston mills again were stopped at Walton Bridge and about thirty arrests made. Messrs. J. H. Spencer and J. F. Billingers wrote (in the Official Handbook of the 1952 Preston Guild) that this incident 'broke Samuel Horrocks' heart and that he was certainly never the same man again'.

These dreadful events happened less than one month before the 1842 Preston Guild celebrations were due to begin. There was much discussion as to whether the ancient festival should be postponed or cancelled. But the Guild is essentially the townspeople's celebration, and to cancel it could have led to more civil disturbance. Moreover the preparations were too far advanced to be stopped. So as peace seemed to have been restored in the town it was decided to proceed with the Guild as planned.

On Monday 5 September Sam Horrocks's carriage, guarded by soldiers, drove out of the Lark Hill gates and took him in full regalia to the Town Hall where at 2 p.m. he proclaimed the opening of the Guild Merchant.

He was now forty-five years old and a very wealthy man; no expense was spared in the lavish entertainment of the guests. Gentry from different

Samuel Horrocks (Junior) of Lark Hill (1797–1846), Guild Mayor of Preston 1842. Artist unknown.
(*Harris Museum and Art Gallery*)

Lark Hill House, Preston, built 1796 by Samuel Horrocks. Now at the centre of
Cardinal Newman College. Lithograph from I. Shaw's sketch *c.* 1850.
(*Harris Reference Library*)

parts of the country had been invited to Preston for the celebrations and
all were graciously received. The Duke of Brunswick, the Duke of Devonshire
and his suite, the Earls of Shrewsbury and of Tranquair, Lord Castlemain,
Baron Audley, Sir Richard Brook, Bart., Sir Thomas de Trafford, Major
General Sir Thomas Whitehead and other high ranking military gentlemen
attended. Wealthy industrialists came from all parts of the country bringing
their wives and daughters in their finery. There was not a vacant bed to be
had in the town, and each day special trains brought thousands more
people on the new railway system to join the throngs. The Mayor and
Mayoress presided over all the traditional ceremonies of the Guild and
guarded by soldiers headed the processions. There were formal and carnival
balls, concerts, theatre performances, trade and religious processions and
organised amusements of every kind.

Eliza Horrocks as Mayoress was hostess to these glittering events. She
and her husband received the guests at the opening of the full dress ball
at the Corn Exchange in Lune Street. It was less than a month since, as
Mayor, he had read the Riot Act that same building whilst surrounded by
a furious mob. What must have been in his mind as he stepped out of his
carriage and into the entrance hall?

A temporary roof had been erected over the open courtyard where trading
usually took place, and the whole of its ceiling lined with white cotton.
National flags hung along the length of the gallery. A local journalist wrote

Newspaper report on the cotton mill workers' revolt in Preston, August 1842. The mayor Samuel Horrocks (seated on horse, upper left) reads the Riot Act, ordering the mob to disperse. (*Illustrated London News, 20 August 1842*)

'Seldom has a greater display of elegance and fashion been seen in Preston'. The ladies were decked in gowns of the most costly materials and trimmings, and hung with jewellery. A long line of carriages bringing the guests filled all the streets leading to the Exchange. Sam and Eliza led off the first dance to Horrobin's celebrated 'Quadrille Band'. The dancers continued in high spirits until three o'clock in the morning, when the stewards had difficulty in persuading the last revellers to leave the ballroom floor.

Tickets for the event had cost half a guinea (ten shillings and sixpence) and were soon sold out. These prices were of course far beyond the means of the working people of the town; but they had their opportunities to enjoy the Guild Festivities. There were dances, sports, competitions, a fairground, circus, magic lantern shows, boating on the River Ribble and other delights for them. The town's mills closed down for most of the week and those of nearby towns also closed on Thursday and Friday to enable their workers to come to Preston for the outdoor sports and the processions.

There was no doubt that his week as Guild Mayor should have been the highlight of Sam Horrocks's life. But the events of the earlier months, his father's death and the workers' uprising had affected him badly and his health began to suffer.

Less than four years after the Guild on the 24 February 1846 he died, at the young age of forty-nine. The local newspaper recorded that his funeral procession was impressive 'with all the display of pomp and power befitting his position.' One hundred and eighty-six attendants from Horrocks's mills walked behind the cortege from Lark Hill to St Paul's Church for the funeral service and burial in the churchyard. His widow Eliza put a brass memorial plate inside the church, inscribed 'In Memory of Samuel Horrocks of Lark Hill who was for many years magistrate and Deputy Lieutenant of this county and in 1842 Guild Mayor of Preston. He was the only surviving son of Samuel Horrocks Esq. of Lark Hill. This monument is erected by his widow as a tribute of affection.' In the previous year Sam had given a chalice and patten to St Paul's Church.

He had hoped that the Horrocks family would always keep Lark Hill after his widow's death and made provision for this in his will. To ensure the good upkeep of the estate and furnishings an annuity of £500 was provided.

All the plate, glass, china, household goods and furniture, and his father's portrait in oils were to be left in the house[23] and kept in good condition.

Preston Guild, September 1842: the Mayoress Mrs Samuel Horrocks hosts a public breakfast party at the Corn Exchange. 'A most select and elegant company promenaded the grand saloon ... it was a magical scene'.

At the Preston Guild of 1992 a committee headed by Mary Hanson Jones and Mavis Rogerson turned the clock back to 1822. They presented in Lark Hill House a dramatisation by local amateur actors of authentic scenes from the lives of the Horrocks family. The audience were invited as if guests of Samuel Horrocks and treated to beautiful singing by the Avenham Singers and Georgian refreshments in the dining room afterwards. This photograph of the cast, taken in the Hall at Lark Hill by Melvyn Carter is reproduced with his kind permission.

His widow Eliza was well provided for. She received a legacy of £1,000, plus the £5,000 capital of the marriage settlement. She was also to receive £2,000 per annum for life, and all the contents (except furniture) of their house and stables. After her death all the remaining estate was to be divided equally between Sam's surviving sisters, his brother-in-law and two aunts and their children. These relatives also all received generous legacies and lifelong interest from a trust fund.

Sam Horrocks's death in 1846 brought to an end the connection of the males of their family in the business which his Uncle John founded in 1791 and named Horrocks and Co. Their involvement had lasted the short duration of 55 years. For another 150 years the Company would trade world-wide under the name 'Horrockses', and dominate the town of Preston.

Thomas Miller became the sole proprietor after Sam Horrocks's death. He was married to Henrietta the founder's niece (his brother Henry to her sister Caroline). Sam Horrocks' widow was Eliza Miller their sister. Thus the Horrocks family was well represented behind the scenes for many years to come in the management of Horrocks Miller & Co.

Eliza evidently did not share her husband's love of the mansion his father had built. After his death she lived there only intermittently. From 1854 none of the family was in residence but a full staff of servants maintained the property in good order. In that year with the agreement of all her late husband's family Eliza took steps to dispose of the Lark Hill Estate at a public auction. The house and grounds, and stables were purchased by a group of businessmen for the parish of St Augustine's for £4,725. The well-built stables were adapted immediately to become a girls' school. Later the house became a female boarding-school and teacher-training college. From 1859 both establishments were run by the French Catholic teaching Order of Religious Sisters 'The Faithful Companions of Jesus' (see *The History of Lark Hill* published by Margaret Burscough in 1979). Thus came to an end the Horrocks family's sixty-two years' residence at Lark Hill.

Eliza Horrocks went to live in Cumbria where she bought a large house and country estate called 'Merlewood' at Lindale near Grange-over-Sands. She lived there until her death in 1872.

Jane Horrocks (1795–1834), daughter of Samuel Horrocks MP

Samuel Horrocks's seven daughters on the whole conformed to the accepted norm for well-to-do young ladies of the Georgian era. Their marriages to professional men were followed by unremarkable lives, apart from the third-born, Jane. Her kinship by marriage to the Lakes poet William Wordsworth introduces to these chronicles the unlikely and interesting connection between the family of a hard-headed Lancashire cotton-master and the Cumberland poetic genius.

A few letters kept by her sister Mrs Eliza Whittaker give a little insight into Jane's life as a motherless teenager in the early years of the nineteenth century.

As her older sisters married and left home much family responsibility fell upon Jane's young shoulders as she took over the running of the Lark Hill household. Some of the problems she faced are revealed in a letter to her sister Eliza. She complained that two incompetent maids had been given notice to leave because the house was 'in a filthy state' and would have to stay so until they could get a new set of servants. There was also trouble in the kitchen. Bella the cook had a 'drunken husband, a worthless character' whom Jane had forbidden to enter the house. Still he came 'making a nuisance of himself from morning till night'. So Bella too would have to go, and Jane must also find a new, good plain cook. Her domestic trials were soon forgotten, however, when she went off to Liverpool with her sister Sarah.

Horrocks & Co did much of their business with Liverpool merchants and Samuel's family had a wide circle of friends in the port. Another of Jane's letters neatly encapsulated the social scene of Liverpool in the spring of 1814. Writing in an amusing style she described the many events arranged for their entertainment. Their hosts, the Aspinalls of Duke Street, invited several young men to a supper party, where Jane 'sat with Stanley son of Dr Percival of Manchester, who made himself very agreeable': again, 'there were 15 to dinner and supper and a very merry party we were'. They visited Mr Bridge's new house in Bold Street and drank tea and supped there. 'A delightful visit we had. Everything was prepared for us in such a comfortable style, and Mr Bridge was very polite and attentive to us all. He speaks highly indeed of Sarah and they always contrive to sit next to each other and have such long arguments together'. Jane walked one morning with Margaret Aspinall on the Botanic Walk and met Mr John Leigh, an old friend. They dined with the Addisons in Lodge Lane, visited the Douglases at Everton and called on Mrs Paton who 'fortunately was not at home'. James Aspinall escorted them to meet Mr R. Jakes, and when time permitted Ann took them shopping. The visit had to be cut short, however, by the imminent arrival home from Westminster of their father. Sarah, an accomplished pianist, and Jane were very disappointed to have to miss two oratorios and other musical concerts in Easter week. They must return to Preston to attend, dutifully, to him.

There was much bantering among the six Horrocks sisters on the subject of gentlemen friends and their attentions and intentions. Should Jane encourage the smitten Mr B. Gregson, whose mother pushed him in her direction, when there was no fear of her liking him? Sarah commented 'Not that it is so great a disadvantage to a young girl to have a "dangler"!' She herself was amused by a visit from Mr Peter Ainsworth (of Smithills Hall) a long-standing family friend. 'He talked much of the folly of girls thinking that because a young man flirted and paid them attention that he had any serious intentions – said in such a manner that I am sure it was intended for me. It entertained me very much to see him so much occupied in pleasing thoughts of himself that he could not read the indifference I felt, or do justice to my character'.

Romance, however, was not in their thoughts when they welcomed another old friend to their home in October 1819. They were all fond of Thomas Monkhouse and were pleased to see him again. He had first come to Preston from Penrith as a sixteen-year-old apprentice in 1799 to learn the retail trade. His master Samuel Crane, a linen merchant, was the old friend of the Horrocks brothers who had supported them during their first years in business. Thus Thomas came to know all Samuel's family at Lark Hill, and watched them grow up. At the completion of his five-year apprenticeship he went to London to work with a merchant draper, Mr Wheelwright of Budge Row. Thomas's family background was interesting. He was the cousin and good friend of Mary (née Hutchinson) and her husband, the Lakes poet William Wordsworth who stayed with him on his visits to London. Thus, as a young man he was admitted to the circle of poets and artists of the period, Keats, Lamb, Coleridge, Southey, Haydn and company. He became a favourite of that group who appreciated his generous hospitality and his quiet kindly nature. On the night of 28 December 1817 when Benjamin Haydn the painter had given the famous 'Immortal Dinner' at his studio in Lisson Grove, London, Charles Lamb partook too freely of the

St Augustine's Church *c.* 1870, before the bell towers were added in 1890. Built across from Lark Hill in 1840 by a group of independent businessmen, the church finally closed in 2002. It is destined to become a community centre and gymnasium.
(*C. Hardwick*)

'Merlewood' Lindale, Grange. (*J. Beckett and A. Gardiner*)

wine. Tom Monkhouse persuaded him quietly to put on his coat and walked him safely home. This was the beginning of a lifelong friendship between the two men. In 1823 Lamb publicly described him as 'the noble-minded kinsman-by-wedlock of Wordsworth'.

Thomas evidently enjoyed his 1819 stay at Lark Hill, for six months later he came back on a second visit, which proved to be a turning point in his life. At thirty-six he was still a bachelor, having suffered two serious disappointments in love affairs. As his cousin Sarah Hutchinson commented, 'now I suppose your regrets are all passed away and the sweet society of the Misses Horrocks made amends for all'. She was right. In the hopes of being third time lucky he made a proposal of marriage to twenty-five year-old Jane Horrocks and was accepted. Theirs was to be a whirlwind courtship, for only three months later on 6 July 1820 they married at Preston Parish Church. Jane was then whisked off to London to her new home in Queen Anne's Street, Cavendish Square. A small group of friends was invited to a celebratory dinner and the cutting of the wedding cake, but the bridegroom, Charles Lamb and William Wordsworth apparently disgraced themselves by falling asleep after the meal.

The reason for the great haste in arranging the marriage soon became known. Thomas was to join the Wordsworths on an imminent tour of the continent and would make this a honeymoon trip with his bride. William Wordsworth had long wanted to retrace his 1790 expedition through France and Switzerland, this time with his wife and sister Dorothy. On 12 July after their brief stay in London Jane and her new husband, with her eldest sister Sarah and maid Jane, found themselves crossing the Channel with the Wordsworths. Dorothy described in her journal how they 'left Calais in two stout carriages and jolted away merry as children and, fresh to the feeling of being in a foreign land drove brightly forward, watchful and gay'. No doubt the elation was sustained as they travelled to Brussels then up the Rhine to Cologne and on into Switzerland. On one happy evening Jane played the piano in their lodging and some local young women waltzed with Thomas 'full of glee and animated by his attentions'. At Berne they were joined by their friend Henry Crabb Robinson and exchanged the carriages for a charabanc to travel via Interlaken to the Wengern Alps.

Their next transfer, to a string of mules for the ascent, proved much too strenuous for young Jane. Thomas and the Wordsworths, brought up in the mountainous Lake District, revelled at the prospect, but the town-bred girl was completely out of her element. Dorothy had already observed 'Mrs Monkhouse is a good, sweet and amiable young woman, but she is not strong and is therefore unable to walk about like her sister and Mr Wordsworth'. She could climb no further. Arrangements were made that she should travel back to Berne with Sarah and the maid. Dorothy was relieved at this for she felt that Wordsworth would be happier with a smaller group. His eyes had been troubling him and Dorothy wrote to Sara Hutchinson, 'If he could take his business more quietly he would receive great benefit from this journey – when our party is smaller I think he will do perfectly well. No people can be more amiable than Mrs M(onkhouse) and Miss H(orrocks) but it cannot be denied that our party is too large for such a country as this'.

The attraction of climbing the Alps proved irresistible for the young husband however: so in the second week of August the honeymoon couple parted. Thomas journeyed on with his cousins and Robinson, crossing the Alps by the St Gothard Pass. They then travelled round the Italian Lakes, walking, driving on horseback or mule until, in the third week of September, five weeks after their parting, the party was reunited in Geneva. The following month saw them in Paris which would no doubt be more pleasing to the Lark Hill group, and perhaps some compensation for the earlier parting. Sufficient to say that Jane conceived a child in the French capital.

The Continental Tour lasted for four months and it was well into November before Tom and Jane finally arrived back in London to begin married life together. Unfortunately the first months were marred by a difficult pregnancy and she was obliged to rest on the sofa, but at the beginning of December suffered a miscarriage. Her father and sister visited them in

London and Thomas was able to see his friends and attend to business affairs again. Their removal to a house at 67 Gloucester Place, Marylebone Lane, began what was probably the happiest year of their lives. She conceived again, and at Christmas 1821 gave birth to her first child, a daughter. Little Mary proved to be a delight to them and all their relations. When she was five months old John rented a house at Rydal, at the foot of the hill from the Wordsworths and there the family spent the summer months. They were joined by Jane's father Samuel Horrocks and some of his daughters who rented Ivy Cottage nearby. Sarah the eldest was already well known to the Wordsworths having accompanied them on their tour of the Continent the previous year.

Although Wordsworth's earlier interest in politics might have turned him against industrialists for their exploitation of the working man, he seems to have accepted Samuel Horrocks as the father-in-law of his nephew. Perhaps it was that Lark Hill House was conveniently situated where he was ready for a break on his journeys south from the Lake district: for we know that he and members of his family visited Lark Hill on several occasions and sometimes stayed overnight. If there was no one at home he would visit young Sam Horrocks and his wife Eliza at 9 Winckley Square. He thought her 'a pleasing woman who plays upon the harp powerfully'. But of her father Thomas Miller he could only comment 'He is a native of Whitehaven and but of vulgar manners'. Their letters show that the Wordsworths were fond of twenty-two year-old Alice Horrocks. In 1820 Dorothy asked Thomas Monkhouse, 'If my friend Miss Alice comes pray remember me kindly to her'. In 1825 after she had married, William Wordsworth wrote of her 'At Chorley I called on Mrs Masters, her husband a credible clergyman and she has a nice little girl'. It is possible that it was Alice to whom Dorothy was referring when she wrote in 1825 'I spell wretchedly but a young friend of mine has begun to recopy my journal.' When Alan G. Hill edited Dorothy Wordsworth's letters, he wrote a footnote to this entry: 'This copy in an unidentified hand is now the only surviving manuscript' (of the 1820 Continental Journal). Was Alice's the 'unidentified hand'?

Before the 1822 summer gathering came to an end in August the Monkhouse baby was christened at Grasmere and given the name Mary Elizabeth. The family group then went home to Lark Hill eagerly looking forward to the forthcoming 'Preston Guild'.[24]

It was twenty years since the last Guild when Thomas Monkhouse had been a nineteen-year-old apprentice living with Samuel Crane and his family in Preston. At this 1822 celebration his situation was quite different. He was now the son-in-law of Samuel Horrocks, Member of Parliament for the Borough and Steward of the Guild, and would be renewing old friendships in his company. The celebrations lasted a fortnight after which Tom and Jane took a short holiday in Blackpool with their infant daughter.

The Wordsworth family all loved young Mary Monkhouse and recorded their feelings for her. When she was three years old Dorothy wrote to her brother-in-law, John Monkhouse, 'She is a child by herself, such an (sic) one was never born before and never will be again. There seems no seed of evil in her, she is constantly happy and everything that is new and everything that is old affords her amusement. It is a great pleasure to see her with her father ...'.

In December 1824 she told Henry C Robinson that her brother had 'written some very pretty small poems which have been composed by him with true feeling, and he has a great satisfaction in having done them, especially that on M. M. [Mary Monkhouse] for her dear father's sake who prizes it very much'.

'The infant M-M-' by William Wordsworth 1824

'Unquiet childhood here by special grace
Forgets her nature, opening like a flower
That neither feels nor wastes its vital power
In painful struggles. Months each other chase
And nought untunes that Infant's voice – no trace
Of fretful temper sullies her pure cheek.
Prompt, lively, self-sufficing, yet so meek
That one enrapt with gazing on her face
(which even the placid innocence of death
could scarcely make more placid, heaven more bright)
Might learn to picture, for the eye of faith,
The virgin as she shone with kindred light,
A nursling couched upon her mother's knee
Beneath some shady palm of Galilee.'

Thomas Monkhouse was unwell in the winter of 1823. His lungs were affected by the polluted city air and he needed to get away into the country. Sara Hutchinson had in 1818 written, while staying with Thomas, 'I sat in the house and could not see the houses on the other side of the street, the fog is not only thick but a yellow colour and makes one as dirty as smoke ... [the days] are often so dark that the houses in the narrow street are forced to be lit up at midday'.

The family spent the summer months at Ramsgate on the Kent coast, but in August Thomas was obliged to consult his London physicians who recommended he move to the warmer climate of Devon for the next winter.

His complaint was diagnosed as a 'derangement of the digestive organs', which could be cured. But he must 'withdraw his mind from business'. When he heard that the property 'Fox Ghyll' in Rydal was to be sold Thomas obtained all particulars from Dorothy Wordsworth, but nothing came of his enquiry.

Instead he took his family first to his brother John's home, 'The Stowe' near Hereford, where his cousin Sara was 'horrified at his ghastly appearance'. When William and Dorothy Wordsworth saw him at Rye two months later, they 'were heartstruck at the first sight of him'; it was obvious to them that 'he was far gone in consumption'.

As winter approached Thomas and Jane with little Mary and Sara Hutchinson went south to stay in a rented house in Torquay. Mary Horrocks, Jane's sister, had recently married Rev. William Birkett whose first parish was at South Tawton, Devon so the two had expected to be able to support each other in their differing situations. But unfortunately Mary became seriously ill and was confined to her bed for several weeks.

A kind letter from their brother Sam shows that they were not forgotten by their family in Preston. He had sent on the coach to Torquay a box full of treats, 'a brace of woodcocks and three brace of snipes, freshly killed so as not to be too "high" for the invalid's stomach, a brace of partridge, a tongue-cheek and a cake of damson cheese.' Sam and Tom Monkhouse had a long-standing friendship and the letter contained anxious concern for his condition.

Although the temperature was mild in Torquay, unfortunately there was constant rain throughout December so the family moved up to Clifton near Bristol where Thomas might benefit from its airy cliff top position and the sulphurous waters of the Pumproom. (It was fortunate that he was too late to be put in the care of the late-lamented Dr Beddoes at Clifton. When Frances Winckley of Preston – later Lady Shelley – was sent to him as a child his 'infallible' cure for consumption was to place the patients in rooms above cow-houses in the belief that the breath of the cows ascending through gaps in the floorboards and inhaled by them would prove a remedial treatment).

Sadly although 'Clifton cheered him enormously' it did not bring about the longed-for cure. Only a week after their arrival he became weaker and suddenly, but very peacefully, he died on 25 February 1825.

Jane 'who had always deceived herself with hope' of a recovery bore the shock of his sudden death 'with perfect resignation': but Dorothy wrote 'they are very anxious about her, she has a cough and is miserably thin'. After the funeral in Clifton the party of mourners travelled on to John Monkhouse's home near Hereford, but Jane 'when a fresh exertion of strength was called for in the journey, poor thing, was hardly equal to it'. She returned to Clifton with little Mary after a three-week sojourn with her brother-in-law.

There is no doubt that Thomas Monkhouse was a well-loved, popular man greatly mourned by all his family and friends. Of many kind memorials written of him, Dorothy Wordsworth's, sent to his brother John, was the most touching. 'He was a man of perfect integrity, not bright or entertaining, but so gentle and gracious that his company was highly prized by all who knew him intimately.' Her brother William considered him one of his 'most valued friends whose death would remove one of the strongest and most important of my facilities for visiting London and prolonging my stay there'.

Thomas left estate valued at £24,000: £7,000 for his brother John; £3,000 to his sister Mary; and £3,000 to trustees for his late brother Joseph's illegitimate son in the West Indies. His widow and daughter were 'well provided for'. Through a technical legal error made in writing his own will Thomas's property at Sebergham near Carlisle although intended to go to his brother John had to be passed down to five-year-old Mary, in trust until her twenty-first birthday. Dorothy Wordsworth considered this 'a grievous circumstance', 'more to be regretted as when she comes of age her fortune will be large for her beyond the needs of any woman of her rank'.

John Monkhouse was his brother's executor and trustee, and, with Sam Horrocks, the guardian of his daughter who was sent to a school in Bath. Her mother stayed on in Clifton, and in the spring of 1825 took Mary up to Preston for a holiday with her family at Lark Hill House. Samuel Horrocks became devoted to his little granddaughter, not wanting to part with her when it was time to return to Clifton. A portrait of that year shows her to be a pretty child, worthy of the praise heaped on her by all her relatives. Her mother appears as a smart, well-groomed lady with the firm, somewhat formidable looks of her father.

After her husband's death she stayed in the rented house in Clifton. At Christmas she returned to Preston for the marriage of her eldest sister Sarah, to an old family friend Dr William St Clare.

In the following year she herself was courted by another doctor, a Clifton bachelor named Paris Thomas Dick, whom she married in 1827 just two years after Thomas Monkhouse's death. The couple moved to Castle Cary in Somerset, but their marriage was not a success. Within a short time Dr Dick was writing making demands of honest John Monkhouse for extra money for his wife and her daughter from Thomas' estate. There was trouble over unpaid bills, school expenses and the whereabouts of a set of books which were supposed to belong to Jane. John's concern led him to take Dr Dick to court for a ruling on payments for the child's educational costs. The demand for £400 was reduced to an award of £150 per annum. It is possible that Dr Dick married Jane to gain access to her legacy income as there seems to have been little affection between the pair. Relations between them became strained, and deteriorated to such an extent that she left him in October of 1832, after four and a half years of marriage. Jane notified her London solicitor Mr Sweet that this was following 'a long-continued series of injuries and provocations'.

We next hear of her living in Blackpool with her daughter and the governess Miss Gregg: John Monkhouse wrote to Sam Horrocks expressing his concern over reports that the two women had apparently taken to drinking excessively. His solicitor advised him to apply for legal guardianship of Mary but John did not want to upset the Horrocks family with publicity about the situation. Although against the idea at first Jane eventually allowed Mary to go with her governess to stay with the Monkhouse family in Herefordshire.

She herself returned to live in Clifton in the New Year of 1834. There in the early summer she tragically contracted typhus fever, to which she succumbed rapidly and died on 14 June in her fortieth year. Her brother Sam travelled from Preston to join John Monkhouse and his sister Mary for the funeral and burial at Clifton. Dr Dick who was then living at College Green, Gloucester did not appear. A scathing letter written afterwards by Sara Hutchinson however, accused him of taking all Jane's money, selling her property, books and silver and leaving Sam Horrocks to pay her debts.

Young Mary Monkhouse was left under the guardianship of her two uncles, Sam Horrocks and John Monkhouse, who with their families worked well together to ensure her welfare and happiness. When she was twenty-four Mary married at Preston Parish Church an old family friend, the Rev. Henry Dew, rector of Whitney, Herefordshire. She was mother to a large family and lived happily into old age.

A different view of Jane Horrocks's life was revealed in a book of letters edited by Kathleen Coburn, published in 1954 by Routledge and Kegan Paul Ltd. They were written by Sara Hutchinson, cousin of Jane's husband Thomas Monkhouse and sister of Mary Wordsworth. Sara was the 'Asra' who had been loved and pursued by the obsessed Samuel T. Coleridge. She had also been suggested by the Wordsworths as the likely bride for William's brother John (who was tragically drowned when his boat the 'Earl of Abergavenny' sank in February 1805).

Sara had been disappointed when her much-beloved young cousin Thomas ignored her advice in his choice of wife. She had tried to steer him towards a different bride, Miss Oaks at Hendon, reminding him that his friend Mr Gee thought her 'a very charming girl' ... 'you would be lucky if you could succeed there'. She gave vent to her disapproval of Jane in correspondence with Edward Quillinan, one of the Wordsworth set who later married Wordsworth's daughter Dora. Kathleen Coburn in editing Sara Hutchinson's letters wrote, 'One of the bonds between Edward Quillinan and her was that they could let themselves go with regards to Mrs Thomas Monkhouse'.

This was done in private correspondence during years when Sara gave the appearance of being a true friend of both Thomas and Jane. She would visit their home and help where she could, nursing anyone who was unwell and generously giving a helping hand. Everyone was impressed by her kindness. But in the ten years from 1824 she wrote at least twenty letters to her friend which contained disparaging remarks about Jane and her Horrocks sisters. A sample, written on 8/4/27 reads, 'All the stories of the Ladies feigned illnesses are wellknown – even little Anne's are all put on, they say, and not one of the sisters are free from using these means of gaining their ends and working upon the feelings of fathers and husbands'. Sara's opinion on this was evidently not shared by Dorothy, William Wordsworth's sister, who wrote sympathetically (31/8/23) 'Mrs M's health has much improved and Mrs Anne Horrocks who has been dangerously ill is recovering'. Again on 13 December 1824 Dorothy wrote, 'The fourth sister has been for some weeks extremely ill requiring constant attendance day and night'. She obviously did not consider them all to be malingerers.

In 1820 when Thomas first became ill with tuberculosis Jane, after several threatened miscarriages eventually lost the baby. When she became pregnant again in 1821 and was troubled by backache, her doctor advised her to rest. This was when Sara began to suspect her of malingering although she spoke kindly of her to Thomas.

In the following two years it appears that Jane could never do anything right for Sara, who in March 1823 wrote 'Mr and Mrs M talk of going to Brighton (for all I can do I cannot bring Ramsgate into favour)' yet the following April she was decrying Ramsgate: April 1824. 'Poor T. M. must be contented to humdrum it up and down in that steam-boat all summer in Ramsgate. I am most heartily grieved that he will not be able to come here even for a short visit. [ie to Grasmere]. Why can he not come and leave his wife, as she has her sister with her'.

A letter of 29 April 1824 reveals that Sara was quite prepared to use the Horrocks family when it was to her advantage. Postage on letters was very expensive and paid by the recipient. Samuel Horrocks as an MP had the privilege of free frankage on letters in his mailbag, which Sara found useful.

Mrs Jane Dick, previously Monkhouse, née Horrocks (1795–1834): a portrait of 1831
with her daughter Mary Monkhouse (1821–1900).
(*The Wordsworth Trust: Centre for British Romanticism*)

'Tell me how long Mr H. will be in Town, because so long as he is I shall
have no scruple in packing off a scrawl like this for him to frank forward,
but not for you to have to pay for it.'

More seriously both she and Quillinan always considered Jane's indisposi-
tions to be imaginary and a source of such anxiety to her husband that
they caused his illness, and even ultimately his death: 'You never said a
truer thing in your life that he was killing himself with anxiety which I
firmly believe to be the cause of his illness since they have been here Mrs
M has generally been very well; yet though she knows that her husband is
happier here [ie in Herefordshire] than he would be anywhere else she is
full of schemes for another removal, This is not to be breathed to anybody
out of our own family, so take care to burn it.' In fact his London physician
had recommended that Thomas should remove to a warmer climate.

Two months later she wrote 'Mrs M. is quite well, and never or scarcely
is seen upon a sofa, this is a blessing indeed for had she been ill also her
husband's spirits would have been worse than ever, anxiety of one kind or
another has I am sure been the cause of his present melancholy state of
body, tho' the Dr's say that the depression of spirits is the effect and not
the cause of his disease. In this I am sceptical.' Sara Hutchinson seemed

Thomas Monkhouse of Cockermouth and London owner of Sebergham Estate near Carlisle. He as born in 1783 and married Jane Horrocks in 1820 at Preston. He died at Clifton in 1825, the father of one daughter. (*The Wordsworth Trust: Centre for British Romanticism*).

unable to accept that her beloved cousin had incurable tuberculosis, and even after his death wrote 'I feel it most bitterly and the truth cannot be doubted that his life has been destroyed by anxiety of one kind or another ...'

She and Edward Quillinan evidently disliked all the Horrocks family, even those they had never met. There is scarcely one uncritical comment about them in their letters. For example Sarah Horrock's husband Dr William St Clare, a well-loved hard working physician in Preston was described as 'a tidy farmer-looking man, about 50, not very refined which used to be a desideratum with the ladies of the family'.

All of the Horrocks sisters failed to please and prompted her opinion 'I am sorry to say the Aunts are not exactly what one could wish them to be.'

About young Mary Monkhouse whom everyone loved she decided 'there is something of reserve about her that does not quite please me ... I have no doubt that she has been prejudiced against her Herefordshire friends'.

The letters continue, in similar vein, until after Jane's premature death in 1834. Until now they have been the only published source of material about her, and the personal opinions expressed in them have been interpreted as facts. Consequently she has, since their publication, been described as the malingering, inconsiderate wife who drove Thomas Monkhouse to an early grave. Readers must decide for themselves whether this is a fair and accurate description of Jane Horrocks.

CHAPTER 4

John Horrocks Junior
(1794–1870)

John Horrocks (Junior) was the second son of John Horrocks MP founder of the textile company, and chosen to be his heir. He was ten years old at his father's untimely death in 1804 and with his older brother Peter was put under the guardianship of his uncle Samuel Horrocks and his father's friend Richard Ainsworth. The two men seem to have divided their legal responsibility for the boys; so that Samuel took care of Peter and Richard Ainsworth of his younger brother. John was then at Mr Pearson's School in Parsons Green, London. Mr Ainsworth employed Alfred Hadfield a young Classics scholar of Oxford University as chaplain and tutor to his own sons at Moss Bank in Halliwell, Lancashire. He brought young John back to Lancashire to be educated with them, in the schoolroom in his own home.

When Rev. Hadfield accepted the incumbency of St Stephen's in Everton, Liverpool, he opened a private school there which soon achieved an excellent reputation. Peter Ainsworth, Jonathan Peel and John Horrocks were among his first boarding pupils.

As his school days drew to an end at the age of sixteen, the question of John's future came under discussion. An academic education was not considered appropriate for in five years he would come of age and inherit his late father's textile company; so he needed to be trained in the ways of industry. Mr Ainsworth found the answer in discussions with a colleague, Charles Macintosh,[25] who was a partner in a Glasgow Company which sold dry chlorine bleach to Lancashire cotton mills. Ainsworth reckoned this product had saved him about £2,500 per year in his bleaching business. Macintosh agreed to take the boy under his wing. He could live with him in Scotland and be introduced to the business world.

On the last day of February 1810 young John Horrocks was taken up to Glasgow and settled in Macintosh's family home 'Dunchattan' in Duke Street just outside the city boundary. There he experienced the stability of a happy family life, and seems to have been well accepted by the four Macintosh children, Alexander, George, Wallace and Mary. John's older brother Peter was at Oxford at this time and kept in touch with him by

Charles Macintosh FRS (1766–1843) of
Dunchattan and Campsie, by R C Bell,
lithograph by J G Gilbert published privately
in his 'Biographical Memoir' by his son
George Macintosh.

letter. They were good friends and Peter was concerned that the new arrangement should work well. When he heard in the summer that John had been kicked by his mare injuring his leg he immediately set off for Scotland to visit him. Finding him fully recovered he stayed in Scotland for the rest of the long vacation. His diary records the carefree weeks they spent together touring the beautiful countryside on whatever transport was available. The tone of the diary was lighthearted and happy as the two brothers relaxed in each other's company. They viewed the castle of Holyrood and enjoyed the theatre in Edinburgh; rode through the Trossachs and on the return journey raced to Stirling on an old cart from the inn at Callendar. Back in Glasgow Peter bought a gold watch for 37 guineas, and each bought the other a gold watch chain.

Unfortunately John left no diaries so we have few details of his early life. We do know, however, that during the next two years he fell in love with Mary Scott Macintosh, his host's only living daughter. Although still under age he proposed marriage to her, and seems to have been accepted as a suitable match by her father. He was a tall good-looking young man with excellent financial prospects. Arrangements for the wedding went ahead, but it appears that John handled some part of them quite badly. He was obliged to obtain the sanction of his legal guardians, and having been forewarned by his brother that they would probably raise objections he wrote a letter to Uncle Samuel which angered all the family at Lark Hill. Aunt Ann-Eliza Robbins hearing of the contents commented 'What a refined imposition, an incomprehensible production.'

Relations between John and his guardians became so strained that neither they nor any of their children were sent invitations to the wedding and the Lark Hill cousins never forgave John for this slight. Charles Macintosh was concerned at this development and wrote inviting Samuel and one daughter to the wedding as his guests. He received a reply declining the 'polite and friendly invitation' as it was obvious that the bridegroom would find his presence 'unpleasant'.

Once again Mr Macintosh wrote trying to persuade him to attend, but Samuel refused. An appeal was made to the other guardian Richard Ainsworth, who was able to persuade him to change his mind. When the young couple married in the drawing room of Dunchattan House on 1 October 1813 both guardians witnessed the event and the marriage was registered in Glasgow's Old Barony Parish records. They spent a two-month honeymoon in York and Bath, then returned north to Penwortham Lodge, Preston[26] which had been left to John by his father nine years earlier.

John's mother was at Penwortham Lodge to receive him back from his honeymoon and meet her new daughter-in-law. That Mary Horrocks was there is remarkable. It was just ten years to the month since she had been shown the door of that house by her estranged husband, and forbidden to return there or to enter any of his properties again. She had lived quietly in Salford and seen her sons only on brief and rare visits but his death meant that she was free to resume her position in the family.

Less than a year after their marriage in August 1814 a daughter was born to the young couple and given her mother's name Mary Scott. But the

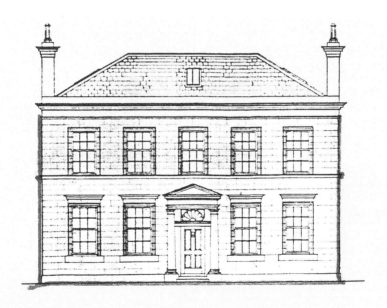

FRONT ELEVATION: DUNCHATTAN HOUSE

Architectual drawing of Dunchattan House, Duke Street, Glasgow, built *c.* 1780 (now demolished). Home of Charles Macintosh. (*Mitchell Library, Glasgow*)

Mary Scott Macintosh of Glasgow (1795–1824), wife of John Horrocks (junior), daughter of Charles Macintosh FRS of Dunchattan and Campsie, Scotland. A portrait painted in Edinburgh *c.* 1822 by S. Andrew (*Horrocks' archives, New Zealand*).

infant died four months later of a respiratory illness, and was buried in her grandfather's grave in Penwortham churchyard. Mary's father became concerned about her health and well-being and advised them to leave Penwortham and return to Scotland. His letters reveal that John had made the decision to sell out his major shareholding in Horrocks and Co. and that arrangements were already in hand to dissolve the partnership at the end of the year 1814. On 13 January 1815 he came of age and entitled to his inheritance. A local directory records that he celebrated with a party at Penwortham Lodge which continued afterwards at the Red Lion Inn, Church Street, Preston.

Legal documents record details of the sale of his father's business thus:

The existing partnership between Samuel Horrocks of Preston, Thomas Miller, John Bairstow, Samuel Horrocks of Bread St London (and Sidcup in Kent), the executors of John Horrocks deceased (i.e. Richard Ainsworth and Nicholas Grimshaw) and the residuary legatee John Horrocks, Junior, was dissolved from the last day of 1814. On 11 February 1815 a public notice issued by the Company announced that the business would in future be carried on by Samuel Horrocks of Preston, Peter Horrocks, Samuel Horrocks of London, Thomas Miller and John Bairstow as sole partners. As residuary legatee of his father John Horrocks Junior would be paid £100,000 for his share in Horrocks & Co and would leave the Company. Articles of Agreement recorded that this amount would be paid over in yearly instalments with 5 per cent interest per annum. Commencing 1 January 1816 payments would be made on the 13th day of each month. The following valuation was made by Mr Hurrill for Messrs. Hughes and Robbins, Solicitors, of London, and the transactions were to be handled by the Solicitors 'Grimshaw, Palmer and Grimshaw' of Preston.

Copy of Deed Messrs Horrocks Miller & Co.

Payable by the partnership to John Horrocks Junior for property:-

Spittal Moss	£8372	18	8¾d.
Canal Street	£4594	7	9¾d.
Dale Street	£9019	15	2¾d.
Frenchwood	£3313	7	4d.
New Preston	£7557	4	2¾d.
Leyland	£ 284	14,	8d.
Freehold leasehold	£33,142	8	0d.

[This valuation is two-thirds of the proper value according to calculations made in 1815].

Plus Mr Horrock's share in the stock of John Horrocks & Co. (steam engines, fixtures, etc.)

£66,857	12	0d.

£100,000

Shares in Horrocks and Co. amounting to 9/20ths of profits had been allotted to John (Junior) since his father's death. When he sold out his allocation was adjusted to 4/24ths for the 12 months to 1816 only, which brought him £3,562. The other partners, Samuel Horrocks, Thomas Miller and John Bairstow took 9/24ths (£8,015), 6/24ths (£5343), and 2/24ths (£1781), respectively. Peter Horrocks with 3/24ths share received £2671.

From the following year, 1817, onwards the shares held were Samuel Horrocks 9/20ths, Thomas Miller 6/20ths, John Bairstow 2/20ths and Peter Horrocks 3/20ths. This arrangement would continue for the next eleven years when Samuel Horrocks (Junior) on his marriage in 1828 joined the board, taking a half share of his father's profits. From that year, significantly, Thomas Miller with 6/20ths share became the major share-holder.

John's decision to terminate his connection with Horrocks & Co was rued by his brother's branch of the family for decades to come. Clara his eldest niece felt that he had 'killed the goose that laid the golden egg' and denied his five nephews rightful access to their grandfather's business empire. She bitterly resented the fact that others freely used her family name to make themselves fortunes whilst her family's inheritance dwindled away.

Mary and John Horrocks were not happy at Penwortham. Coming from a loving family in Glasgow Mary had expected to be welcomed warmly by her husband's relations in Preston. But his behaviour both before his wedding and in suddenly withdrawing his money from the business had not endeared him to them. Mary had been a very young bride, too inexperienced to cope easily as mistress of a large household. She needed her own loving family around her to give her support.

The death of her first child affected her badly, so when she became pregnant again the couple decided to return to Scotland to be near her parents. Before they left John had a stone tomb, enclosed by iron railings, erected over the family grave. The inscription reads 'John Horrocks late of Penwortham Lodge in the County of Lancashire, Esquire, and Representative in Parliament for the Borough of Preston. Died on the 1st day of March Anno Domini 1804 aged 36 years. This memorial of Mortality was erected in filial veneration by his son John Horrocks of Penwortham Lodge, Esquire who with the loss of a father has also to lament the loss of his infant daughter Mary Scott Horrocks who died 11th December 1814 aged only four months, whose remains together with those of her grandfather lie buried beneath'. (In later years his mother and Aunt Mary Whitehead were also interred there.)

John and Mary's first home in Scotland was the Charlotte Square house in Edinburgh which they had previously rented for the 'season'. There, on 19 June 1816 twin boys whom they called John and Charles were born. Their happiness at the birth was once again marred, this time by the death shortly afterwards of Mary's beloved younger brother. Wallace had sailed for the Cape of Good Hope, with the expectation that the sea journey and warmer climate at his uncle's residence there would cure his pulmonary consumption. He never reached the Cape but was taken off the ship at Madeira where he died at the home of a friend. This was a grievous blow to the family who had earlier lost their older daughter Frances from the same disease.

In 1817 John heard of an estate in Dunbartonshire which was vacant and likely to suit his increasing family. Tullichewan Castle had been built in 1808 by Robert Lugar for John Stirling of the nearby Cordale estate, on 422 acres of land purchased from Buchanan of Ledrishmore and the Colquhouns of Luss. The castle stood on a hill overlooking the southern end of Loch Lomond, a most beautiful outlook. To the rear was the small town of Alexandria. The house was a copy of a mediaeval castle, but John Stirling never moved in. When John Horrocks bought it in 1817 he and his family were its first occupants. Over the next five years their numbers were increased by the birth of four more children, two sons George and James Dunlop in 1820 and 1821, and two daughters, another Mary Scott in 1818 and Eliza Macintosh in 1823. Mrs Flaxman, a London friend of their grandmother wrote, 'I rejoice to hear Mr and Mrs Horrocks are so agreeably settled in a beautiful and magnificent country, rendered more engaging by domestic happiness and an interesting little family. Long may their happiness and yours increase'.

Charles and John Horrocks (b. 1815), twin sons of John Horrocks (Jnr), Edinburgh c.1822 (*Horrocks' archives, New Zealand*)

But not everyone was impressed by the Horrockses. Elizabeth Grant of Rothiemurchus wrote in her *Memoirs of a Highland Lady* (1817–1818): 'The gay set in Edinburgh was increased by the advent of — and Mr and Mrs Horrocks. Mr H was the very rich and extremely underbred son of a Liverpool merchant, a handsome little man married to a Glasgow beauty, a cold reserved woman who did not care for him a bit. They could do nothing better than give balls' – a scathing comment on the couple.

During the following years the family lived happily at Tullichewan with holidays in Edinburgh or with the Macintoshes at Dunchattan House. Mary returned to her parents' home for the birth of her first four children; but the youngest, Eliza, was born in the Charlotte Square house in Edinburgh.

Tullichewan Castle, Alexandria, Dunbartonshire – built 1808, demolished 1954.
Owned by John Horrocks Junior 1817–1841. Sketched by a family member.
(*Horrocks' Archives, New Zealand*)

The baby thrived but Mary who had a delicate constitution was weakened by a severe chest infection in the winter. She appeared to make a good recovery and in the spring went back with her family to see her parents' new home 'Crossbaskets' in High Blantyre south of Glasgow. Her husband and brother then took a short holiday in Paris, from where they returned laden with gifts for the children. At the same time their grandfather Charles Macintosh was called to London to be made a Fellow of the Royal Society in recognition of his contribution to the early development of the science of chemistry.

A governess's journal of the following months records how the Horrockses returned to Tullichewan Castle and its beautiful grounds. She tells that the children had their own little gardens and tools and enjoyed playing in the woodlands and riding their pony. Poor local people came up to the house and were fed and given clothing and flannel gowns made by Mary. The family knew them all and had their favourites, old Mary Sloane was little Mary's whilst the boys were intrigued by a strange man called Ellie who lived in the woods and was fed in their kitchen. In the evenings Mama played the piano for the little ones to dance whilst Papa played with the baby on his lap. On a visit to Edinburgh he took his boys to see caged wild beasts. At 'the Panorama' they viewed 'the Coronation of George IV' and 'the Carnival of Venice'. John and Charles had their portraits painted and Mama herself painted five year-old Mary's likeness. Their mother chose to spend much more time with her children than was usual in those days.

Tullichewan Castle Stables, Alexandria, Scotland. This is the only remaining building.
(*Photograph, John Horrocks of Wellington, New Zealand*)

She taught them to read at an early age and stimulated their interest in nature and religion.

Those were happy days for the Horrockses, but sadly they were to be very short-lived. The dreaded illness tuberculosis, which had taken the lives of her brother and sister, had been lying dormant in Mary. She became very ill and was taken to be nursed by her parents in their home. She succumbed quickly and was soon confined to her bed. The local doctors could not help so they called in Dr Hamilton who had treated her in Edinburgh. There was no cure for the disease and two days after his visit Mary Horrocks died. She was twenty-nine years old. All the family were utterly devastated; they were devoted to her and loved her dearly. Her parents, suffering their third family bereavement, coped with their grief in their own quiet, dignified way. Charles Macintosh was a gentleman, greatly respected by all who knew him. Among his letters of condolence was one from the Earl of Montrose, his friend through their shared interest in science and chemistry:

'Dear Sir,

It is with utmost regret that I received your letter and lament with you most justly the loss of your gentle and amiable daughter. It is indeed a heavy loss which time alone can cover. I remain with greatest esteem, dear Sir

Yours sincerely,

Montrose.'

John Horrocks appears to have been so affected by his wife's death that his whole personality changed. Mary had been a steadying influence who brought out the best in him. He had lost this lifeline and guidance and in the following years returned to the unthinking careless behaviour of his bachelor days. Leaving his children with their grandparents and a reduced staff to manage Tullichewan Castle he began a new life in the south of England.

Like his brother Peter before him he joined the wealthy hunting set and rode with the Duke of Somerset, the Duke of Beaufort's Hunt and followed Earl Ducie's hounds. Clara tells us that he was regularly invited to Badminton and returned hospitality at two hunting lodges he bought, 'Forest Lodge' at Bracknell and another one at Faringdon, both in Berkshire. His children rarely saw him. They were left in Scotland for the Macintoshes to bring up, and spent their holidays either at Crossbaskets or at Uncle Peter Horrocks's house in London. Whilst the cousins there looked forward to these visits they did not care for their Uncle John. The girls particularly found his behaviour and language boorish and vulgar, and were embarrassed by him. As he would not mend his ways Peter was obliged to stop his visits and an estrangement developed between the two brothers, which was never settled. To his credit John did not forget his duty to the poor people around his Scottish Dumbarton estate. In November 1827 when he was in Rome, he wrote to his agent Robert Fleming in Glasgow:

'Dear Sir,

During some weeks of last winter, you in the most earnest, kindest and active manner carried into effect those measures which I thought well calculated to bring relief to the doors of the suffering and poor around Tullichewan. The season of winter is again come round and I again call upon you for your benevolent exertions. My wish is ... that the really distressed poor in the villages of Bonhill, Alexandria and Renton may be relieved according to the system adopted last year. No coals were given, I recollect, but if a few carts would be proper, pray let them be ordered and distributed on the present occasion. I'll thank you to commence in the distribution of stockings, flannel petticoats etc as soon as you can procure them, and in addition to the above let there be given this year forty pairs of shoes between 20 old men and 20 old women, the shoes ought to be strong and of good leather. The distribution of oatmeal I wish to commence on 20 December and to continue until the last day of February.

Be very particular in your list and do not suffer one poor object to be left unrelieved!!

It will be a great consolation to me to receive your answer to this communication. I have sent a duplicate of this letter to you … [to avoid] the possibility of my letter being lost from miscarriage!'

He spent that winter touring the cities of Italy, buying marble statues and other works of art. He wrote 'I am busy with antiquities and my delight is great at what I behold.' His agent was told to go to Glasgow docks on a certain day to collect some valuable packages, which he had shipped from Leghorn and 'to prevent the Customs House officers from damaging the contents'.

Back home in Berkshire he continued living the highlife, based at Forest Lodge, nobody suspecting he was a widower with six children. The ladies loved him and called him 'Mad Horrocks' as he amused them with his unconventional rakish behaviour. He had his father's dark, handsome looks and could be quite charming in company. Liaisons with married women – Mrs Astley and Mrs Lockhart in particular – no doubt caused tongues to wag. But his longstanding romantic friendship with Elizabeth Arbuthnot of Newtown House, Newbury seems to have been condoned by her husband, Edward. This couple, with their brother-in-law Mr Charteris began to visit his Scottish home, Tullichewan Castle, which had become like another hunting lodge. The Horrocks children were still at Crossbaskets House with their Macintosh grandparents, and the childless Arbuthnots became very fond of them. After one visit they persuaded John to take Mary and young James back to Berkshire where they could live with them at Newtown House. The wealthy couple sent the children to good schools and were hoping to adopt them. But as James grew older the arrangement ended suddenly and he was packed off home to Scotland. His patrons had been very amused by his talent at mimicry and would encourage him to 'take off' his father. Unfortunately when he began to mimic them and make fun of their per-sonalities, they were mortally offended and considered it an 'insolent affront'. This episode brought their parenting of James to an abrupt end, but Mary spent the rest of her life as if she were their own daughter. As a child she was sent to a good boarding school in the north of Scotland. She was married from Newtown House and went back there to the Arbuthnots for the birth of her children.

Although the Macintosh grandparents valiantly strove to bring up their grandchildren in the way their mother would have wished the four boys became quite unmanageable, full of tricks and mischief and more seriously, untruthful and wilful.

Crossbaskets is a four-storey house with a castellated roof. One of their favourite pranks was to climb to the rooftops and race up and down the

Crossbaskets House, High Blantyre, South Glasgow. Home of Charles Macintosh FRS (note the roof parapets where his Horrocks grandsons used to play).
(*Reproduced by kind permission of the present owner*)

stepped castellations as if they were a staircase, putting the fear of the Lord into their grandparents below. Unfortunately the uncles spoiled and petted them, laughing at their outrageous antics. Their father on his visits alternately chastised or ignored them; so they grew up without the influence of loving but firm role models. There is no doubt that all the boys were extremely bright and could have done well academically if they had applied themselves to their studies. At school at Eton, the twins were always in trouble, for breaking rules, being out of bounds and missing homework study. The punishment for such offences was flogging by the headmaster. They were identical twins and found it amusing to take it in turns to be flogged; until Dr Hawtrey discovered their ruse and punished both of them together for each other's misdemeanours. Their total neglect of studies angered him exceedingly, but no one could persuade them to apply themselves to their books. At the end of their college days the only distinction they could claim was that John was Captain of the Boats and Charles Captain of Cricket.

In Scotland things came to a head in the summer of 1832 when the twins' wild behaviour led to them breaking down their grandparents' coach-house door. This was the last straw for the Macintoshes, who gave up on them and banned them from Crossbaskets House. Their father, brought from Berkshire to deal with the offenders interviewed them in grandfather's study. Apparently the two headstrong wilful boys faced him in an unrepentant attitude. In a letter he wrote to them shortly afterwards we read of his great distress at 'the revolting and disgusting manner' in which they had repaid 'the kind and affectionate offices of the blood relations under whose roof you are living'; of his 'despair at the hearts which can for a moment imbibe such feelings'. He had 'heard of their bathing scenes and most abominable and disgusting language' and considered them 'most brutal blackguards, wanton and cowardly'. Strong words indeed, but ineffectual. The twins left Scotland for their final year at Eton 'in sulky and improper frame of mind maintaining a thick silence with consummate obstinacy and no expression of sorrow or regret'.

Their grandfather, extremely concerned at the boys' misbehaviour and general misconduct, asked his son's advice about their futures. Sandy was a high ranking army officer (later General Sir Alexander Fisher Macintosh KCB) and well known at Court. He suggested that the discipline of army life would tame the twins and give them honourable careers. He would use his influence for them in the right quarters. The Macintosh family had a record of illustrious military service. General Sir John Moore of Corunna was an uncle, and a cousin was Brigadier General Andrew Dunlop who with his nephew Captain Robert Vans died of fever while in charge of the troops at Antigua in 1804.

The two boys should have been proud to have followed in their footsteps. But a letter of August 1832 written by their father reveals that they rejected their uncle's offer and had other ideas for their future; they planned to go to Oxford University and then study law at the Temple and live in London. Seething with anger he wrote to them, 'Who are you to give yourselves such airs, and despise Scottish gentlemen as unworthy of notice? Your plan is to set at defiance all projects for your benefit, which do not embrace Oxford and the Temple ... Years ago you put yourselves in opposition to me and my wishes. I am determined to bring you to your senses and humble your minds to a just and proper consideration of the duty you owe to me and your Uncle ... I tell you once for all to cast out of your minds, and quickly too, these rash and magnificent ideas, and obtain proper and rational ones that are more suited to your station in life and which can only be achieved by application and study. Where is the money to come from to keep you in London and its fashionable society? Not one farthing from me! ... I shall act for myself as regards your professions, and recollect, I hold the pursestrings! ... You shall have £50 from me on leaving Eton and will leave like the sons of a gentleman.

'Come down in your ideas or you shall beg ... You shall not come here [ie to Tullichewan] at all. I shall come to Crossbaskets at the proper time

Lt General Sir John Moore, hero of the battle of Corunna, cousin of Mrs Macintosh. The sculptor was John Flaxman of London, 1818. (George Square, Glasgow)

to decide for you, as you are incapable both from want of judgement and want of good feeling to do so for yourselves. You have begun the contest – you know what sort of person I am when unjustly opposed – so judge for yourselves and take the consequences.'

There is no more mention of Oxford and the Temple. Their father got his way and in December 1830 the twins were taken by Uncle Sandy to the Pavilion Palace at Brighton and introduced privately to the King. A few months later in their eighteenth year both were offered army commissions by him. John would join the 85th Regiment as Ensign, and Charles the 15th Regiment of Foot. Clara comments 'Thus they entered two crack regiments under the very best auspices for success and promotion, more so, than almost any other young men.'

A few years later their brother George was commissioned as Lieutenant in the 78th Highland Regiment and went to serve at Scinde in India.

James, the fourth son of John Horrocks, did not follow his three brothers into the Army. He had become an expert at fly-fishing and enjoyed travelling in Italy and Germany where he became well known among the Lakes fishing sportsmen. On one occasion at Ishel in the Tyrol as he walked along, fishing rod in hand, he was seen by the Emperor Francis Joseph who, struck by his handsome looks and bearing, enquired who he was. The answer came back 'Grandson of John Horrocks'. One of the party of Imperial Officers was the Archduke Albrecht whose secretary happened to be a friend of Peter Horrocks, the young man's uncle, so the Grand Duke was informed all about the late John Horrocks and his achievements. In 1841 young James went off to pursue a career in Singapore where he stayed for over five years.

With his sons at last off his hands John Horrocks found himself alone on his rare trips to Tullichewan Castle. His daughter Eliza, in 1843, married

John Graham Rogers of Glasgow and they went to live at College Lawn, Cheltenham.

Her two daughters married well, Mary Scott Macintosh to Edmund Harford of Evesham House, Cheltenham, and Eveline to John Forrest whose father was Inspector General of Hospitals and honorary physician to Queen Victoria.

Nothing is known of their son Charles Macintosh, born in 1857.

Cousin Clara did not care for her Rogers relatives, who she felt had become snobbish after moving south. Eliza and John's marriage lasted for nearly fifty years, until their deaths in 1891 and 1892.

Mary Scott Horrocks, John's second daughter named after her mother, lived for most of her life with her adoptive parents, the Arbuthnots of Newtown House, Newbury. She was pursued by John Wylde, the vicar's son, who loved her and wanted to marry her. (His sister Millward later became Mary's stepmother when she married John Horrocks.) Her husband-to-be, however, was John Stratton the son of a wealthy coal merchant of Farthingside Lodge, Northamptonshire. When the couple married from Newtown House she was given £15,000 by the Arbuthnots and bought Turweston Hall in Buckinghamshire. Over the next few years they had several children of whom only two survived, Elizabeth and Laura. Sadly, like her mother before her, Mary contracted tuberculosis and died in childbirth aged thirty-three in 1851.

The Macintosh grandparents lived on at Crossbaskets with their bachelor son George until their deaths within a few months of each other in the winter of 1843/1844. Charles had worked at his Campsie laboratories producing thousands of tons of alum[27] for the textiles industry. During his lifetime he had made numerous discoveries in the chemicals field and gave his name to a long list of inventions. The most famous one, which made 'Macintosh' a household name, was his method of producing waterproof fabric by compressing a film of dissolved rubber naptha between two layers of cloth. Another of his discoveries was the manufacture of a perfect, dry, Prussian-blue dye. His ingenious process produced a simple salt which reduced by half the cost to calico printers and dyers.

Both the surviving Macintosh sons, Alexander and George, were bachelors but their sisters' children were given the name Macintosh as a forename, a tradition which has been continued by their descendants to this day.

Clara described Alexander (Sandy) as tall and dark-haired, an excellent soldier, who rose from Colonel of the 93rd Highlanders to become General, Knight Commander of the Bath and Knight of Hanover. His nephews thought him a strange man whose personality was marred by a violent temper. He was often angered by their careless undisciplined behaviour and ingratitude and they were obviously incompatible. Little is known of his brother George. He possibly worked in the family chemicals business. After his father's death he edited all his business papers and from them compiled a biography entitled 'Biographical Memoir of the late Charles Macintosh FRS' which was printed for private circulation.

He died unmarried in 1848. His brother Alexander was the last chief of their branch of the Macintosh clan.

The 1841 census shows that there were new owners at Tullichewan Castle. John Horrocks had met the woman who would become his second wife and she lived in Berkshire. The marriage took place in July 1842 when he was forty-seven years of age, and his bride was Millward Wylde, the unmarried daughter of the Vicar of Speen, Newbury. They took a house in Chapel Street, off Park Lane in London and put Tullichewan Castle on the market. (The castle was demolished in 1954.)

The Macintosh family were becoming concerned that their grandchildren would receive no inheritance from their father if he sold the castle and never returned to Scotland. There was no love lost between any of them by this time. So Charles and his two sons 'forced' John to hand over a sum of money (probably £5,000) to each of his children for marriage settlements.

John's own marriage to Millward seems to have been successful, and once again he had found a wife who would keep him on the straight and narrow and bring some happiness into his life. 'Aunt Millie' was a kind-hearted person who became quite close to some of her step-grandchildren. A photograph of John taken in his later years shows an undistinguished old man, with no hint of the dashing handsome fellow who had inherited £100,000 of his father's fortune and squandered much of it on high living. When he died in December 1870 he left estate 'under £16,000' to Millward and was buried in Kensal Green Cemetery.

His widow lived for another thirteen years, becoming blind before her death in 1883. She had inherited Wylde family money and her estate totalled nearly £50,000. To her step-children she left bequests totalling £14,000, about the same amount their father had left at his death. The balance of her estate including her house at 14 Cadogan Place, London was left to her brother John. None of the 'Wylde' money went to the Horrockses.

In 1842 when John Horrocks sold Tullichewan Castle, their childhood home, three of his sons, John, Charles and George were serving officers in the army and James was working abroad in Singapore. It was expected that the army would provide lifelong careers for the older brothers. Although soldiering had not been their own choice they seemed to have settled well. John was to be made Colonel, and Charles's promotion at twenty-two years made him the youngest Captain in the British Army.

Early in 1842 John went abroad on what proved to be a significant trip to Weimar in Saxe-Germany. He was so charmed by the place that on the spur of the moment he made a decision to stay and not return to his regiment. He sent his Army commission papers back to England with a letter of resignation bringing his military career to an abrupt end. There was no explanation for his action but Cousin Clara who knew his character well wrote: 'there was no other reason but that he would not be under any rule or discipline, and should do as he chose. All of us – the Horrockses and the Macintoshes – were dreadfully cut up and angry, none more so than Uncle Sandy.'

(There was a curious family connection with Weimar which had probably prompted John's visit. He was close to his aunt, Countess de Colville, daughter of William Macintosh (1738–1809) and called his first son Charles Colville. His great-uncle William had died in Eisenach, Weimar, incarcerated in a dungeon there on the orders of Napoleon Bonaparte. His story is extraordinary. Years earlier, in 1781 he had gallantly offered to help a Scotswoman by escorting her back to England from India. She had been the widow of a British officer, afterwards divorced by her second husband the notorious French statesman and ex-Bishop Prince Talleyrand. Through them William Macintosh became caught up in Napoleonic intrigue. He was duped into acting as agent for the exiled Bourbon family and sent to communicate with Napoleon respecting their return to France. He angered Napoleon by rendering 'certain services' to Lord Whitworth's British Embassy in Paris and his mission failed abysmally. He fled penniless to Eisenach, and was discovered to be there by Napoleon on his 1808 visit to nearby Erfurt. He was arrested, imprisoned and died in the following year. Following the restoration of the Bourbons, William's daughter, now married to Lord Colville, went to France and was successful in recovering some of his seized assets there.)

Meanwhile John's twin Charles had fallen in love with their cousin Amelia, daughter of Peter Horrocks. He had taken her to her first ball when she was sixteen and his regiment was stationed at Windsor. Two years later he asked her mother's permission to propose marriage. There was strong opposition from all her family, especially from her brother John Ainsworth, the head of the family since his father's death. He was home on leave from Australia to sort out his mother's finances, and refused to allow the marriage, knowing Charles to be charming but as undisciplined and unreliable as his twin. The couple threatened to elope if they could not wed, so in January 1843, having got his way, Charles married Amelia at Chertsey Parish Church. John Ainsworth formally gave the bride away, then watched in dismay as Charles' twin John, who had come home for the wedding, began to pay attention to her sister Augusta. She, however, refused his proposal firmly, and he had to return to Weimar alone. Very shortly afterwards in October 1843 he married his landlord's daughter Carolina Hahn. His twin could not attend the wedding as Amelia was seven months pregnant and gave birth to a baby daughter, Amelia Clara in January 1844, at her mother's house.

Although she was living on an annual income of only about £600 Peter's widow Aunt Clara subsidised the lives of not only her own children and their husbands but also the family of her brother-in-law John who had abandoned them completely. Her daughter Clara wrote 'Beomond was always the refuge for the destitute and unhappy amongst our kith and kin'. It was certainly the only home that John, Charles and George ever had after leaving Scotland to join the Army.

In 1844 Charles became very ill and the doctors advised that he and

Amelia Horrocks who married her cousin Charles. Portrait painted in 1846 in Weimar by F. Remde when she was twenty-one years old. They were the parents of Brownlow Horrocks of New Zealand to whom Clara sent all her family records. (*Horrocks archives, New Zealand*)

George should go to live at the seaside. So Aunt Clara took a lease on a house at No. 1 Warwick Square, St Leonards-on-Sea. She gave up her own home, put her furniture in store and leased 'Beomond' to a tenant. All the extended family moved to the large house by the sea next to her daughter Alicia who, on 10 December, married her fiancé William Wilkinson in the Parish Church.

Before long they were joined by John and Carolina from Weimar and his brother James from Singapore, all expecting and receiving free board and lodgings. Alicia and her husband William Wilkinson, who was on leave from India, had his mother and two sisters with them, so that the Horrocks's family now totalled seventeen members.

When their friend Dr Gilbert, Bishop of Chichester called, seeking lodgings for his large family, the party moved further along the road to a house where Queen Adelaide had once lived, and the Gilberts took up residence at No. 1. That turned out to be one of their happiest summers. There were

John Horrocks Junior (1794–1870). John Horrocks of Tullichewan Castle sold Horrocks & Co. 1815. Married: 1) Mary Scott Macintosh of Glasgow; 2) Millward Wylde of Berkshire. (*Horrocks' archives, New Zealand*)

nine daughters in the Bishop's family, and he had also brought two nieces and a governess and four of her ex-pupils; so that there were now thirty-six in their group. Charles soon recovered his health and the twins and James became the life and soul of the party. Young Clara wrote 'All the girls for fun used to walk together in a "crocodile" up and down the Parade, in our lives we never had greater fun! In the evenings all the Bishop's party came and the menfolk played Charades. We laughed until tears ran down our faces. The twins and James (always mimics) "took off" their father and his manservant Dan James'.

When John and Carolina had to return to Weimar Charles missed his twin greatly. He returned to his regiment in Manchester, but had lost interest in an army career and soon sold out his Commission. Next he took Amelia and their baby daughter and went to begin a new life in Weimar. They lived there for ten years during which the two brothers began what could be described as a Horrocks 'dynasty'.

Over thirty years after their great-uncle's tragic death the twins, John and Charles Horrocks, chose to make their home close to Eisenach. They soon came to the notice of the Grand Duke of Sachsen-Weimar through a shared passion for dry-fly fishing, and were invited to join him in the sport. Over the following years they spent many happy hours in his company fishing the mountain lakes. (In 1874 John published a book on fly-fishing printed in German Gothic script, which he dedicated to the Grand Duke).

The twins had many adventures shooting and hunting with the Imperial party and the friendship extended to their wives and families. The Grand Duke's son became a lifelong friend, and made the long journey to the Baltic coast to stand in person as godfather to John's first grandchild.

John Horrocks would live for the rest of his life in Saxe Germany where he was always known as 'Jack'. He married three times and had seven children, two sons and a daughter by Carolina Hahn, a son and daughter by Isabella Zwierlein and a son and daughter by Maura Dimme who outlived him.

Clara wrote that he treated his first two wives very badly. He would throw coal from the fireside at Carolina and used her like a servant. Both died young, Carolina in 1847 and Isabella in 1853. His third wife Maura, however, was from a different background and would stand none of his bullying. She was a very young working-class girl, a 'cutter out' at one of the largest shops in Weimar selling ready-made clothes. She thought she had made a 'catch' and was a great spendthrift. His family were horrified at his civil marriage and cut themselves off completely. 'We are furious, it is too bad,' commented Clara. 'She rules him completely and seems bent on spending his money and depriving his children of any.'

In 1872 John's younger brother James had died childless in Italy and left him £9,000. Clara's assessment of Maura Dimme proved accurate, and the bequest did not last long. Two years after her comment John Horrocks died on 23 June 1881 in Weimar. His estate valued at £374 less threepence was left for his son Lindsay to sort out. There was no money to honour marriage dowries rightfully due from his estate to the aristocratic husbands of his two older daughters, who were mortified and angered by the default. His widow Maura soon found herself another husband, a banker from Berlin who took her two infants as his own and gave them a good education. None of the family ever saw them again.

Charles Colville Horrocks

Charles Colville, John's first-born son, followed family tradition by having an eventful life. His bachelor great uncle, General Sir Alexander Fisher Macintosh (Sandy), the last male of their branch of the Macintosh clan, picked Charles out to be his heir. Having failed to influence the lives of his nephews the twins, he began to groom Charles Colville at an early age to succeed him.

At eleven years old the boy was taken from the Saxe-Coburg Gotha school to England to be educated. He would be placed opposite the General at the great banquets held at his town house, and expected to converse with all the important guests. He was sent to Sandhurst and was then commissioned in the 83rd Regiment and posted to Armagh in Ireland. There he fell in love with a beautiful young girl, Helen Alice Miller, daughter of General William Miller KCB, CB of Mullingar. Unfortunately her family had become impoverished, so Helen could not expect a marriage settlement.

Like many young officers of his day Charles had a tendency to overspend his army allowance, and knowing how his uncle disliked him owing money, kept this from him. He asked permission to marry Helen as the regiment was leaving Ireland, but was forbidden to do so.

He sailed off to Gibraltar and there received a letter from his guardian enquiring if he had any debts. Unknown to Charles the General was dying and was drawing up his will. At first he was tempted to lie about his financial situation so as not to offend his guardian, but he replied truthfully that he owed £300. On receipt of the letter his great uncle in a rage took a pen, struck out the name 'Charles' as heir, and replaced it with the name of his niece Eliza Macintosh Rogers. Eliza was married to a wealthy man and living in style at College Lawn, Cheltenham. Charles's legacy was reduced to the interest on a Trust fund of £1,200.

Shortly after this Charles turned up at his Aunt Clara's cottage in Chertsey with Helen. He had left the army, and gone back to Ireland to marry her in Armagh Cathedral. With the refund of his army commission he had bought boat tickets to Australia.

He told Clara that they had gone cap-in-hand to Cheltenham to ask their Rogers relatives for some financial help. Clara was furious to hear that they had been refused. All that John Rogers would give them was £20 on their arrival in Australia. His wife Aunt Eliza had inherited all the Macintosh fortune, a large house in Weybridge and a London property.

So with £8 in his pocket Charles and Helen sailed for Brisbane on the 'Young Australia' on 12 April 1869.

On landing he discovered that the Governor of Queensland, Major Black-hall, had served with his father in the 85th Regiment, and applied to him for a job. He was placed in the Education Department in Brisbane, taking care of the Aborigines, emigrant Chinese, and Fiji 'coolies' (contracted labourers) at a salary of £300.

The young couple found it difficult to settle in Australia. Helen came from a big Irish family and missed them badly. They felt themselves crushed by heat and incurable homesickness, and were heartbroken when each of their first five children died in early childhood. Seven more children, all of whom survived, were born to them, Cecil Colville, George Macintosh, John Galway, Charles Francis, Phyllis, Madeline and Beatrice. Charles was particularly close to his sister Melanie Ysenberg and she was the only family member with whom he corresponded.

He was often short of money, although his salary increased when he was made head of the Department, so would welcome a legacy of £1,000 from his step-grandmother in 1885 along with some pieces of silver. Charles died in Brisbane in October 1897 when he was fifty-seven and his youngest child was nine years old. He would, no doubt, at times have pondered on how his life was transformed by the youthful candour which deprived him of the Macintosh fortune.

Lindsay Horrocks

Charles had a younger brother Lindsay, born 1847, who had also been educated in England by Uncle Sandy and was training as a Cadet on the P & O Mail Steamers to Australia. He sailed after his brother to Brisbane and had many adventures in his few years in Australia. But eventually he persuaded a P&O captain to give him free passage back to Europe. Clara described Lindsay as 'a most charming fellow, amusing, merry-hearted and affectionate like his German mother'.

He was one of several of that generation of Horrockses (Augusta, her cousin-husband George, their son Alexander, Arthur's son Eardley, etc.)

who were talented musicians with remarkably good singing voices. One of his posts in Australia was tutor to a family. When his father heard of this he 'laughed heartily at the idea'. But Lindsay was prepared to work at anything to earn a wage and also spent many months labouring with a team on a sheep farm. After his return to Europe he headed for America to try his fortune in New York but could not make any money so returned home.

All of the family enjoyed Lindsay's company. We hear of him in Marseilles with Uncle Edgworth, at Clara's Chertsey cottage, and in Russia with his sister Isabella. At one time he was employed by Lord Macdonald in the Hebrides. Ultimately his wanderings came to an end. He settled down and married a vicar's daughter, Harriet Turner. They had two daughters, Helen and Muriel, and lived at 50 Abingdon Road, Kensington. Lindsay was very close to his step-grandmother Millie, and was made an executor of her will. She left him a legacy of £4,000, some of her table silver and half of her 'Eagle' cutlery. He was thirty-four years old at the time of her death and no doubt appreciated the windfall.

When Lindsay died at Bournemouth in 1913 he left 'over £6,000' to his widow, Harriet. She lived until 1919 and her estate of 'over £16,000' went to her daughter Muriel.

Arthur Wellesley Horrocks

Arthur Wellesley, John Horrocks' third son, was born in October 1849 and named after his godfather Lord Charles Wellesley, son of the Duke of Wellington. John and Lord Charles had served together in the 15th Regiment of Foot. Arthur's mother was Isabella who died when he was three years old. He was educated in Weimar and in 1870 joined the 94th Regiment which was attached to the 'Red Prince', father of the Duchess of Connaught, and became known as 'The Fighting Regiment'. Arthur fought bravely in the fierce battles at Wörth, Gravelotte, Sedan, Artenay, Orleans and Beaugenay. At Gravelotte he came across his brother-in-law Ferdinand Ysenberg, and the two shook hands before going into battle. Count Ysenberg was wounded and saw his cousin Prince Maximillian killed at his side. Arthur was wounded in the head at Sedan, after two narrow escapes when bullets lodged in his uniform. He was taken by his father's friend the Grand Duke of Sachsen-Weimar into his own hospital to recover. At the end of the fighting both he and his brother-in-law Ferdinand were awarded the Iron Cross and received them from the Imperial Crown Prince at Versailles. Arthur was promoted Lieutenant and the regiment returned to Eisenach. Three years later he transferred to a Hanoverian regiment stationed in

Osnabruck. He married Anna Wolff, only child and heir of a Berlin Professor. They had one child Agnes Millward, named after her English step-grandmother. Clara wrote that she had lost patience with Arthur who 'would not study so as to rise' ... 'He and his wife are always quarrelling and separating – he is so bad a sort of husband and but for the little girl Anna would leave him altogether' ... 'He is always in debt and has given Lindsay great trouble in settling his father's affairs'.

The daughters of John Horrocks of Weimar

There were no such problems with John Horrocks's first two daughters, Melanie born to his first wife Carolina, and Olga Isabella born to his second wife Isabella, who both married high-born men. Melanie, born in 1848, raised the family into noble circles by marrying Henry Ferdinand Count Ysenberg-Peilpseich in Offenbache, Hesse. The couple met and fell in love in Baden-Baden. Ferdinand was the son of Princess Lowenstein Werthern, first cousin of Queen Victoria's mother. To Clara's chagrin Melanie was a morganatic[28] wife because her father 'failed to have her enobled before marriage'. Family papers record that Count Ferdinand expected to follow his bachelor cousin as prince, when Melanie would have become a princess. But in the event, because of his marriage to a commoner he was superseded by a cousin who had married into the nobility. Ferdinand was made Count of Budingens, a lesser family title, whose castle was near Bad Nauheim in Germany. Princes of Budingens still occupy the fairy-tale castle there; but the descendants of Melanie and Ferdinand lived in a large manor house nearby at Nieder Florstadt.

The couple had three sons. Carl August was named after his godfather, heir to the Grand Duke of Sachsen-Weimar who travelled a long distance to stand in person at the christening. While he was still a young boy Carl served as page at the golden wedding ceremony in Berlin of the Emperor and Empress of Germany. His two brothers were known as Fritz and Max, although all the children were given six or seven baptismal names. Their first daughter Frida was born at her grandfather Horrocks' house in Weimar in 1870 where Melanie and the children lived while their father was fighting in the French War. John Horrocks described her as a beautiful child, and thought Melanie 'the best and dearest of daughters'. When her husband returned from France he was made Commandant of the Fortress at Coblenz and the family made their home there on the Baltic Sea Coast.

A second daughter, Malvine, was born in 1881. In 1883 when Clara wrote out her family's pedigree the two older sons were students at the German Military Academy near Emms; 'fine hearted and clever boys'. (In 1955 Edith

Horrocks, great great-great-granddaughter of John the Lancashire cotton manufacturer was serving as an Australian nurse in the British Army of the Rhine in Germany. She sought out and visited her relatives Gilbert and Vera Von Budingen and their Aunt Sophie, descendants of Melanie and Ferdinand, at Bad Nauheim and Nieder Florstadt. She was given a great welcome and came to love her German relations.)

John Horrocks's second daughter Olga Isabella also became 'a very great lady' on her marriage in 1871 to Freiherr ('Free Lord', a very ancient title) Ferdinand Von Nolde of the Castle Furstein in Kurland, not far from Riga. The Von Noldes were neither royal nor mediatised[29] so Bella's marriage was not morganatic like Melanie's. Her husband was immensely rich, with lands the size of a principality and an annual income equivalent at the time to £30,000. The Von Noldes had two daughters. After sixteen years of marriage Ferdinand died in Decemeber 1887.

Five years later Bella married for a second time, another Freiherr, Behr Von Tetelmunde. He died without children three years later in March 1895. Cousin Clara has the last word about Olga Isabella: 'Bella is an ill-natured parvenue, and a stuck-up specimen of the rich woman suddenly made so.'

The children of Charles Horrocks

Charles and his cousin Amelia had four children born to them in their Weimar years – Marion, Henry Charles, Alice and Edith. A second son and fifth child Leonard Cecil Brownlow was born in Ostende in November 1851. (This son, known as Brownlow after his godfather Lord Brownlow, is important to this family chronicle. In later life he settled in New Zealand and his Aunt Clara became concerned that his children might never know about their Horrocks relatives in Britain, so she compiled an extensive family pedigree and sent it to him in 1883. She also bombarded him with letters to add to the family history, all of which he dutifully kept. They were passed down through generations and have now generously been made available to the author of this book.)

In 1856 Charles and Amelia left Weimar and for the next ten years lived on the Belgian coast at Ostende. There they had six more children; Eveline Cecilia, Florence Mary, Bernard Macintosh, Cyril Spencer Gatwicke (born in Bonn), and Maud Elizabeth. Another son Leslie Macintosh was born in 1858 but survived for only two months.

Little is known of Charles and Amelia's later years when they returned to St Leonards-on-Sea where they had lived so happily at the start of their marriage. Amelia outlived Charles who died in 1885. At that time their youngest child Cyril was nineteen years old. He died unmarried seven years later. The oldest son Henry, born in 1846 and educated by his uncle Alexander Macintosh, became a Captain in the Royal Marines Light Infantry and sold out in 1882. He served for some time on the China Station and then went to Ashanti during the war with the King of Ashanti, and was decorated with a service medal. He died unmarried aged forty in 1886. The two sons Leonard Brownlow and Bernard Macintosh, always known as Brownlow and Mac, emigrated to New Zealand.

When Brownlow arrived in the young colony in 1875 he was already an experienced traveller. He had spent his youth in various parts of Belgium, England and Germany before deciding to try his hand on an Argentinian cattle ranch near Rosario on the River Plate. When a family friend, William Lettson heard of this plan he advised him strongly to keep well away from the Indian frontier, then a dangerous place for a white man. Needless to say, like most young men, Brownlow ignored the advice and was 'very lucky to escape with his scalp when the Indians did come, as Lettson had warned him they most certainly would'.

After travelling in America he returned to Europe and spent the next few years in Germany and England. Then he set sail once more, on the long sea journey first to Australia and then to New Zealand where he settled permanently.

For the first eight years Brownlow worked in the town of Bulls, Rangitikei for the busy stock auctioneers Messrs. Stevens and Gorton. In 1883 he married Alice, daughter of William Brown of Wellington (sometime Registrar General of New Zealand). The couple took possession of a 600-acre farm on the Junction Road near Taranaki, North Island, an original province which had been settled in 1841, the year of Brownlow's birth. They called the farm 'Penwortham' after the place in Lancashire where his illustrious English grandfather John Horrocks had built his family home 'Penwortham Lodge'. (When this name appeared in the Domesday Book it was spelt Peneverdant and referred to an already long-standing settlement.)

No doubt the young couple would be able to put to good use the £1,000 legacy they received in 1883 in their step-grandmother Millward Horrocks' will. Brownlow's younger brother Mac received a similar bequest, and spurred on by letters from New Zealand decided to emigrate himself. He bought some land near to Penwortham Farm where he established his own farm, named Beomond after his grandfather Peter's house in Chertsey, Surrey. In 1888 when he was thirty-two years old Mac married Ethel Buchanan, and over the years they raised a family of three sons Charles, Leslie and Vivian, and a daughter. At Penwortham Farm Brownlow and Alice were also parents to three sons, Lindsay, Leonard, and Henry, and two daughters. A third member of their family, Edith Laura, also left England

and joined her two brothers in New Zealand where she married James Deuchar and had a son also named James.

At the time of the First World War (1914–1918) the Horrocks brothers left Taranaki and established a second Penwortham Farm of 500 acres on the river Wanganui, just outside the town of that name. In 1979 the old homestead was destroyed by fire, and replaced by a third Penwortham farmhouse built in the modern style. There Andrew Macintosh and Fiona continue the Horrocks' line in this new millennium.

Other descendants of Leonard Brownlow and Bernard Macintosh Horrocks live in Wellington, Masterton, Remeura and Hawkes Bay, all in North Island.

Charles and Amelia's youngest son Cyril Spencer Gatwicke, born in Rhemish Prussia in 1866, was at school in St-Leonards-on-Sea when Clara compiled her family tree, and nothing more is known of him. Their seven daughters all married and had children who were scattered across the globe. Young Amelia married Bernard Croft of Berkshire; both of their grandfathers had been friends at Oxford University. Marion's husband Joseph Barnes bought Dulwich School at Notting Hill, London. Clara commented 'They commenced the Autumn term with 80 boys and could have had more if they would take shopkeepers' sons.' Alice and her younger sister Florence emigrated to Rosario, Argentina, despite their brother Brownlow's earlier experience with the native Indians there.

Maude and Eveline Cecilia stayed in Ostende where they were born, until in later years Eveline moved with her husband Victor Feyht to Mons to live with his parents. Edith Laura followed her two brothers to New Zealand.

George Horrocks (1820–1891)

George Horrocks, the third son of John of Tullichewan Castle, born in Edinburgh in 1820, lived all his early life in the shadow of his older twin brothers. He had a much quieter nature preferring the solitude of fishing and country pursuits to their noisy pastimes. Nevertheless he enjoyed watching and sometimes joining in their daring antics. In later life when shown a photograph of Crossbaskets, his grandparents' Scottish house, he recalled with a grin that he had secretly played up on the roof there with his brothers.

His grandfather found him much more amenable than his three brothers and gave him a job in his laboratories to learn the clerical side of the business; Clara felt that this was a golden opportunity for George. There were no male heirs to take over the Macintosh company, so he would become the obvious successor to his ageing grandfather. George, however, 'found a clerk's life extremely distasteful, and left'.

The Macintosh family did not give up; Uncle Sandy obtained a commission for him in the 78th Highlanders as Lieutenant. The regiment was due to set sail for India, but before embarking marched through London to the docks. The men magnificently decked in kilts and feathers paraded proudly behind their pipers. Within two years the 78th Highlanders were decimated fighting at Scinde in the Punjab. Many more died from an epidemic of cholera and 'Scindian fever' which struck the men in their canvas quarters.

George was repatriated to England a very sick man almost blind and deaf. At Portsmouth some of his troops carried him to a hotel, and his father and relatives were sent for. When the message was read out to the family at Beomond his brother Charles callously responded 'I cannot go to him, I am off to Weimar tomorrow to shoot with Jack.' So it was left to his cousin John-Ainsworth to go to his assistance. As soon as he could be moved young John found him lodgings in London with a nurse and brought his grandfather's old friend Dr Sir Benjamin Brodie to see him. Then followed a remarkable scene. George's father, who had not seen any of his boys for years and had abandoned all responsibility for them, arrived. He stood at the foot of the bed, looked at his son and said, 'George you had better go to the hospital' then turned and without another word left the room and the house. No offer to help John with his bills was forthcoming.

When he had recovered sufficiently both men returned home and George transferred to the 8th Company of the 64th Regiment at Birmingham. About two years later when Clara and her family were renting 'Dillon House' in Datchet George was brought to them having had a relapse and thought to be dying from a recurrence of 'Scindian fever'. The family took it in turns to nurse him, and during one night when his cousin Augusta was sitting at his bedside he whispered something to her. She was astonished to hear the words 'Augusta if you would promise to marry me I know that I should live'. Thinking there was little chance of his recovering Augusta soothed him with 'Yes, I will be your wife, so get better now!' For the past eleven years Augusta had lived in hope that she would eventually be able to marry her true love, the Baron Victor Von Andrian Werburg of Goritzia who was expecting to be heir of his wealthy uncle.

George, knowing that if he were to die the money paid for his army commission would be lost, sent his papers back to the army for a refund. Thanks to the loving care of his Aunt Clara and her family he made a remarkable recovery, and began to consider Augusta, who at thirty-one was five years his senior, as his fiancée. When she received the news that Victor's uncle had left him only a small portion of his money, insufficient for him to marry her, Augusta ended the long engagement and married her cousin George.

The wedding service was performed at Datchet Church by the Queen's

Chaplain the Rev. Gossett who said afterwards that he had never been at 'such a merry wedding'. Clara, the only bridesmaid, loved the informality of the day – 'We just walked to the church in our everyday dresses'.

The newly-weds lived happily together in a small cottage at Remenham Hill, Henley where in the spring of 1847 their first child, Gabrielle, was born. They then left England and for the next ten years lived abroad first in Switzerland near to Lake Lausanne, then in Mannheim in the Rhineland and later at San Servain near Samur in Belgium. Clara often lived with them helping them with their children Adrienne (1849), and Beatrice (1853) and working as the family's seamstress.

In 1856 their only son was born and named after Uncle Sandy, Alexander Macintosh. (Clara wrote ruefully 'General Alexander never spent a penny on him or his sisters'. In fact he died when the boy was still very young.)

Augusta Horrocks was a very clever woman and a talented musician. She had been educated at her Preston home, Penwortham Lodge, by good tutors and separately coached in classical subjects by her father. She taught all her children at home until Alex was old enough to go to college. He spent some years under Dr Benton at Wellington then went to Dr Burny's at Gosport. He was a good scholar and performed well in all subjects.

After a spell in the Surrey Militia, Alex was commissioned in the 103rd Dublin Fusiliers and served with his regiment in India for six years until 1890. When he was forty-four he married Elizabeth Fox, but the heat of India had ruined his health in the same way that his father's had been affected. He died aged fifty-four and left £5,000 to his widow.

George and Augusta's first daughter Gabrielle died a dreadful death from typhoid fever contracted when she was on holiday in Italy with her elderly Great-Aunt Clara, Peter's widow. The two had arrived fit and well at Castella mare near Naples from Switzerland in 1872, when she was twenty-five years old and Clara eighty. A month later Gabrielle died and was buried in the Protestant burial ground under 'Capo di Monte' near Naples. Clara was grief-stricken by the harrowing experience.

We know nothing of the second daughter Adrienne except that she was born in Switzerland, near Lake Lausanne in 1849 and received a legacy when she was thirty-four from her step-grandmother Horrocks.

The third daughter (Augusta) Beatrice was born at the Chateau Boverie, near Namur in Belgium. In 1888 she married Rev. Lorimer Strong and had twin daughters Paulette and Irene but like many of the women of the Horrocks family she died young, aged thirty-eight, in Normandy just before her third wedding anniversary.

Her parents lived their later years at St Johns, Ryde, in the Isle of Wight. They called their house 'Dunchattan' after the Macintosh grandparents' home in Glasgow. When his stepmother Millward died in 1885 she left George £2,500, some table silver and half her 'Eagle' cutlery (the other half went to his nephew Charles Colville of Weimar). His son and two surviving daughters were each bequeathed £1,000.

Clara tells us that Augusta had a very happy married life with her cousin, probably more so than if she had married her first love, Baron Victor. George Horrocks died and was buried in Normandy aged seventy-one in 1891. He and his daughter lie in the same grave. Augusta outlived him by eight years and died aged eighty-four in 1899.

James Dunlop Horrocks (1821–1872)

James was the fourth and youngest son of John and Mary Scott Horrocks, born in Glasgow in 1821. When his father sold Tullichewan Castle James was working abroad for five years in Singapore. During that time he matured from a handsome twenty-year-old youth to become an experienced man of the world. Clara felt that he 'had returned a dreadful man'; 'He could be most charming and was fond of poetry and fishing, but at times became like a devil'. When he was due to return to Singapore he shocked everyone by trying to persuade Millie, his young stepmother, to leave his father and go to live with him in Singapore. He wrote from Gibraltar hoping to entice her to join him, but was unsuccessful. Eventually he returned to England, and when he was thirty-four married Florence, heir of a Lt. Col. Craddock, 'and treated her most shamefully and cruelly'. There were no children of the ten-year marriage, and when Florence died on Christmas Eve 1864 at South Audley Street she left James almost £5,000.

James was consorting with loose women in London, and directly after his wife's death he disappeared from England with a seventeen year-old girl called Marie. None of the family knew where they went, but eventually they were discovered to be living in Athens. The two travelled through Greece and Italy and reputedly were thrown out of hotels along the way, until they settled near Pisa. Marie died aged twenty-four in 1871 and a year later James too died. They were buried together in an unmarked grave in the Protestant cemetery outside Pisa. Nothing more is known of them.

Suprisingly James left an amount of money 'under £9,000' in his will, bequeathed to his oldest brother John (Jack of Weimar).

James was undoubtedly the 'black sheep' of the family and does not appear in Clara's 'Pedigree of the family of Horrocks'.

CHAPTER 5

Peter Horrocks (1791–1841)

We must now return to the year 1804 to discover how Peter Horrocks, brother of John and first son of John Horrocks MP, fared after his father's premature death. His story proves just as interesting as his brother's and at times reads like a novel. From scenes of elation when he and his family rise to the heights of social success, we are dragged down to voids of despair when they are crushed by tragedy. So many aspects of life in the first half of the nineteenth century features in one family's story. We are taken from student days in the Oxford of 1810, and life as the son of a Lancashire cotton master to the London scene of 1830. Then follow six years in Europe culminating with acceptance at the Imperial Court of Vienna, and at Prince Paul Esterhazy's palace in Hungary. Through his three sons who were pioneers in the opening up of Southern Australia we are treated to memorable scenes of stoic bush life in the years following their emigration in 1838. Thanks to family diaries, journals and letters we are able to share in these fascinating events.

When John Horrocks died prematurely in 1804 he named his younger son heir to his business company and the residue of his estate. Thirteen year-old Peter, the older son, was bequeathed £50,000 to be paid without interest on attaining his majority. There was no explanation for this arrangement, but no doubt John had given serious consideration to the matter before composing his will, and was satisfied with the decision. All education and maintenance costs were to be paid from the estate and legal responsibility for the boys was in the hands of two guardians, Uncle Samuel Horrocks of Lark Hill and Richard Ainsworth of Halliwell, cotton bleacher. For the next four years young Peter was left to continue his education at Dr Locke's school in Farnham. He was very happy there and developed a friendship with his master which continued into his adult life. Next door to Dr Locke's was a school for young ladies. It was not long before he noticed a very pretty young pupil there who became his friend. At the age of eleven he had met Clara Jupp who would become his wife. In his last summer at Farnham, 1807, Peter's mother came down from Salford and took him to

Brighton for the month of August. After her divorce she had lived apart from the family and had limited access to her two sons. The death of her husband freed her from these restrictions, although the boys were still under the care of legal guardians. Peter was always very close to his mother.

In October 1808 he left Dr Locke's school and was taken by his Uncle Robert Robbins to Oxford University and entered as a gentleman-commoner of Trinity College. Thus began three years which his daughter Celia later described as 'happy carefree days of complete freedom'. There is no mention in his diaries of examinations or that he ever took a degree: but he emerged from school and university with a good grounding in Classical subjects and modern languages. His Oxford diaries, which record the three years up to his twentieth birthday, reveal that he had a restless personality, full of energy which he burned up by constant pursuit of vigorous horseriding.

Although he became 'madly fond of hunting' he rode quite recklessly and fearlessly, and 'was never a good horseman'. This is borne out in his daily jottings:

25 November 1810: 'Several of us rode up Headington Hill when I had a fortunate escape of my life falling off my horse (the large chestnut). He maliciously got me under him and trampled on me with his forefeet and tore my coat all to tatters'. Constantly thrown and kicked he was lucky to survive without serious injury.

26 November: 'Rode 29 miles to follow Sir Thomas Morton's hounds in pouring rain ... Soaked to the skin went to the Red Lion Inn at Banbury, stript off completely and got into bed. Borrowed a pair of slippers, a hat and a shirt from the landlord, a greatcoat and waistcoat from my man Tom, bought a pair of stockings and ribbed trousers, and after dinner came back by Woodstock 29 miles.'

After breakfast the next day 'hunted with Symmond's hounds near Lord Abingdon's ... The day following, having ridden 28 miles to Wooton, immediately joined the hunt with Corbett's hounds. In full cry after a second fox was sighted my horse's hind leg slipped into a ditch and he broke his back, hurting the spinal marrow. A farmer at the village of Libbford lent me three horses and a gate, so that we pulled him up to the barn where I had everything made as comfortable as possible for him. Gave the farmer's wife a £1 and half a guinea to the man, hired a pony to take me to Chapel House ten miles off where my horse Sussex was and rode back to Oxford. Taken very ill on my arrival, sent for Stephans who soon relieved me, my illness was occasioned by too much fasting and exercise'. Nevertheless he was soon back in the saddle and reporting "My black horse fell three times – a narrow escape of my life', and 'My little chestnut knocked up'.

Fortunately for him and the horses, at the end of that week he went up to London for an assignation with his sweetheart, Clara Jupp. Much of his time at Oxford was spent riding down to her home at Goring in Sussex or taking the coach to London when she was in town. Because they were so young and Clara's parents were not wealthy he had to battle with both his Uncle Samuel and her father to be allowed to continue his courtship. The young couple determined to meet whenever possible, and friends and relations connived to help them do so. Clara was a beautiful girl with a good background, descended from a Saxon family who appeared in the Domesday Book. Some of her forbears had been High Sheriffs of Arundel, and all were 'of good Sussex stock – the Gratwickes, Olivers, Dukes, Spencers and Jupps'. Peter Horrocks had made his choice and never wavered in his love for Clara.

His journal shows him to have been of a generous nature, often presenting gifts to relations and friends. Grouse, woodcock and barrels of oysters were dispatched from Lancashire for him to his southern friends. At Hamlets the London jewellers he bought rings for his Lark Hill cousins Eliza and Sarah, a gold case, a pencil and trinkets for his friend's sisters and a gold seal for his cousin John Knowles. He delighted in showering presents on Clara – 'a set of coral ornaments and a ring with my hair in it; a gold chain for her neck; some Woodstock gloves; velvet for a pelisse [cloak], and a twelfth-night cake from Farrances'. When they were apart he wrote twenty-page letters, impatient for the day when they could marry and set up home together. He was still beholden to his guardians who held the purse strings, so was careful not to displease his Uncle Samuel. As he returned to Lancashire for the long vacation of 1810 he was carrying as gifts for him 'a copy of Brown's book and a pocket map of England'.

Happy days were spent that summer with his brother riding across the moors at Edgworth and shooting with Peter Ainsworth at Halliwell. They dined at Lord Stanley's and at his cousin's, Mr Hornby, and made trips to Lytham where their friends Jonathan and Bolton Peel spent their summers. The vacation ended at his mother's house on The Crescent at Salford, where he sought and obtained her approval to his love match. While there he visited the Moseley Billiard Tables and bought a cue to be sent to Oxford.

In February 1810 Peter was recruited by Lt. Col. Hutton, and accepted a captaincy in the Militia of the Lower Blackburn Hundred. Three months later he returned north to Blackburn and, dressed in his regimentals, marched with his troops to Moor Park, Preston, where their patroness Mrs Parker presented the regiment with new colours. His commision meant a commitment to be available for military service in any national emergency, but, like his father before him, he was never called on to fight.

Peter spent his three years at Oxford in a constant round of socialising with many friends, and by the time he left he had reportedly spent the enormous sum of £8,000. In his final year he pursued his leisure activities with the usual phenomenal stamina and bravado: 'Nearly shot my own feet by a rabbit as it came within a foot of me. Fell over into a ditch and nearly broke my thigh and arm'; 'On the anniversary of Lord Rodney's victory dined with my uncle at the London Tavern with 270, including Sir Sidney Smith'; 'Met Lord Stanley and rode down to Westminster Bridge and back to Blackfriars before breakfast'; 'Met Clara and her friends and went to the Lady Mayoress's Ball'; 'Took a tour of Warwick Castle with my cousin Sam' (who was at Eton); 'Saw Sir Francis Burdett taken to the Tower and dined with Mr Ainsworth at the Adelphi'. (Burdett was the radical left-wing Whig whose publications led to riots in London.) He loved entertaining. His visiting Lark Hill cousins were 'lionised'; his father's business partners, family friends and relations from the North of England too were welcomed and shown the London sights.

As his university days came to an end Peter had to consider his future. One option was to enter the legal profession, but an 'enquiry after chambers in the Temple' seems to have been unsuccessful, so he decided to return to Lancashire and was offered a home by his father's sister, Aunt Mary. Uncle John Whitehead had recently died, so his widow had left the Mill Manager's house at Spittal Moss and moved to a new home in fashionable Winckley Square, Preston. Peter was content to have a base there until he came of age and gained his independence. He had visited the house on his last visit home and presented his aunt with some chairs for the entrance hall. After accepting her kind offer it was time to wind up his Oxford connections.

On 17 March 1811 having said farewell to Clara in London he arrived back at Oxford in a post-chaise at 6pm and went to chapel in the evening for the last time. The diary ends on the 19th when, having taken his name off Trinity books he 'called on the President to take leave, breakfasted with Harrison, then left Oxford for good in a tandem'.

Peter's stay at his Aunt Whitehead's home was shorter than expected. His guardians interviewed him on his arrival in Preston and tried to lay down the law as to his future plans. They were adamant that at twenty he was too young to marry and withheld their permission, threatening to make him a Ward-in-Chancery. Peter's response left them dumbstruck. He would bide his time until he was twenty-one, then withdraw all of his inheritance of £50,000 from Messrs Horrocks and Co. – a dire threat to the firm's financial stability. The outcome was that he left the meeting freed from any personal constraints by his guardians. He then found a small estate for rental near to his Uncle Samuel's Lark Hill house. Frenchwood House was

Frenchwood House, Preston, leased from the Starkie family of Huntroyde by Peter and Clara Horrocks from 1811 to 1817. Lithograph of 1855 by Worthington & Co. London. (*Published in Hardwick's History of Preston*)

vacant following the death of its owner Thomas Starkie, a lawyer. Built about thirty-five years earlier the house stood alone on a high ridge facing south over the Ribble valley; several acres of grounds behind the house led down to a gateway with a porter's lodge. Directly opposite this entrance were Lark Hill House and Horrockses' Frenchwood Mill.

Peter took a long lease on the property and was now able to bring forward arrangements for his wedding. On 11 November 1811 he married his beloved Clara in London at St George's Church in Hanover Square, then brought her to Preston to begin married life at Frenchwood House. They were both twenty years old. Four months later Peter came of age. Celebrations included a splendid party at his new home, when his bride was introduced to northern relatives and friends. She was already three months pregnant with her first child, another Clara, who eventually became the Horrocks family scribe, and in her writings provided background details for this book. Over the next four years three more daughters were born at Frenchwood, all brought into the world by Dr William St Clare, an old family friend.

At the time of his brother John's marriage in Scotland in 1813 a rift began which divided the family. There had never been much love lost between the two boys and their Uncle Samuel. He was a stern hard-working man, and as guardian of their inheritance disapproved of the boys' lifestyles and attitude to money. For his own reasons John did not invite any of his Horrocks relations to attend the wedding. Peter who would not take sides against his brother was caught up in the friction this caused. Letters writen by relatives at the time refer to the estrangement: 'As we were coming from my Aunts this morning Peter met us. He did not speak of course but his countenance bespoke a mind ill at ease' ... 'So Peter hath a daughter born. I saw the event announced in the newspaper' ... 'the Merediths did not see Frenchwood [House] he said they had nothing like an invitation'. Cousin-in-law Charles Whittaker who was to be in Glasgow on holiday wrote 'I dare say Master John Horrocks would start if we met ... I do not intend calling on the young man.' Peter, with his genial nature, was not happy with this situation and soon restored his friendship with the cousins. There is no evidence, however that his brother was ever reconciled or kept up any relationship with his Lancashire kin from that date. When he came of age in 1815 and sold the family business John moved to Scotland and began a new life there.

There were big changes in the Preston business in 1815. A new company, Horrocks, Miller & Co. was formed with Samuel Horrocks and Thomas Miller the senior partners. On his father's death young Peter had inherited £50,000, which was still invested in the company and brought him 3/20th share of profits. This, his only source of income, in the first year yielded £2,671. He had no home of his own and was still leasing Frenchwood House from the Starkie heirs.

Before John left Preston for Scotland he drew up a legal document bargaining and selling his house and lands at Penwortham Lodge to his solicitors for a nominal five shillings. From August 1815 they would hold the property at an annual payment of one peppercorn. The house stood empty until April 1817 when other legal charges on it were altered. The mortgage of £10,000 which since 1803 had produced an annuity of £500 for the boys' mother, Mrs Mary Horrocks, was discharged. A new, similar bond endorsed by Peter and his Uncle Samuel guaranteed the annuity payments to Mary for the rest of her life. So it came about that Peter could move his family out of Frenchwood House and return to the beautiful home his father had built.

Penwortham Hall, as the main house is now called, is in two distinct sections. The main stone building with a pillared, canopied entrance faces west. The south-facing side of the block is brick-built and covered in ivy. The extension was added sometime before 1820, as Arthur, Peter's son, writing in Australia in 1868 recalled from his childhood both the stone pillared entrance and the ivy-covered side entrance. He wrote of 'the grand entrance where visitors rolled in, in their carriages, under its splendid arches; the handsome entrance hall, large dining room with its noble library, the massive mahogany folding doors leading into the elegantly furnished drawing room ... Then there was my beloved mother's dressing room upstairs most beautifully furnished, its winding staircase leading from the hall. In all, twenty rooms upstairs with my father's dressing room and visitors' bedrooms, a back-stairs leading to the ivy entrance. Underground were kitchens, lobbies, storerooms, cellars, scullery, pantry and gunroom. Outside, the stabling in line, stables for twelve horses, loose boxes, harness room, large hay-loft, coach house, brewery, laundry, wash-house, drying room; fowl-house, cowhouse for six cows. The stable yard was some hundred yards in length all surrounded by a high brick wall with large double-folding entrance gates. This range of buildings was hid by a splendid plantation of oaks, elms and other forest trees'. Arthur remembered 'how beautiful it all was – never to be forgotten – with its shrubberies, ornamental walks, flower gardens, plantations, and hedges all in order'.

Those were halcyon days for Peter and Clara and their family. On 22 March 1818 a longed-for son and heir was born 'amid great rejoicing', and christened John Ainsworth. Three more sons, Arthur, Eustace and William Scott arrived in quick succession, followed by two more daughters Amelia Elizabeth and Ann-Eliza. Their next child died in infancy, then in June 1829 came a fifth son, Edgworth, the last of the family to be born at Penwortham. Clara the eldest child wrote fondly of her 'supremely happy childhood and girlhood ... We were born just before and after the battle of Waterloo. Our brother was named Arthur after the Duke and we used to dress him in laurels and decorate his little carriage with bay leaves and twigs, and push him around shouting "Up for Wellington!", and "down with Bony and the other Monsuerrs"(sic). At election times we sang and shouted all over the grounds "Orange and blue should always be in view, but green and white should never be in sight".

Her brother Arthur's memoirs record how he too loved Penwortham Lodge. 'I was born and lived in luxury ... The household consisted of a butler, two footmen, one boots, two lady's maids, two house servants, a cook, needlewoman, scullery maid and nursery governess. Outside staff were a coachman, three stable boys, a groom, head gardener, under gardener and six labourers ... I had my own pony, a grey, my brother John had a black one. We raced to Preston every morning for a few years ... to get the papers and letters for my father ... He had his hunting hack, park-horses, carriage-horses for my mother, three fillies for my sisters and two extra ponies, with an old horse for the stable boy to ride on errands.'

Arthur was writing as a man of fifty who had fallen on hard times in Australia. He remembered nostalgically 'the most distinguished assemblages and brilliant entertainments at the old hall'. His father, the host, was 'without exception the most elegant and finished man in manners and bearing I ever met in society, at that time or afterwards. He spoke French beautifully, was a good German Scholar, and in Latin and Greek a master hand. He stood six feet, with a noble countenance, and when he and my beautiful mother with my four pretty elder sisters entered either a drawing or ballroom, dressed for the evening, they always created a sensation and were admired by all and much courted'. A portrait of Amelia, painted in Weimar aged thirty, shows that she was indeed beautiful and elegant.

The year 1822 saw the proclamation of Preston's Guild Merchant, an ancient tradition in the town recalling the granting of its first-known Charter in 1179. This prestigious event is celebrated every twenty years and this would prove to be the only time in his life that Peter Horrocks was in his home town for 'the Guild'. His Uncle Samuel, Preston's MP, was elected steward and all the Horrockses participated fully in the celebrations. Peter filled Penwortham Lodge with visitors and spared no expense in ensuring that all enjoyed the memorable occasion. Six members of the Ainsworth family from Smithills Hall; three univeristy friends and sister-in-law Kate from the south of England; and one of the Peel girls, made up the house party. The Lark Hill cousins and their father joined them at a grand dinner party to set off the celebrations.

Each day the group came into town to witness the events. Some of their ladies, beautifully dressed, walked with the Mayoress in her procession to the Parish Church. Aunt Mary Whitehead, splendid in figured lace over white satin, flounced and beaded, and with an ostrich-plumed turban, accompanied her Lark Hill nieces. Their dresses were of white net decorated with flowers and each wore a headdress of white ostrich feathers. The Carnival Ball was enlivened by Peter Horrocks and a group of friends, including the Hon. Edward Stanley and his cousin Edmund entering into the spirit of the Guild. Dressed as female ballad-singers they 'regaled the patrons with impromptu renditions, causing much hilarity'! At the formal Guild Court a number of Horrocks men renewed their status as Free Burgesses of Preston, and Peter registered himself and his three infant sons in the Roll. His Uncle Samuel took him as his guest to one of the prestigious formal dinners given by Peter's former guardian, Nicholas Grimshaw the Guild Mayor. Such was their status in the town that no event of Guild Week was complete without some member of the Horrocks family attending.

All through his life Peter had a touch of wanderlust, and during his time at Penwortham travelled in Europe. After his return boxes of books would arrive, well-bound volumes of the Classics in Latin, Greek, French and German. Often there would be five copies of each book, one for himself and one for each of his four daughters. In this way he built up libraries for Clara, Celia, Augusta and Alicia; so that Augusta, at her marriage in 1846 owned and treasured eight hundred books. Clara recalled how he would reward them for lessons well done by inviting them to choose a volume from his own collection. In 1823 his library was catalogued, and contained nearly two thousand books covering every subject. It was common in those days for gentlemen to own beautifully bound books forming part of the décor of their houses. They were rarely taken from the shelves. But Peter was proud of his library and encouraged his children to use it. Thus the older girls learned to love literature and became academically accomplished. He employed tutors for them but coached them himself in Latin and modern languages using the same text books as the scholars at Eton College. His daughters were fortunate to have such an enlightened father at a time when a classical education was usually available only for boys.

His sons were sent away to a school in Chester but apparently were not as well taught as their sisters. Augusta had an aptitude for Ancient Greek and for several years was tutored separately in this subject. She had always been a bookworm and would often be found hiding under a sofa reading her father's books. (In later years she taught her own children at home until they were old enough to go to college.) All the children learned to play the piano, violin and harp to a very high standard, and music became an important part of their lives. The younger children formed a separate group in the family and were taught by two local clergymen, Edmund Shuttleworth and William Birkett (who later married their cousin Mary Horrocks of Lark Hill).

Life was not always serious for the older children at Penwortham Lodge. Occasionally we get a glimpse of the lighter side of their daily life when their young cousins, the twins John and Charles, came from Scotland and lessons were abandoned. Clara and Celia never forgot one day when the four sisters and their brother John took their visitors to play across the fields. They wandered into Penwortham churchyard, where the twins pulled out a pack of cards and began to play a game on top of one of the gravestones. Suddenly there came a tremendous clap of thunder and brilliant flash of lightning. The children were petrified, convinced that it was the hand of God punishing them for being so wicked as to play cards on top of a tomb. As the heavens opened they ran out of the graveyard and raced home through the pouring rain, terror-stricken.

The children at Penwortham Lodge loved their adventurous cousins and nicknamed them 'The Furies'. In 1827 Celia, Clara and their parents spent a two-week holiday at Tullichewan Castle, their Scottish home. On the drive up through the Lake District they called on Lord and Lady Lowther at the Castle and on William Wordsworth the poet (their cousin Jane's uncle by marriage). This was their last visit to Tullichewan, but the Scottish cousins would figure largely in the future lives of their Penwortham cousins.

There had always been a close friendship with the Lark Hill cousins too, whom Clara describes as 'our constant companions at Penwortham Lodge'. Peter and Eliza were particularly close, and if it were not for the arrival of beautiful Clara Jupp on the scene were thought likely to marry.

In February of the year 1829 Peter and John's mother died at her home on The Crescent in Salford. Twenty-six years had passed since their father, the great cotton-master, had divorced her for 'suspected infidelity'. No evidence has ever been discovered as to the identity of the supposed co-respondent, and she never remarried. Banished from Penwortham Lodge she had lived the rest of her life quietly with her servants, maintained by an allowance of £500 per annum from the mortgage on her old home. She had received nothing in her late husband's will and left estate 'under the value of £800'. Compared with the wealth of her family the will reads pathetically. Eleven cash legacies totalled £327. Her possessions included nothing of value, and were shared between a niece and nephew and her domestic staff, who were also to be supplied with funeral clothes. Her son John was not mentioned in the will, but Peter was the residual legatee and executor.

His mother's death led to big changes at Penwortham Lodge. The mortgage of £10,000 which provided her annuity had to be repaid to the solicitors who held the deeds. Samuel Horrocks brought pressure on his nephew to wind up her estate and settle his share of the debt. Peter was in a dilemma. His only capital was the investment in Horrocks & Co. which provided his income. This fluctuated from one year to the next depending on trading results. He could not afford to buy the estate and no assistance was forth-coming from Horrocks and Co. To his distress he was obliged to give up his home. His daughter in later years recalled how he loved the house and had travelled all over England seeking out specimen trees and rare plants for the grounds, which were now in their prime. He had expected to live out his days there. His wife was expecting a baby in the summer and they must leave as soon as possible after her confinement. Peter had many commitments which tied him to Lancashire. He was a Deputy Lieutenant of the County and President of the Preston Agriculture Society, a magistrate, Chief Constable of Leyland and an Officer of the Blackburn Militia.

He counted many Lancastrian families – the Peels, Parkers, Masters, Ainsworths and Starkies – among his friends. Since his Oxford days he had been close to the Earls of Derby and Sefton who would regularly visit Penwortham Lodge and invite Peter and Clara back to their homes. But his popularity led to jealousy on the part of his Uncle Samuel and Thomas Miller at Messrs Horrocks & Co., until a distinct antagonism grew up between their families. It did not help matters when the Penwortham estate was bought by William Marshall, husband of Thomas Miller's eldest daughter Ann. (In 1832 when an earlier hall in Penwortham was demolished William Marshall changed the name of Penwortham Lodge to Penwortham Hall. The road alongside became known as Marshall's Brow.)

Peter's farewell to Penwortham Lodge and his many friends was at a great ball for over 400 guests. The event was spectacular and long remem-bered by all the family. Young Arthur could describe it in detail nearly half a century later: 'The 30 year-old house and grounds had never looked more beautiful. Illuminated by the blazing lights of chandeliers the entrance hall and passage to the below-stairs kitchen, now transformed into a supper-room, were hung throughout with scarlet cloth. The double mahogany doors between the drawing room and library were thrown open for the guests to stroll about and listen to the music. The large dining-room was cleared of furniture for dancing; and tea, cofee, punch, wine and cake were served in the Study'. The children were allowed to stay up for the celebrations. Clara was seventeen years old and she and her three younger sisters wore their first ballgowns made of Horrocks's fine muslin trimmed with white satin over white satin petticoats. Hers was tied behind with a broad sash and she wore a fresh white rose in her fair hair. She opened the ball with Edmund Peel, twin of Joseph, and wrote afterwards that if she had been able to stay at Penwortham she 'would have become the wife of one of the Peels or of young Tom Miller'.

Before the end of the autumn all ten children with a new baby brother 'Edgworth' were on their way south to London with their parents, transported in two carriages. Their new home was to be at No. 5 Albany Terrace, close to the gateway of Regent's Park. Arthur described how during their two years in London his father 'kept his carriage and cab and was the gayest of the gay, with balls, dinner-parties, drives in the park, concerts, theatres and no end of pleasures ... The best masters were engaged to finish his own education and that of his four eldest daughters in music and language'.

The boys were sent to Dr North's school in Regent's Park and there Arthur had a serious accident which left him physically disabled for the rest of his life. In 1830 at the age of eleven, he was skating on a frozen pond in the park with his older brother and some schoolfriends, when the ice broke and John fell into the freezing water. Arthur laid down full length on the edge of the ice and was attempting to pull him out when some school fellows tried to help by dragging his legs, but pulled his hip out of joint. John survived unscathed, but eminent surgeons Sir Astley Cooper, Brodie and Clark who attended Arthur were unable to mend his injury completely. A lumbar abscess developed on the joint, causing permanent damage. He was never able to mount a horse again, a great trial and terrible affliction which altered the course of his life.

The Scottish twin cousins ('The Furies') were at Eton then, and spent all their holidays at Albany Terrace so that when Peter's own four sons were home from school too there would never be less than thirteen children in the house. Clara remembered the 'terrible din in the dining room', and how the twins led the whole family a dance. The four older girls would at 8am be in the library-room with their father, reading their lesson books while he shaved before breakfast. They would then be expected to study until midday. But the moment they were left alone the boys would barge in and start their pranks. Clara at eighteen would try to keep her dignity and ignore them. They called her the 'Angora cat' and tormented her, winding a skipping rope round her waist and pretending to saw her in two. Then there would be games and noisy cushion fights when even the infants joined in the fun. The children all adored their cousins. The two boys vowed that they would marry Clara and Celia and John called his spaniel at Eton 'Clara'. (In fact two of their brothers Charles and George did, in due course, marry two other of the sisters, Amelia and Augusta who would have been aged five and fifteen years old at this time).

Peter Horrocks moved in high circles in London and made some influential friends during his two-year stay. His son Arthur wrote 'My father was a Freemason for many years, a member of the Provincial Lodge of St John. It was of very great service to him on different occasions, particularly on the Continent. He was very attentive to the different lodges he visited in many parts of the world' (i.e. in Europe). His new friends included members of the Rothschild family, Samuel of Regent's Park Crescent and his son-in-law Baron Solomon de Wörms. The older girls of the family spent many happy hours in their home playing with the infants Anthony and Henry. Years later in 1883 Clara and Celia were still in touch with the Rothschilds and were invited to dine at their 'most regally grand house in Florence'. Other friends were the Arbuthnots, Sir George Pocock, the Bolingbroke family and the Davisons of 'Pierrepoint' ('No children ever enjoyed themselves so much as we did there!'). Clara describes their time in London in 1829–30 as a 'golden era when everything was beautiful'. While visiting her Lark Hill cousin Mary and Rev. William Birkett at Wantage Rectory she went to a grand ball at the magnificent residence of Baron Thomas Throckmorton. There she saw King George IV's mistress the Countess of Jersey, and remembered years later her own first dance with Prince Nicholas Esterhazy. Her partner was the son of Prince Paul Esterhazy the Ambassador from the court of Vienna, who had become a good friend of the Horrockses. His friendship would in due course lead Peter away from England to begin a new life in continental Europe.

Meanwhile the older members of the family were caught up in the whirl of London social life, with invitations to balls and to some of the grandest houses. The wife of Admiral Sir George Knowles took young Clara to Queen Adelaide's first Drawing Room and introduced her to King William who complimented her on her prettiness. Peter was a Deputy Lieutenant of the county of Lancaster and proudly wore his scarlet and gold uniform with feathered cocked hat at such events as the Levées of King George IV and William IV. The house at Albany Terrace was often filled with guests as Peter repaid hospitality. All the family, but especially the four older girls, developed social graces and savoir-faire which would serve them well in years to come. But there was one event which Clara remembered all her life and which made her and the rest of the family 'more than sad'. They were all very fond of their father's dearest and oldest friend Peter Ainsworth. Clara had only happy memories of the Ainsworth family of Smithills Hall in Lancashire stretching back to her childhood when she was given rides on the backs of their huge hunters at Halliwell. The friendship between the two families had survived through three generation, but came to an abrupt end in 1830. The reason was not recorded. Clara just wrote that her father 'fell out with Peter Ainsworth after a quarrel in the Trafalgar Square Union Club'. The two men never met again, but when he was seventy-nine years old and Peter already dead, Peter Ainsworth called at the home of Celia Horrocks and her husband Colonel John Temple at Heathfield, Ascot.

Peter Ainsworth
(1790–1870), bleacher, of
Moss Bank and Smithills
Hall, Halliwell near
Bolton. Son of Richard
Ainsworth and friend of
Peter Horrocks.
(*Smithills Hall, Bolton
Museums, Art Gallery and
Aquarium, Bolton
Metropolitan Borough
Council*)

Unfortunately the couple were away on holiday; so the opportunity for a reconciliation between their families was lost. Peter Ainsworth died the following year.

It appears that Peter's extravagance was not matched by any increase in income during 1829–30 and he was seriously overspending. He really could not afford London life, and would have to leave for a cheaper haven for a few years to refill his coffers. The whole family – parents and eleven children – left England for France where they leased a chateau at Wimille near Boulogne. There in November 1831 an eighth daughter, Anna Maria, was born. Shortly after this, a curious episode occurred which affected Clara so much that she still felt resentment in her old age. Young Sam Horrocks of Lark Hill called on them at Wimille with his wife Eliza (Miller) and her sisters Mary and Catherine, daughters of Thomas Miller: 'We killed the fatted calf for them, and Mama gave Sam and Eliza her bed and slept on a mattress in my room'. Peter was away in England but by chance met

Sam and party at Dover. No thanks were offered for the kind hospitality which his wife and children had shown at the chateau. Instead some comments were made by the Miller girls which 'cut him up': so that he returned home angry and had his first ever row with his family. Clara and her sisters were upset and vexed, and from then hated Eliza, but more especially Catherine Miller: 'She turned out to be a wicked mischief maker, we never could forgive her, she has been our greatest enemy due to jealousy to this day' (i.e. in 1883).

In 1832 Clara and Celia returned to England for a holiday with their parent's friends, the Davisons, at their country house 'Pierrepoint'. The son of the family, Crawford, was in love with Clara and proposed marriage to her, but her father advised against it as she was so young. At the time, it seems that she was smitten by a young Guards officer who became deeply in debt and tragically shot himself. Clara was destined to be disappointed in several love affairs. The lack of a dowry was a great drawback, and she seemed to attract men who had insufficient income of their own and needed to marry an heiress. At her coming of age in 1833 she was able to claim an inheritance which had been left to her nine years earlier by her maternal grandfather William Jupp. She sold the property Field House, her mother's old family home in Goring, Sussex, and shared the proceeds between her mother, brothers and sisters. From this bequest she kept £1,000 for herself as a nest egg. Crawford never gave up hope of marrying Clara; but his father, who had been a wealthy West Indies merchant, lost all his money with the emancipation of slaves. Despite Government compensation he never recovered financially, and was forced to live in very reduced circumstances. He had to sell some of his possessions and Peter bought from him the superb old family coach and horses, together with its various leather trunks and boxes.

In 1834 the lease on their rented chateau ran out, and the family decided to leave France and take up their long-standing invitation from Prince Paul Esterhazy to visit Vienna. The Davison's big coach was prepared for the long journey and all their possessions packed in its many trunks and boxes. With great excitement they set off, Papa and his four older daughters in front in his small carriage (a mail phaeton), and everyone else in the coach behind.

Prince Paul had supplied Peter with a passport 'extraordinaire' and papers for the police and customs men at the Austrian border. Their route took them via Brussels, Aix-la-Chapelle, Erns, Nassau and Frankfurt to Nuremburg-Regensbrig on the Danube. There they stayed with Princess Esterhazy's brother, Prince Tour and Taxis, in a splendid palace on a hill. They passed through fortified towns where the guards saluted them and presented arms.

At Lintz, where Prince Paul's brother-in-law Count Ugarte was Governor, the Regimental band of about forty-five men, many carrying torches, serenaded them in the square outside the hotel. Peter was taken to the theatre by the Count. On the following day, at Passan, they were invited into the library at a monastery, where the monks and Abbot were 'quite struck' that the older girls could easily read Latin. At last the eventful journey ended in May at Unterdobling where a chateau had been leased from Baron Lang.

Dobling, seven miles from Vienna, had recently become very popular with the bourgeoisie who built themselves elegant and stylish houses like smaller versions of baroque palaces. Here Peter and Clara's thirteenth and last child was born in July 1834. The Esterhazys had recently arrived back in Vienna and the two families were happily reunited. Prince Paul put Clara under the care of his own doctor who attended at the birth. An old friend Dr William Jacobson, Bishop of Chester, baptized the baby and named him Crawford Davison, after Peter's London friend. The sequence of girls and boys in the family meant that the children divided neatly into three groups. First came the four daughters, now aged eighteen–twenty-two years, all educated and so attractive that heads would turn when they walked into a room. Next were the four sons aged eleven–sixteen years, and finally a mixed group of five infants and youngsters.

John, the oldest son who been left behind at school in Paris, walked out one day when the master threatened to beat him. With the only coin in his pocket he bribed a coach driver to take him from France to Switzerland. When he arrived at the border-crossing he hid under a leather tarpaulin and so arrived safely in Geneva. There he had the good luck to meet a friend of his father, Captain Tweedale, who lent him some money. Soon afterwards he bumped into another friend, Lord William Scott. Together, with knapsacks on their backs, the pair went off on a walking tour of Switzerland. At the monastery on the Simplon Pass John bought a large St Bernard dog as company for the rest of his journey. One day as Prince Paul and his son Nicholas were sitting in the Horrocks's drawing room the door opened and in walked young John. They hardly recognized the tall bearded young man dressed in a blue cotton blouse and covered in dust from head to foot. On a thick stick he carried a bag and behind him was a huge dog with a large bundle in its mouth. He was given a great welcome and delighted everyone with tales of his recent adventures.

Peter's friendship with Prince Esterhazy gave him immediate entry to the Imperial Court circle. He was introduced to the old Emperor Franz I and to the Princes Kiethersuck, Leichenstein and Swarzenberg.

Thus began 'three glorious years' when he and his family were accepted and entertained lavishly by the aristocratic Viennese. They moved from

Unterdobling to a house within the city, which became known as 'the little embassy'. At that time the British Ambassador Earl Cowper was replaced by Sir Fredrick Lamb who was still in England. Peter Horrocks bought all Earl Cowper's horses and took over his servants. His son Arthur described his father's new establishment as a splendid house containing enough rooms to house a regiment, and a ballroom with a waxed floor: 'All the court circle visited our house'. He always remembered how his father's unique English carriage and livery attracted attention and how the family loved riding in the beautiful Prater parklands along the banks of the Danube. The Esterhazys constantly entertained them at their palace in the aristocratic district of Tein. Prince Nicholas persuaded Peter that young John was now old enough to accompany his sisters on their outings so dancing lessons were arranged to enable him 'to share in all their gaieties'. Invitations were extended by many of the Austrian and Hungarian nobility to these new friends of Prince Esterhazy. The Horrocks girls with their genteel English style and striking looks stood out among the more flamboyant Viennese. The family group led by their tall handsome father occasionally accompanied by their mother always attracted attention. They were invited to endless balls in the old palaces and returned the hospitality in their own home. There the girls would entertain and surprise the guests with their musical talent. Celia would lead, at the piano, accompanied by Clara, Augusta and Alicia on the harp, violin and flute. They pleased everyone by including Viennese waltzes in their repertoire and were rewarded with requests to play at balls in many a nobleman's palace.

An invitation to perform at an amateur concert in the palace of Prince John Razzamovsky resulted in Celia and Augusta playing piano duets, with Clara on her double-action Erads harp. A celebrated violinist (Movoury) paid them the compliment of accompanying them. In the audience was the old Emperor Franz with all the Royal Archdukes, only two weeks before he died. Prince John loved the Horrocks children and would sit them on footstools around his chair in his library, talking with them in perfect English about their lives in England. His older children's social confidence in such surroundings more than rewarded Peter for the effort he had expended in their education and upbringing. He must then have reflected on the transformation in his own lifestyle. Here he was a welcome guest at the Imperial Court of Vienna, the son born forty-four years earlier to a simple Lancashire quarryman. He was of course living on money inherited from his enterprising, hard working, successful father. Like his hosts he had never been expected to earn a penny from his own labours. Whereas they were rich men who could afford such a lifestyle, his only income was from Horrocks & Co. shares. He was unwisely living for the moment. Mere self-interest might have warned him to curb his spending, but no. The invitations continued to pour in, for performances at the Grand Opera House, to Strauss orchestral concerts and to even more balls.

The death of the Emperor Franz I caused a lull in the 1835 season. The menfolk of the Horrocks family became involved in the Court mourning obsequies, paying their respects to the Emperor's body which lay in state at his palace. They followed the funeral procession to the Capuchin church for the Requiem service, and witnessed the coffin being placed in the Imperial Crypt.

The coronation of the new Emperor Ferdinand brought an end to the mourning and an invitation for them to attend the impressive Installation ceremony. The Chancellor, Prince Metternich, and his beautiful wife Princess Melanie honoured the older Horrockses with invitations to the splendid celebratory ball in their palace. There they waltzed under hundreds of candles in the white marble ballroom, a dazzling spectacle. (Later they were guests at the palace again for the wedding of Prince Metternich's daughter to Count Sandon).

A great coronation treat for the Horrocks boys took place on the Glacis outside the city. They were taken up to the walls to observe the Military Review where 30,000 mounted soldiers gave a magnificent display of horsemanship and military drill. As a disabled boy Arthur was not always able to share in his older siblings' activities. The Military Review thrilled him and his brothers and remained the highlight of his young life.

In the midst of this round of pleasure came more and equally brilliant celebrations when Prince Paul Esterhazy came into his inheritance after his father's death. Peter and his four daughters (their mother unable to travel because of her confinement) were invited to the 300-roomed Palace at Eisenstadt in Hungary. The Esterhazy family estates there covered the extent of a three-day journey and contained ninety castles and chateaux. Five hundred special guests, all noblemen and their wives and thousands of peasants were gathered in the town for the celebrations. The only other English guests were the Duke of Norfolk and his brother Lord Edward Howard, Marquis of Westminster. The evening of the Prince's Installation as Lord Lieutenant of Hungary was the high point of the visit for the four Horrocks girls. They were in the Princesses' party and their arrival at the Palace caused quite a stir. Their father wore his splendid Lord Lieutenant's uniform whilst the girls were dressed alike in becoming gowns of fine white muslin. Each wore her hair in long ringlets with topknots trimmed with sprigs of heather. Their simple, natural beauty and English style charmed everyone. Many noble guests surrounded their group and pressed for an introduction by Prince Paul who confessed himself to be delighted by them.

In contrast to their demure style the Hungarian noblemen in their colourful uniforms and costumes were graced by most beautifully gowned and bejewelled ladies, their diamonds sparkling under the chandeliers.

The 500 guests were seated at the table with a servant behind each chair, while Strauss and his 'band' played waltz music in the gallery above. As the evening progressed toasts were drunk to the Prince and his family and then came the call 'To the English ladies and their father'. The Horrockses stood and raised their glasses which everyone attempted to touch in response. Among much gaiety glasses clinked, clashed, were broken and replaced several times before the family was allowed to sit down.

The celebrations continued in this vein for over a week. Daytimes were spent at leisure, the men out in the forests on boar hunts or shooting hares on the wide plains. Never before had Clara and her sisters been so courted and complimented. Their large English coach 'with Papa on the box' attracted attention and interest wherever they went. A young Englishman named Hindley Allix-Wilkinson, a late arrival at the Palace, fell seriously in love with Clara and would pursue her for many years afterwards. They never married. Due to his lack of money he needed a rich wife, which she unfortunately was not.

Prince Paul Esterhazy had always been impressed by young John Horrocks. He invited him to join the elite corps of the private army which provided his personal bodyguard. But John felt he was too 'English' to fit into the Hungarian military and turned down the honour. It is not revealed how his parents felt about this; but the refusal seems to have somewhat affected the great friendship between the men of the two families, although the daughters remained friends, particularly with Princess Marie (later Princess Chorinsky). Peter Horrocks had limited funds, and the support and influence of the Esterhazys could have been invaluable to him. The families would meet again in following years, but young John's close friendship with Prince Nicholas does not appear to have survived.

Back in Vienna the city seemed to have lost its appeal without the presence of their Hungarian friends; nor could the expense of the heady social round be maintained indefinitely. So, wisely but regretfully, the Horrockses packed their bags and left Vienna in June 1835. An advance party of Arthur, William and Eustace, the St Bernard dog, and two German servants went ahead. They were to travel 'Veterino', keeping the same carriage and horses throughout the journey to Trieste. Their route took them through the hilly country of Burgerland and the splendid mountainsides of Styria down to the Adriatic coastlands. At Trieste they were to report to the British Consul for further directions from their father.

After three happy weeks enjoying the 'particularly nice society' there they set off to travel the forty-five miles north to Goritzia where Peter had now settled his family in an ancient palace rented from the Attem family. The boys were intrigued by the old house and especially enjoyed exploring the garret, full of memorials of centuries past. Suits of armour lay alongside rotting paintings of forgotten barons who had once worn them. The females of the family were not quite so impressed and viewed the damp and draughty bedrooms with dismay. The Attem Palace stood in beautiful hilly countryside which was soon transformed by the coming of spring. Slowly, the family made new friends and were invited to their homes. The Goritizians were an agricultural peasant community, farming land rented from the few local aristocrats. They were all Catholics, living in parishes run by monks from the hilltop monasteries. Their journals reveal that the Horrockses considered the Goritzians to be living in a time warp. They viewed their devotion to the old wayside shrines and Via Dolorosas, and their prayerful response to the Angelus bells with disdain and repugnance.

Social life for the newcomers was limited to visiting the two or three 'acceptable' (although Catholic) families and in return offering hospitality, which was not always taken up. The young people made friends and arranged dances and balls where they could dress in their finery and display their musical talents. But Goritzia could never compare with Vienna. As they were driving to one ball attired in silk gowns one of the girls sighed and recalled how they had previously driven in the same carriage wearing the same outfits; but on that occasion their venue had been the Palace of the Austrian Chancellor, Prince Metternich!

Fortunately the land around was ideal for horseriding, a sport which they could enjoy for most of the year. Each day Peter would take two or three of the children off on an expedition, riding long distances exploring the countryside. A favourite venue was Trieste forty-five miles way where they would catch up on the world's news and stay overnight in a pensione. Shorter trips would take them up rugged hillsides to visit the monasteries and churches. Sometimes the monks would be friendly and take them inside for refreshments, but not always. A group of English strangers disturbing their solitude and devotions would sometimes be an unwelcome intrusion.

As time passed the Horrockses extended their circle of friends to include most of the families in the district. Two or three prominent aristocrats became particularly close and romantic associations developed between their handsome sons and the Horrocks girls. Sadly, Augusta was left heartbroken when her unofficial engagement to Victor Von Andrian was forbidden by both sets of parents. The heirs to ancient Catholic baronetcies could not be wedded to English Protestants. Religious difficulties were compounded by the fact that the girls would not be able to take dowries to their bridegrooms. Once again Peter was becoming impoverished. Nevertheless he made one last grand gesture sparing no expense on a lavish Farewell Ball when the lease on Count Attem's house expired. As their stay in Gorlitzia drew to an end four hundred Italian and German guests danced to the music of military bands on the beautiful polished floor of the State room, and enjoyed supper in their large Court room.

Peter then left the country and with his nineteen-year-old daughter Alicia began the long trip in his travelling carriage, back to England. His original intention had been to stay in Italy, either in Milan or Venice. These plans were quickly altered when Venice was overcome by an epidemic of cholera. During the previous months Peter had suffered from acute rheumatism in his legs, which was painful and debilitating. The doctors could not help him, and he began to think that he might gain relief from the mineral waters of an English spa town. So the family would be relocating not to sunny Italy, but to Cheltenham. Clara was pleased to be returning home to England. Domestic life abroad had been hard and very tiring for the mother of such a big family. For the past six years she had lived in rented houses watching her husband and older children enjoying an impressive social life. Young Clara rarely mentions her mother accompanying them to the balls, or travelling to such events as the Esterhazys' Hungarian celebrations. There were always the six or seven infants and young children to be cared for, and after her last baby was born in Vienna she was expected to remain at home for several weeks recovering from the effects of her confinement. The thought of returning to 'normal' life in England was very pleasing to Mrs Clara Horrocks.

For her older daughters the prospect of life in Cheltenham held no joy; they were bitterly disappointed not to be transferring to Italy. All of them would miss the high social life enjoyed in continental Europe, and Augusta would be parting from her beloved fiancé Baron Victor Von Andrian. As friends of Prince Paul Esterhazy they had risen right up the social ladder and been accepted in Viennese aristocratic circles. It was as if they had been acting parts in a play and were now recast with a shift of scene to a town they thought small and boring with 'mediocre' society.

As they went off to Venice to sell some of their horses and begin the long journey home the girls knew that life would never be the same for them again. The ball was over.

Peter's first halt in England was London where he and Alicia lodged for a while with their friend Crawford Davison in Great Portland Street. There he was very surprised by a visit from his long-estranged brother John, who began to babble an apology for his very bad behaviour in the past. Alicia was in the room at the time, and was not the least surprised that the apology was not accepted. Both she and her father doubted John's sincerity and preferred not to meet him again. There was no reconciliation between the two brothers.

After three months in London Peter succeeded in renting a house for his family in Berkley Street, Cheltenham, and they were all reunited there. They were soon visited by old friends from the past and began to have some social life. At a county public ball five of the Peel family accompanied the four older girls, John and Papa, and Clara opened the ball partnered by the Chief Steward in a quadrille. The locals, however, thought the girls rather strange. The style of their clothes and their Viennese waltzing was quite foreign, and somewhat shocked the sedate ladies of Cheltenham.

Young John was now nineteen years old and thinking about his future. He was very much like his grandfather, a good all-rounder, intelligent and a capable mechanic, who would have succeeded well in the textiles industry. So he made his way north and persuaded Messrs. Horrocks & Miller to take him on. Expecting to be trained in one of their factories he was disappointed to be placed in a retail shop in Manchester selling cloth by the yard. Meanwhile back in Cheltenham his family were delighted to

Augusta Horrocks in Goritzia aged twenty-one in 1835. An academic, articulate beauty she became engaged there to Baron Victor von Andrian. After waiting in vain for twelve years for him to receive an inheritance she married instead her cousin George Horrocks.

welcome one of their Preston friends. John Bairstow, now an old man, was first an apprentice and then a partner in Horrocks & Co. for many years. When they had lived at Penwortham Lodge Peter's children had loved the three Bairstow sisters and their brother, and now gave him a great welcome, so that he was sorry to leave their home. Mr Bairstow was a very wealthy bachelor, and Clara evidently had hopes of some of his fortune coming their way. Years later she wrote 'When he died he left £100,000 to Preston charities – we think Catherine and Eliza Miller influenced him so that he turned against us – we never knew why.'

There was certainly bad feeling stirring up against Peter and his family in the boardroom at Horrocks & Co. at this time, and decisions were being made which would have far-reaching and shocking consequences. Uncle Samuel and Thomas Miller (Senior) had watched him and his brother John spend their adult lives in self-indulgence and high-living. It is not surprising that accounts of the older nephew's years at the Imperial Court of Vienna and his rise in society provoked resentment in the older men. They had spent the last decade working hands-on in the counting house and running Horrockses' factories, with little time for such leisure and pleasure-seeking. The only record of Samuel ever taking a holiday had been years ago when he rented a cottage in the Lake District for a family break. Their disapproval of Peter was increased when he applied to withdraw £2,000 from his investment in their company. He was paid the cash, plus a further £300.

In June 1836 a letter arrived for Peter at Cheltenham like a bolt from the blue. It was from the Horrocks & Co. partnership notifying him that he was to be dismissed as partner. On a certain date the whole of his capital investment would be paid out to him. His connection with his late father's business was to be severed. He was instructed to attend at the head-office of the company in Bread Street, London to sign the necessary legal documents.

Clara wrote 'This terribly sudden and bad news almost killed my father and laid him up'. She and Celia who were returning from a stay in Suffolk arranged to meet him at Bread Street to give him support. They were not received well by Uncle Samuel and were shown straight upstairs to his living quarters where they found old Mrs Miller lying in one of the bedrooms. She flung her arms around their necks in greeting then burst into hysterical weeping, berating her husband, and telling the girls that things were very bad for their father. She was horrified and distressed that he was to be given very little money above the value of his shares. According to Clara she thought that Miller and Mr Horrocks were behaving shamefully and ungratefully to the son of the man who had been their own sole benefactor.[30] She would never be able to forgive them.

From here Peter's story begins to read like a cautionary tale in the manner of Dickens, as he returned to Cheltenham a chastened and worried man to consider the future. He had never been good at managing his finances and must now find a rock-solid investment to replace Horrocks & Co. He was eventually in November 1836 paid £40,000 by the firm; £35,499, 6s. 3d. for the value of his shares and £4,000 to round up the sum in lieu of notice.

Clara tells us that among his friends was a man named Bainbridge who owned a large shipbuilding yard. He prevailed upon Peter to entrust him with £13,000 for shares in the huge steamships he was building. Another £12,000 was spent on a house for himself and family. Peter had never owned a home of his own outright, and decided that at forty-seven years old it was time to buy one. He found a suitable freehold estate named 'Beomonds' in Chertsey, Surrey.[31]

The large spacious eighteenth-century house stood in twenty-six acres of rich meadowland watered by the River Bourne. The grounds included ornamental pleasure gardens and kitchen gardens, with a cottage, two tenements, stables and other outbuildings. 'Beomonds' was ideal for the Horrockses, and their twelve children soon brought the old house to life. Their parents found good friends in the neighbours, Lord Paget, Colonel and Lady Wood, Lady Frances Hotham and others. Clara tells how they always followed the formal lifestyle, dressing for dinner and leading their family and guests two by two into the dining room. Their butler, John Green, a Lancashire man, proved a valuable asset to the family and in later years figured prominently in the lives of some of them. Other domestic staff included four female servants and one male, all under the age of twenty-five, a governess for the children and a groundsman.

The Horrocks family was reunited under one roof at Beomonds when young John returned from Manchester, 'sacked without notice or explanation' by Horrocks & Co.. Arthur, after a short spell in Bury learning the cotton industry, had taken a post in Antwerp at the head office of the City firm, Messrs Clegg and Bros where he lived the life a gentleman in a hectic social whirl. Not surprisingly this was short-lived and he returned home when the office closed down. During his absence his father had gone to the famous mineral spa of Carlsbaad in Germany with two of his daughters.

John had been visiting the Jupp grandparents at Goring in Sussex and came back full of enthusiasm for news he heard there. Life would never be the same for him or any of his family as he shared his excitement with them. He had heard discussions of the recent founding of Port Adelaide in South Australia, named after the King's German-born Queen. Tales of this great pioneering venture stirred his imagination and he was determined to go there himself. His father listened carefully and was persuaded that there were fortunes to be made in the new colony, if the venture was properly planned. He decided to back John with some of his remaining capital and made application to the South Australia Company for an allocation of 1,000 acres of land near to Adelaide, for a sheep farm.

Months were spent planning and organising the undertaking. John Green, the family's manservant, concerned for the boy's welfare, insisted on accompanying him to Australia. They would also take his younger brother Eustace, a shepherd, and a joiner with his wife and family. A huge amount of baggage would be shipped over. A large marquee and bell tent for their first shelter, and all necessary equipment and stores were packed. A number of wooden cases contained, besides such essentials as tools, a framed picture of Queen Adelaide and a church bell. At last in October 1838 the day of embarkation arrived. The group set sail from St Katharine's dock in London on Captain Fell's ship the 'Katharine Stuart Forbes', only to be stranded in the Channel for six weeks by a fearful storm. Their long voyage ended the following March when they sighted Australia and anchored in Holdfast Bay. The ship could not reach land so they were taken in by boats, one of which unfortunately capsized throwing the carpenter's wife into the sea. The poor woman was nearly drowned and died soon afterwards from severe shock.

John Ainsworth Horrocks set foot in Port Adelaide on 22 March 1839, his twenty-first birthday, an auspicious day to start his great adventure. He was, however, thwarted from the outset on discovering that everything was at a standstill around the port. Proper authority had not been received from England for the surveying and marking-out of land allocations. Many immigrants were stranded at the port, unprepared for the long delay. Their money and supplies soon ran out and ships from home with replenishments took months on the voyage. John was struck with sympathy at their plight and doled out cash to some deserving cases, two of them sons of Lord Petre.

He became very frustrated, and when an explorer named Edward Eyre told him of good land he had seen about a hundred miles north decided to investigate. He bought a horse and set off alone with some provisions, a blanket and his gun, to find the place. Eyre was right. The grassy land on the River Hutt was well watered and timbered; so naming it 'Mount Horrocks' John squatted there. His bed was a hollowed out gum-tree which served for several weeks until his team arrived and set up the marquee and bell tent as a base camp. Peter Horrocks had provided £6,000 to be laid out on sheep, oxen and mares which cost alarmingly high prices. Three thousand sheep had been ordered from Sydney and the men set to, making a settlement as they began their long wait for the flocks to arrive. Young

Beomonds House, Chertsey, owned by the family of Peter Horrocks (1837–1872), now demolished. (*London Borough of Lambeth Archives*)

John had never before laboured in the field, and knew nothing about farming; so he came to rely heavily on John Green for practical advice.

Eventually the Government Surveyors finished mapping the land north of Adelaide and marking it out in eighty-acre sections. Then began the official allocation. John was very disappointed to discover that someone else had also applied for 'his' land and they would have to draw lots for it. On 2 December 1839 he was relieved to be granted his first allocation of five hundred acres which contained the camp and settlement. Unfortunately his second allocation proved to be land ten miles away which was useless to him without more capital. Undeterred John threw all his energy into developing the first settlement which he called 'Hope Farm' – from the Horrocks family motto 'Industria at Spe' (Work and Hope). The surrounding land was to be called 'Stanley', the family name of his father's English friends the Earls of Derby. The village would be called Penwortham after his old home in Lancashire. All these names survive to this day.

As time passed two men named Gleeson and Hawker and other immigrants came. The workforce grew to twenty and two agents, John Oakden, nephew of his mother's friend Osmond Gilles, and a man called Campbell were employed. While visiting Adelaide John heard of an honest man named Theakston gaoled for debt. Hearing that he was a skilled stonemason and sculptor he bailed him out and gave him a job at Hope Farm supervising the quarrying of stone. The great need of permanent living quarters was eased by their building a stone four-roomed farmhouse (which still stands today). In time the whole 'section' was fenced, and fifty acres of land were ploughed and planted with wheat which produced a splendid crop for some years.

The problems around Port Adelaide lessened as the Land Company surveyors measured and allocated new sections. A continuous trail of immigrants then began the long trek to their 'runs' up country. Penwortham, fifty-three miles from Gawler became their first port of call. Everyone who halted there was given a 'shakedown'; a hearty dinner, bed and breakfast free of charge. Numerous poor travellers received this hospitality, often up to thirty each night, and rarely less than one hundred and fifty a week. Tales of John Horrocks' philanthropy spread and he acquired the nickname 'King of the North'.

He was a natural leader who worked hard with his men, inspiring them to develop and build up the station. There were many problems to be overcome. Most worrying was the fluctuation in the market-price of sheep. Stock bought at high rates, cattle £11 and sheep £2 10s. per head, were sold at a loss when prices fell. It became obvious to John that there would not be the quick high returns from sheep farming that his father expected. He was also very concerned about his younger brother, now nineteen years old. Two years of heat and hardships in the colony had ruined his health. Although 6 foot 2 inches tall like his brother, Eustace did not have John's physique and stamina, and was obviously unsuited to bush life. A solution came when a third brother, seventeen year-old William who had been sailing in a merchant ship in the Indian Ocean, arrived in South Australia on a short visit. He took Eustace back home to England, hopeful that the long sea journey might restore his health.

When Arthur, the second son in the family, heard that John, whose company he greatly missed, was now alone in Australia he changed his own plans and set off to join him there. In the spring of 1840 Arthur had sailed to Ile de France, Mauritius, at the invitation of the wealthy Rowlandson family, lifelong friends of his mother. He spent four months there which he later recalled as the happiest most carefree time of his life. He described the island as 'one of the most beautiful in the world' and his hosts 'generous, kindly and hospitable'. In later years he commented ruefully that his decision to leave them altered the whole course and prospects of his life.

Landing in Sydney with letters of introduction to Messrs. Smith & Co. solicitors, he was fortunate to meet up with two of his old friends from England. He had been at school with Augustus Yates, Sir Robert Peel's cousin, and took lodging with him for his six weeks' stay there. Lieutenant Rooney of the 96th Regiment, who had been in Vienna with the Horrocks family, was overjoyed at seeing him. He insisted on entertaining both men nightly in the Officers' Mess, and took them off to the races, on picnics and to the theatre. Arthur was worn out by the whirl of late nights when he sailed off at last to Adelaide, via Melbourne and Hobart. He arrived at Penwortham village at three o'clock on a brightly moonlit morning to a great welcome by his brother and John Green.

So began Arthur Horrocks' new life as an Australian which he described as 'bush life, the stern reality … without fiction, romance or good society'. Although crippled and unable to ride a horse he made a valuable contribution to the new settlement. With John Oakden and his team he spent months in the hills splitting timber to build a stockyard and boundary fences.

The following year they constructed a six-roomed building of pine covered in bark, an enclosed stockyard for 1500 cattle, and stone stables for the horses. There were now about twenty men living and working on the station and Penwortham village's population was growing. They needed a place to relax and an inn was the obvious answer. In 1841 the 'Derby Arms', named after Horrockses' friends the Stanley family, was opened, no doubt to great rejoicing by the men.

Meanwhile William and his ailing brother were enduring the long voyage to England. The months on the high seas affected Eustace badly so that he finally arrived home in a pitiful condition. His shocked parents were advised to send him to the warmer climate of the Channel Isles to be nursed back to health. Then came the tale of woe which William had to report to his father concerning the lack of profit from the Australian venture. Despite the back-breaking work in establishing the sheep station John was unable to send a penny back home. It would probably be years before he was financially secure. Peter's investment of about £10,000 had foundered. Worse news followed. The first great steamship from Bainbridge's yard sank in the Atlantic on its maiden voyage taking his investment of £10,000 to the bottom of the sea. The second vessel, in which he had a £5,000 share, suffered the same incredibly unfortunate fate. He was devastated and filled with anxiety by these terrible blows which left him almost bankrupt. Clara wrote, 'Poor Papa becoming daily weaker, weaker in head and health, and more broken-hearted and morose.' His distress turned into deep despair until he could cope no longer.

On 7 June 1841 at two in the afternoon Peter Horrocks went out on to the lawn of Beomonds House, and committed suicide by cutting his throat.

The dreadful nature of his death was kept secret within the immediate family and never alluded to anywhere in their papers. At an inquest held on 9 June the jury passed the verdict which appears on the death certificate, 'Self-destruction in a fit of temporary derangement'. His last Will and Testament made nine months earlier was proved in the Prerogative Court of Canterbury, Doctors Commons, and administered in November 1841 by Charles Barry Baldwin the sole executor. Beomonds House, its contents and land were left to the widowed Clara, and after her death to any unmarried daughters. His portrait and that of his father, with the silver plate which had belonged to his mother were to go to his eldest son, John Ainsworth. A codicil to the will, dated March 1841 instructed that the sum of £300 should be paid to Mary the widow of his old manservant John Tuffrey.

Reeling from the dreadful blow of Peter's death Clara was totally incapable of handling the family's financial affairs. Her four older sons were living abroad and not able to help. In desperation she wrote to John and begged him to come home from Australia. His brother Arthur agreed that he must go, and he himself went to work for a Mr Frederick Hayes at the Murray River. The farmhouse at Hope Farm was let to John Green who, with the agents, would manage the farm in his absence. In July 1842 young John sailed for England via Valparaiso. On that coast his boat 'The Dorset' was miraculously saved from shipwreck on the rocks in a violent storm. Reflecting on his safe delivery he made a vow to God that in thanksgiving he would build a church on the Australian settlement.

John was given a great welcome home by all his family: but sadly there was more lamentable news to be told. Besides the tragedy of his father's death the family was also now mourning the loss of two of their young brothers. Eustace had lived for only a few weeks after his father and was buried on the Isle of Jersey in St Saviour's churchyard. Little Crawford, eight years old, had fallen down a small staircase in their home and died from injuries to his head. Both these brothers were like their mother with her gentle nature. Crawford, the baby, had been born in Vienna and was cosseted by all the family, who mourned his loss deeply.

John Horrocks' stay in England extended to nearly two years largely spent in attending to his mother's financial affairs and trying to raise funds for his proposed church. But he was dogged by innumerable setbacks. His family seem to have been singularly unfortunate and naive in their choice of financial advisers, and fell victim to swindlers. In making his will Peter Horrocks had appointed his 'friend' Barry Baldwin as sole trustee. This man proved to be 'a dishonest rogue who caused many an anxious moment' to the widow and John. Arthur in his memoirs wrote 'He turned out to be a scoundrel who cheated me, my mother and us all of at least £10,000.

He died rotten in Paris as England was too hot to hold him.' His sister Clara had a contretemps with Baldwin and considered him a 'most unworthy trustee'. She could not forgive him for wrongfully keeping her grandfather's treasured ceremonial sword, 'borrowed for Queen Victoria's Levee in 1843'.

Baldwin was not the only embezzler to steal from the family. While John was absent from Australia his agent Campbell there was found out defrauding him at the sheep station. As a result all the sheep, bought at a high price, were having to be sold 'for a song' just to feed the workmen. There was no money left. Devastated by this dreadful news John contacted some of his rich uncles to beg for financial help to save the Australian farm. A trip to Preston to Messrs. Horrocks & Co. yielded nothing. His uncle Samuel Horrocks had recently died and his estate was not yet settled. But an old family friend there, Mr Thomas Lowndes-Gorst kindly gave John £300 for his own travel expenses. (This would not be the last time that this gentleman would help Clara's family out financially.)

Uncle Oliver Jupp, his mother's brother, offered practical help and promised to ship him the machinery for a cornmill which was being built on the settlement. His sister Celia organised the shipment of the mill parts and also sent a large number of grape vine cuttings, English and Madeiran, and some hawthorn berries. All the plants, wrapped in flannel and packed in sand, survived the journey and were in 1843 the first vines to be planted in the Hutt River district. Her sister Clara made John a loan of her £1,000 'nest egg'.

In March 1844 he returned to Australia on the ship 'Will Watch' and found that the situation in Penwortham was a bad as had been reported. He was advised to take out a lawsuit against his agent, Campell, for recovery of his money. Meanwhile having collected subscriptions in England and locally he was able to claim a matching figure from the Governor of the Colony to build the church. Several acres of his land were given for a graveyard. The church of St Mark, finally completed in 1854, stands as a memorial to John Ainsworth Horrocks to this day.

When the mill parts and machinery arrived in Australia a dreadful disappointment lay in store for John. They were made in two halves which should have fitted together. As they struggled in vain to bolt them together the men realised that they would never be able to do so. The two halves did not match and their task was impossible. John's hopes were dashed to the ground, and for the first time he could not control his frustration. His man, John Green, said it was a pitiful sight to see him seated on a stone, his head buried in his hands, his great heart almost broken.

His luck did not improve. Although when the case came to court he won the lawsuit against Campbell he could never recover any of his money. He was almost destitute, with an empty stockyard and no prospects for his sheep station. Casting about desperately for ideas to earn some cash he went to Adelaide and offered his services to the colonists there. He volunteered to seek out for them suitable farming land in the unmapped area to the north of Port Augusta. If they would sponsor him and pay all expenses he would lead an expedition to survey and map the land. They were convinced enough to agree to the scheme and collected voluntary contributions to finance it. John returned to Penwortham to plan the project. He would include the two best workmen, Kilroy and Theakston, in his team. They would take with them an artist named Gill, and two men to look after the animals and tents. One of these was an Aboriginal named Jimmy Moorhouse and the other a Mr Garlick.

The expedition was provided with cash to buy provisions, cattle, horses and ammunition for their potentially dangerous enterprise. Before they left John made two fateful decisions. He had received a letter from his mother beseeching him to sell up everything in Australia and return home to England. He put it to one side 'to be considered after the expedition'. The second was to exchange six of his cows, worth £15 each, for a camel, said to be the first one to be imported into Australia. This was to be an experiment which he hoped would enable him to explore territory inaccessible to horses.

The team's first foray was into the barren desolate country to the west of Lake Torrens. Marking it unsuitable for farming and inhabited by unfriendly natives who were very troublesome, John took Gill and Kilroy to explore the high land nearly 150 miles from their base at Depot Creek. They set out on 28 August 1846 with 356lbs of provisions and water loaded on the camel. After five days walking over 65 miles of difficult terrain, mostly heavy red sandhills, they arrived at a salt-water lake. Kilroy pointed out a beautiful bird which he thought they should shoot for their wildlife collection.

In Horrocks's own words we read what happened next: 'My gun being loaded with slugs in one barrel and ball in the other I stopped the camel to get at the shotbelt which I could not get without his laying down. While Mr Gill was unfastening it I was screwing the ramrod into the wad over the slugs, standing close alongside the camel. At this moment the camel gave a lurch to one side, and caught his pack in the cock of my gun, which discharged the barrel I was unloading, the contents of which took off the middle fingers of my right hand between the second and third joints, and entered my left cheek by my lower jaw, knocking out a row of teeth from my upper jaw'.

The trio were in a terrible dilemma, stranded in inhospitable country, the leader badly injured. Kilroy undertook to return to the depot for men and horses, whilst Gill stayed with his friend and cared for him as best he could. The rest of the story makes very sad reading. Young John was carried the 160 miles back to Penwortham village where he was tended lovingly by John Green, his brother Arthur who had been brought home, and the rest of the men. His friend Dr Nott came from Adelaide and desperately tried to treat the injuries. But without the necessary medical equipment the situation was hopeless. It was typical of John that despite his great pain and discomfort he managed to send a report of the blighted expedition's findings to the committee who had sponsored him. He died on the evening of 23 September 1846 aged twenty-eight years, and was buried in his own churchyard in Penwortham village.

Once again the Horrocks family had lost the young man who was the brightest hope of his generation, and so dearly loved by them all. His loyal 'man', John Green, planted a white hawthorn sapling, grown from the English berries, over his grave. Green was a remarkable man who, through all their pioneering years in the new Colony was at the Horrockses' side, a tower of strength, completely dependable. Young John greatly valued his advice and companionship, and consulted him on all matters. Grief-stricken

John Ainsworth Horrocks of Penwortham, South Australia (1818–46). Portrait *c.* 1845 by unknown artist. (*Copy from Horrocks Archives, New Zealand*)

166

John Horrocks with Kilroy and the artist S. T. Gill, Australia 1818–1880, *Travelling through the bush and sandridges, August 30, 1846*. Adelaide watercolour, pencil on paper 18.6 × 30.3 cm.
(*Art Gallery of S. Australia, Adelaide Gift of Mrs Howard Davenport 1939*)

at his death, Green stayed on in Australia and in later years lived in his master's first-built cottage in Penwortham. He took an active part in the building of St Marks and lies buried in the churchyard there, next to his beloved master.

Arthur Horrocks was a beneficiary in his brother's will. He was left the 500 acres of the second allocation of land which lay ten miles from Penwortham. He sold this not having the capital to develop it and went to live with John Oakden at Cadlunga near Mount Horrocks. He spent some happy years there, during which he courted Ann Jacob of Morooroo. She was a friend who had sailed to Australia from Winchester in England in 1839 to join her brothers William and John. They were near-neighbours of the Horrockses. John Jacob had been at John's deathbed reading prayers and scripture readings, and at the funeral had led the religious obsequies. So there was already a close family link.

After their marriage in 1850 they moved into the farmhouse at

S. T. Gill Australia 1818–1880, *Invalid's tent, salt lake 75 miles north-west of Mount Arden*
c. 1846 Adelaide watercolour, pencil on paper 21.4 × 34.2 cm.
John Horrocks lies injured in the tent, awaiting help from the base camp.
(*Art Gallery of S. Australia, Adelaide Morgan Thomas Bequest Fund 1944*)

Penwortham, farming the fifty acres. Although crippled by his childhood
accident Arthur worked hard on the land and was one of the team that
built the church of St Mark and the parsonage. His sister Clara sent money
from England to pay for the altar rails of the new church. John's godmother,
Sarah Ainsworth of Smithills Hall, Lancashire, also sent gifts; a bible,
communion books and church linen. (Sarah was the eldest daughter of
Peter Ainsworth. She married the Hon. Arthur Annersley, second son of
an Irish Peer, the Earl of Moutinnos. A few days after their wedding the
bridegroom was drowned when swimming in the sea off the cliffs at
Blackpool.)

In the year 1858 Arthur's income from Hope Farm was seriously reduced
by unforseeable events. The Victorian goldfields were discovered, and drew
people like magnets. Men left the land in their thousands, sold up and
made the trek there, hoping to make fortunes. Arthur was left without men

to do the heavy work, so decided to try his luck at making some quick cash. He joined his solicitor's brother Mr Moulden and the two men made the long journey to the Bendigo diggings north of Melbourne.

After seven months away he returned home, wiser but not much richer with £180 in his pocket. The venture had proved difficult and at times dangerous. He had survived a narrow escape from drowning but could not afford the enormously inflated price of foodstuffs at the goldfields. One bag of flour cost £25. He was relieved to be back to the normality of family life with his wife and family, and accepted the fact that he would never become a rich man. Years later he wrote in a short biography 'I never took kindly to a colonial life, and even now after 29 years the feeling and recollection of the Old World is strong in me'. Nevertheless he threw all his energy into running the farm, and was proud to be a founder member of the Northern Agricultural and Horticultural Society. He also served as Councillor for Clare district and became well known in the community. He and his wife became the parents of five children, all born at Penwortham and named after their father's brothers and sisters, Charles, Eardley, Arthur John, Clara and William Crawford. Their descendants still live in South Australia and are very proud of their pioneer ancestors, John, Eustace and Arthur Horrocks.

Arthur died in 1872 and is buried in North Adelaide cemetery. Ann, his wife, died two years later at her brother's home in Jambierton, South Australia and is buried there.

John Horrocks's death in 1846 caused long-term repercussions which directly affected the development of Penwortham township, Australia. In his will he left his sister Clara the three sections of land which had been let to William Robinson. She had lent him her £1,000 'nest egg' and this was in settlement of the loan. The village section was left to his English mother, also named Clara, for her lifetime and afterwards to any of his sisters then unmarried. This land was not to be sold for twenty-one years. This last restriction meant that the Penwortham, South Australia estate had to be 'put in Chancery' in England and administered by trustees, one of whom was Arthur Horrocks. As the years passed local people were unable to buy any of the land and grew tired of waiting. Some moved into the next valley and trade declined. Thirteen years passed before the restriction was lifted. The long delay had reduced its value when the population of Clare township overtook the numbers in Penwortham.

Many of the old buildings have now gone. The flour mill was burned down in 1869. The Derby Arms Inn closed as a licensed hotel in 1890 and after some years was demolished for road-widening. In 1915 a new railway cut through the area. John Horrocks' station house stood in its path and was demolished. The parsonage land was also affected, and after many years without an incumbent the house was sold in 1923 and later demolished.

In 1946, the centenary of his death, three stone cairns were erected in memory of John Horrocks. The first was built at Penwortham, about 200 yards from his grave. The second on the roadside near Gulnare, ('Gulnare' was his pet dog) and the third at the head of Horrockses Pass. A thousand people attended the ceremony.

In September 1996 the 150th anniversary celebrations, organised by the Mount Horrocks Historical Society at Green's Cottage in Penwortham, saw the unveiling of a commemorative plaque and the laying of a wreath on the two graves. The marble plaque was unveiled by Mrs Pamela McTaggart, great-granddaughter of Arthur Horrocks, and wreaths laid by John Green's granddaughter Mrs Hazel McGee. A memorial service was held in St Mark's church for John Ainsworth Horrocks, one of Australia's most remarkable pioneers.

Edgworth Horrocks (1829–1908)

Edgworth was a younger son of Peter and Clara Horrocks, born just a few months before they left Penwortham Lodge in 1829, and educated at the Charterhouse School under Dr Augustus Saunders. During the Crimean War he joined his cousin Charles as Lieutenant in the 1st Lanarkshire Militia. When that regiment disbanded he was promoted Major in the Highland Borderers and served until 1875. In June 1869 he married Mary Westcar, daughter of one of his father's Oxford friends, at St James, Piccadilly. They had one daughter Clara Elizabeth born at their home 'Mascalls' in Kent in 1871. She married Frederick Morgan of Hungershaw Park, Tunbridge Wells, and had two sons and one daughter. (A descendant of theirs was the high-ranking army officer named Morgan who worked with General Montgomery in producing the strategic plan for the 1944 'D-Day' invasion of Europe.)

Edgworth, named after the village in Lancashire from which the Horrocks family originated, was the longest-lived of the sons of Peter and Clara, and the only one to stay in Europe for all of his life. He was a thoroughly good man who took responsibility for his widowed mother after the deaths of his four older brothers. She lived with him and the younger sisters in a rented house near Louvain in Belgium, until he joined the army and eventually bought the house 'Mascalls' at Paddock Wood in Kent. Until his marriage whatever cash he had seems to have gone towards supporting his female relatives, who were constantly in debt and needing handouts. Clara was exasperated by their irresponsible attitude to money and felt that they fleeced Edgworth, preying on his generosity and good nature. His wife Mary had always expected to be her father's heir, but in middle age her parents gave birth to a son who inherited the family money. Although he died young he willed everything to a friend on the understanding that any children would change their name to Westcar. Mary and Edgworth did not receive a penny of her intended inheritance.

After his army service Edgworth became severely disabled by rheumatism in his legs (like his father before him), but nevertheless created a most beautiful garden at 'Mascalls'. He had to restore the fabric of the house and succeeded in making it a haven where Clara and other relatives were always welcome.

Edgworth was the only member of his family to keep in touch with the Preston relatives. He was very friendly with Frederick Marshall the son of Ann (née Miller) who

Arthur Horrocks aged forty-five in 1864, with his son Eardley. Six years later his sister Clara brought Eardley (and his sister Clara Ann) to England for a prolonged visit.

lived at his own birthplace 'Penwortham Lodge' (Hall). On one occasion when travelling from Aldershot to his regiment in Hamilton, Edgworth fell ill at Penwortham Lodge where he broke his journey. Frederick Marshall saved his life by careful nursing.

When Edgworth died in 1908 he left nearly £12,000 to his daughter Clara. Edgworth and Arthur were the only two of Peter Horrocks' six sons to reach maturity and have children. Of their brothers, John Ainsworth died in Australia aged twenty-eight, Eustace in Jersey, Channel Isles aged twenty and Crawford Davison at Chertsey aged eight.

William Scott, born in 1823 had visited his brothers in Australia in 1841 whilst sailing on a merchant ship and taken Eustace back home to England. A neighbour in Chertsey, Lord Hotham, obtained a Cadetship in the 21st Madras Native Infantry for Eustace, but he was too ill to accept it. So nineteen-year old William took his place and sailed for India in February 1842. He was promoted to Ensign, but in December 1844 contracted cholera, and died after an illness of only four hours. His brother officers erected a tombstone over his grave at Hulladghie, Madras.

Clara Horrocks (1812–1909) and her sisters

In contrast to their brothers the daughters of the Horrocks family were very long-lived. Clara died aged ninety-seven in 1909. Four of her sisters, Augusta, Celia, Amelia and Ann-Eliza lived into their eighties, Alicia and Anna-Maria beyond sixty. Their mother, Clara, survived for twenty-four years after her husband's death. Left virtually penniless she had to leave Beomonds House in Chertsey and let it to tenants. Her daughter Clara went to Messrs. Horrocks & Co. in Preston, cap in hand to ask for an annuity for her. She was turned away; but their friends Mr Clegg and Mr Gorst who had helped them in the past were touched by her plight and agreed to pay her £250 per annum from their own funds, and to settle the outstanding debts. She lived on this and the rent from 'Beomonds', and travelled around Europe staying with different members of her family until settling with her younger daughters at Teruven outside Brussels for many years. Occasionally she was relieved by contributions from her children who had married fairly well, or received bequests from relatives.

She herself had close relatives who were very wealthy. On her mother's side was William Gratwicke of Ham Place, Angmering in Sussex who left over £150,000 when he died aged ninety in 1821. He had one daughter who died shortly after him so his estate went to the descendants of his two sisters, Amy and Philadelphia. One of these was the William Jupp who had made Clara's daughter of the same name his heir in 1822. Gratwicke's will was contested by the Sussex relatives and (as the tenant of Ham Place had life tenancy) dragged on in the Chancery Courts until 1871 when Clara (Junior) received her one-sixth portion of £24,000.

Perceiving this to be family money Clara, who was by now fifty-nine years old took £6,000 for herself and shared the rest equally between her mother and surviving brothers and sisters, and the four families of her Jupp aunts and uncles.

It is interesting to discover that William Kinliside Gratwicke had been a very successful racehorse breeder and owner. He won the Derby twice with 'Frederick' in 1825 and 'Merry Monarch' in 1845, and was narrowly deprived of a hat-trick when his 'Sittingbourne' ran second to 'West Australian'. He also won The Oaks three times with 'Cheerful', 'Hesse Hamburg' and 'Ebony'; the Cambridgeshire with 'Landgrave', the 1,000 guineas with 'Governess' and the Steward's Cup with 'Maid of Kent'. In 1845 when Clara's family were living at Windsor Alicia and her husband treated them to a visit to the Derby at Epsom Racecourse. They were all delighted to see their cousin William Gratwicke's horse, Merry Monarch win the race and 'so very proud when he came across to receive our congratulations'.

It is clear from Clara's letters and writings that she was an intelligent, articulate woman who cared deeply about her family and its connections. As the oldest and longest surviving of John Horrocks's grandchildren she remembered very early events and had listened intently to conversations and discussions even in her childhood. For many years in the 1870s and 1880s she wrote regularly to her nephew Brownlow in New Zealand, recording all that she could remember of the Horrocks story.

As she grew older a bitterness crept into her writings as she reviewed the fall of her branch of the family from wealth into near-penury. She tells how on several occasions she had been mortified to have to go begging to the partners of Horrocks & Co. in Preston for money for her destitute mother and siblings. More often than not she came away empty-handed or was insulted by the pittance offered to her.

In 1850–52, when the family were lodging at Louvain in Belgium, in desperation Clara wrote to the Miller family telling them that her mother was unwell and young Edgworth's physical and mental health was suffering and had brought on epilepsy. 'To my dying day I shall never recover from these begging letters to the Millers, never! It was all dreadful, and worse still to receive and read their letters in reply and touch the small sum of a £5 note. They are humiliations never to be got over.'

She came to despise Thomas Miller who had been treated with such charity by her grandfather, and owed all his success in life to John's generosity. Now he was the sole owner of Horrocks & Co. but treated his benefactor's impoverished daughter-in-law with contempt. She resented the fact that he traded worldwide using the name 'Horrockses' whilst her family received nothing from this valuable asset.

Whilst this was true, Clara ignores the fact that the two Miller sons and their sister Eliza had all married Horrockses, the founder's nieces and nephew. It was also a fact that the Millers had worked all their lives in the cotton mills of Preston, whereas her father Peter and his brother John had lived the lives of idle-rich gentlemen, frittering away their share of John Horrocks's fortune. Perhaps she never knew that her grandfather in his will had specifically excluded her father from ever inheriting Horrocks & Co. or the Penwortham Lodge estate. He had directed that if his second son John did not live to be twenty-one to inherit, these assets should pass direct to Uncle Samuel of Lark Hill or his heirs. She admits that in selling Horrocks & Co. when he turned twenty-one 'Uncle John killed the goose that laid the golden egg', but she was completely unknowing about the workings of big business and always harboured the suspicion that her branch of the family had somehow been cheated of a bigger share in Horrockses' phenomenal success.

Clara knew that her father, Peter, had invested his inheritance in the business, but was tolerated as a shareholder only as long as it suited the partnership to keep him. In her opinion his ousting from the company was the indirect cause of his subsequent failure to manage his finances, and ultimately his death. For this she could never forgive them.

There had always been a close friendship between Clara and her sister Celia and the two often lived together in the 1840s and 1850s. When she was forty-three Celia married, as his second wife, a widower Colonel John Temple, brother of Sir Grenville Temple, 10th Baronet of Stowe (Clara could not resist commenting that the couple received over 200 wedding gifts!). She and her husband, who was retired from the 60th Rifles, at first rented the impressive Potters Park residence in Surrey and later lived at 'Heathfield', Ascot.

The family were all very fond of another brother-in-law 'Willie' Wilkinson who had married Mary Alicia at St Leonards-on-Sea in 1844 and shared the happy season they spent there. He was a kind generous man who enjoyed arranging treats for his 'in-laws' such as visits to Ascot and Epsom for the races, which were otherwise beyond their means.

When Alicia and Willie sailed for India to rejoin his regiment, the 21st Bombay Native Infantry, they looked forward to a long and happy life together. But Willie soon found himself in one of the most bitterly fought battles of the century, which General Napier won against tremendous opposition to keep Scinde and so the whole of the Punjab. Willie showed conspicuous gallantry in the fierce fighting and on three separate occasions was congratulated by Napier. When he saw his own Major about to be attacked by the great Chief Belooch he leaped in and killed the man with the thrust of his sword. General Napier had Belooch's great sword engraved with Willie's name and presented to him after the battle. He offered him promotion to Major in 'Jacob's Horse' regiment or to any post he preferred.

Three years later in 1851 while he was visiting a friend in Janna near Bombay, Willie was struck with a severe attack of gastroenteritis and within a very short time died, most unexpectedly and tragically for his family.

Maria-Alicia, distraught and already weakened by the heat of India, had to travel from Lahore 800 miles up the Punjab in bullock carts. She and her four-year old daughter Clara Harriet were escorted all the way by Willie's fellow officers. On her return to Europe she went to live at first in the

Chateau at Namur in Belgium with her sisters Clara and Augusta and Augusta's husband. Later she settled in Louvain with her mother, brother Edgworth and sisters Anna-Maria and Ann-Eliza.

Mary-Alicia lived until she was sixty-nine, and died on 14 January 1885, probably at St Leonards-on-Sea. Her experiences in India had affected her health, and Clara described her as 'nervous and highly excitable'.

Anna-Maria, Clara's youngest sister who was born at Boulogne in 1851 at the beginning of her parents' European travels, spent much of her life on the Continent. After her father's death she lived for many years with her mother and siblings at Louvain in Belgium. She was thought by Clara to be spoiled, ungovernable, and a spendthrift. She and her next-older sister Ann-Eliza led Clara and her mother a merry-dance. When they were still young teenagers in St Leonards-on-Sea it was discovered that they had secretly been buying on credit in the shops, and run up large bills. Clara and the older sisters had somehow to clear a debt of £500, and (although Augusta refused to) began by selling their treasured libraries of books given to them by their father.

Clara managed to beg money from Mr Clegg and Mr Lowndes-Gorst in Preston and some from her Jupp Aunts in Sussex, until the debt was repaid. The sisters' conduct did not improve as they grew older, until Clara grew exasperated and wrote of them, 'They were our family's Disturbers of the Peace and expected me to get money for them to pay their debts. They spent all Edgworth's capital and expected me and Celia and Augusta to give them ours. They became unscrupulous until no one would give them a farthing. It is all very sad. Their conduct has been the cause of the separation between us older sisters and our younger ones.'

She explains that whilst their father had governed and educated the four older daughters to a very high standard, after his death his widow could not manage the younger girls. Celia taught them to read and write. 'Their mother was not capable of teaching them anything, ruling them has become an impossibility in her, have them ruled [by us] she will not permit.'

The poor widowed Clara must have found life very difficult. Her husband and four of her sons had died. Arthur was at the other side of the world in Australia, and Edgworth was too young to help much. Her younger daughters were causing such trouble that their older ladylike sisters wrote them off as 'ungovernable'. Over this, the family split in two, never to be reunited.

Eventually when she was thirty-two Anna-Maria married Captain Charles Nassau Martin of the Royal Engineers who was nearly thirty years her senior. They lived mostly in Dublin where he was stationed and there had two sons Charles Francis (Frank) and Charles Rudinge, and a daughter Frances. After their move to Woolwich a second daughter Eileen was born. Captain Charles was promoted Major in 1872 and following army reforms retired as Lieutenant General in July 1882. He fought with distinction throughout the Crimean Wars and just before peace was signed was shot in the hip by a Russian firing from a hidden pit. He received every English and Turkish medal struck for that war, but suffered severely from a rifle ball that could not be extracted from his leg. On his retirement the family went to live in Mannheim in Baden where Charles died. Anna-Maria died in 1900.

Ann-Eliza the other 'ungovernable' daughter, born at Penwortham in 1826, did not marry and lived with her mother in Belgium. Clara hints occasionally that they were influenced by the local Catholic community and their priests and became too close to Rome for her liking. Not much is known of their last years, but by 1865 Mrs Clara Horrocks, when she had reached her ninety-first year, was living back in her native and beloved county of Sussex. She died at the home of her niece, yet another Ann-Eliza, née Oliver, the wife of Reginald Warren of Preston Place, East Preston, Sussex on 30 August and was laid to rest in the churchyard of the parish church of East Preston.

After her mother's death Ann-Eliza stayed in Belgium and is not mentioned again in Clara's writings. There was a fourteen-year age gap between the two and it is clear that they simply did not like each other. We do not hear the younger girl's view of her older sisters, but it was as if they were from two different families: the older girls academic and somewhat snobbish and maybe sanctimonious, the younger end resentful and frustrated by their poverty. Each set coped in opposite ways with the tragedies which had blighted their lives.

As the years passed Ann-Eliza outlived all her brothers and sisters. She died at Teruven in Belgium in June 1920, the day after her eighty-fourth birthday.

As the family began to split up they had to decide what to do with their house 'Beomonds' in Chertsey which their father Peter had bought in 1837. When he died in 1841 he had left the house on trust, first to his wife Clara and, after her death, to any unmarried daughters. Edgworth and his solicitor conveyed the property to the unmarried sisters, but in early 1872 they agreed to sell it. There were three cottages on the estate, one of which Clara kept as her 'bolt-hole' where she could spend quiet times away from her sisters and their families.

In 1870 she brought her brother Arthur's children Eardley and Clara Ann from South Australia to Europe for a prolonged visit hoping to set them up in promising futures. She tried unsuccessfully to persuade the management of Horrockses in Preston to employ young Eardley and was disgusted by their refusal. Clara Ann's visit had a happier conclusion. She married James Grieves McLaren of Edinburgh from her Uncle Edgworth's home 'Mascalls' in Paddock Wood, Kent. Her husband worked in Calcutta and Clara Ann had four children there, another Clara and three boys.

When Eardley returned home to Australia he took with him a gift of £800 from Clara. This came from the sale of the land in South Australia which John Ainsworth had left to her on his death.

In that same year Celia's husband John Temple died, after thirteen years of marriage. At forty-three she was left a financially secure widow. She had always been close to Clara and once again became her companion. Together the two moved about Europe, much more relaxed and contented than had been their earlier lot.

They parted for the year 1884 when Celia went to visit their cousin Countess Melanie Ysenberg, daughter of Uncle John, and her husband Ferdinand, in Baden-Baden. She was persuaded to prolong her stay and was fêted and entertained like royalty by the Ysenbergs and their aristocratic friends. Ferdinand was then Commandant of the military establishment at Metz.

Celia's last decade was spent in Europe with Clara, until her death at eighty in January 1894.

Clara spent much of her time researching her family tree, then retreating to Chertsey to sort out and record the huge assortment of notes she stored in boxes at her 'wee hut'. She had become increasingly deaf, a great affliction, and could communicate only by asking people to speak clearly through a long tube which she held to her ear.

Most of her remaining years were spent in the South of England with relatives and occasionally in boarding houses. Of her eleven younger sisters and brothers, only Ann-Eliza outlived her, by a matter of months. Clara died aged ninety-seven on 1 September 1909 at 'Mascalls'.

She appointed her nephew Frederick Beverley Morgan executor of her will and left estate valued at just under £2,500.

There is no need to look at Clara's portrait, photographed at Folkestone in 1884, to know the strength of her character. It speaks out for itself from her letters to Brownlow and in her 'Pedigree of the Horrocks Family'. There were flaws in her personality, it is true. She was judgemental, a social snob, harboured grudges and was unforgiving. But these traits surfaced only after her father's death. She loved him dearly and was embittered by the events that led to his suicide.

She was called on then to develop new strengths to cope with her family's

Clara Horrocks (1812–1909), the first born child of Peter and Clara (Jupp). Compiler of Horrocks' family pedigree and records. Photographed in 1884 by Lambert Weston, Folkstone. (*Horrocks Archives NZ*)

sudden change of fortune. Her mother was overwhelmed, not only by the loss of a loving husband but also by her total inability to handle their enormous financial problems.

It was Clara who, although mortified at the prospect, went to Preston to beg for money from the partners at Horrocks & Co.; not once but on a number of occasions when there was no one else to turn to. The double humiliation of being forced to beg for help, only then to be turned down, stayed with Clara for the rest of her days. Her later resentment of those who rejected the family is quite understandable. Yet she herself was a generous woman who did not hesitate to share her own rare windfalls with her mother, brothers and sisters.

Thanks to her 'steady perseverance' in recording her own family memories she provided valuable material for these Chronicles of the Horrocks Family.

To Clara go the author's gratitude and the closing lines:

'Our story is a romance in itself of a position in life lost through our own faults because the males of the family have not the steady perseverance of the females.'

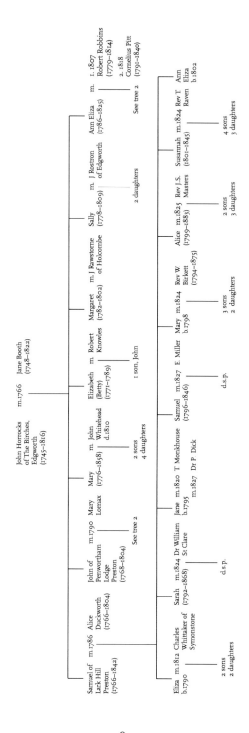

John Horrocks   m.1766   Jane Booth
of The Birches,   (1748–1822)
Edgworth
(1745–1816)

Samuel of   m.1786   Alice
Lark Hill   Duckworth
Preston   (1766–1804)
(1766–1842)

John of   m.1790   Mary
Penwortham   Lomax
Lodge
Preston   See tree 2
(1768–1804)

Mary   m. John
(1776–1858) Whitehead
            d.1810

            2 sons
            4 daughters

Elizabeth   m.   Robert
(Betty)   Knowles
(1771–1789)

            1 son, John

Margaret   m. J Rawstorne
(1782–1802)   of Holcombe

Sally   m. J Rostron
(1778–1809)   of Edgworth

            2 daughters

Ann Eliza   m.   1. 1807
(1786–1825)   Robert Robbins
                   (1779–1814)

                   2. 1818
                   Cornelius Pitt
                   (1791–1840)

                   See tree 2

Eliza   m.1812   Charles
b.1790   Whittaker of
                 Symonstone

            2 sons
            2 daughters

Sarah   m.1824   Dr William
(1792–1868)   St Clare

            d.s.p.

Jane   m.1820   T Monkhouse
b.1795   m.1827   Dr P. Dick

Samuel   m.1827   E. Miller
(1796–1846)

            d.s.p.

Mary   m.1824   Rev W
b.1798   Birkett
                 (1794–1875)

            3 sons
            2 daughters

Alice   m.1825   Rev J.S.
(1799–1883)   Masters

            2 sons
            3 daughters

Susannah   m.1824   Rev T
(1801–1845)   Raven

            4 sons
            3 daughters

Ann
Eliza
b.1802

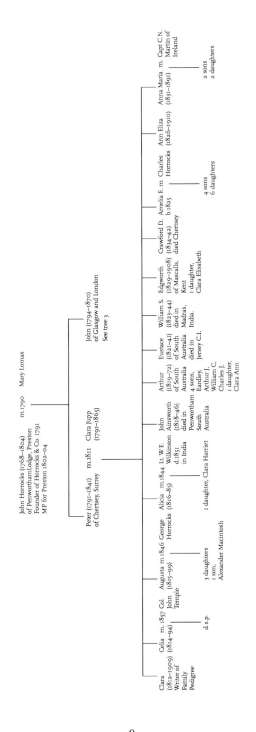

John Horrocks (1768–1804)
of Penwortham Lodge, Preston
Founder of Horrocks & Co. 1791
MP for Preston 1802–04   m.1790   Mary Lomax

Peter (1791–1841)   m.1811   Clara Jupp
of Chertsey, Surrey   (1791–1865)

John (1794–1870)
of Glasgow and London
See tree 3

Clara   Celia   m. 1857 Col   Augusta m 1846 George Alicia m.1844 Lt. W. E.   John   Arthur   Eustace   William S.   Edgworth   Crawford D. Amelia E. m Charles   Ann Eliza   Anna Maria m. Capt C. N.
(1812–1909)   (1814–94) John   (1815–99) Horrocks   (1816–85) Wilkinson   Ainsworth   (1819–72)   (1821–41)   (1823–44)   (1829–1908)   (1834–42)   b.1825   Horrocks   (1826–1910) (1831–1891)   Martin of
Writer of   Temple   d.1851   (1818–46)   of South   of South   died in   of Mascalls,   died Chertsey   Ireland
Family   in India   died in   Australia   Australia   Madras,   Kent
Pedigree   Penwortham   4 sons,   died in   India.   1 daughter,   4 sons   2 sons
                                                                                             South   Eardley,   Jersey C.I.   Clara Elisabeth   6 daughters   2 daughters
                                                                                             Australia   Arthur J.,
            d s.p.   3 daughters   1 daughter, Clara Harriet   William C.,
                     1 son,   Charles J.,
                     Alexander Macintosh   1 daughter,
                                                                                                          Clara Ann

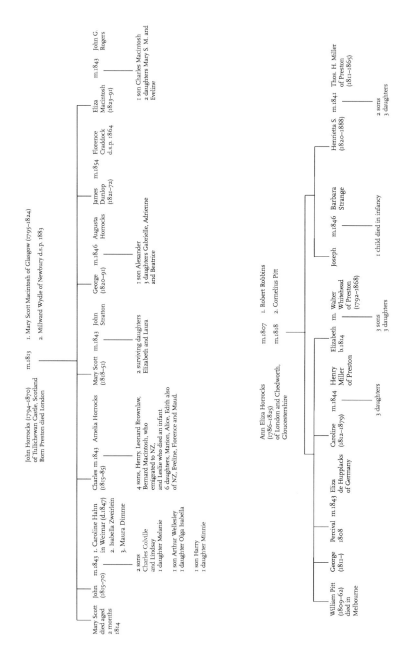

Notes

1. Boons means service in kind or labour
2. Grandfather Robert Peel and his son were calico printers and later cotton manufacturers in Blackburn, until their mill was destroyed by anti-machinery workers. They moved their business to Burton-on-Trent and Bury. Grandson Robert Peel, made a Baron in 1800, later became Home Secretary, then Prime Minister. The Peels were well known by the Horrocks family.
3. Roving and carding; in this process cleaned cotton, having been beaten to loosen the fibres, was dragged through cards studded with metal wire. The short broken fibres were discarded and the longer lengths drawn out in parallel lines to form a single, strong, continuous length of fibres ready for spinning.
4. In the last years of the eighteenth century, John Watson was a successful cotton master and Lord Derby's chief agent for the Whig political party in Preston. He had the mill on Moor Lane and others outside the town at Roach Bridge and Penwortham. In these last two he employed apprentice or orphan labour reputedly from the Foundling Hospital in London. Joseph Livesey the moral reformer described these children as "the most pitiful objects I think I ever beheld". Watson owned other industrial and domestic properties, all bought on credit. From 1791 to 1804 John Horrocks became his main competitor in both business and political life. In 1807, following adverse trading conditions which affected several Preston manufacturers, Watson was made bankrupt and detained as a debtor in Lancaster Gaol. He died in London in 1813 leaving effects worth 'under £20'.
5. Attorneys acted for others in Courts of Law. Proctors were qualified to act for others in civil or ecclesiastical Courts. Notaries were officers authorised to attest and witness legal contracts.
6. There was little cash about in those days. A discounter would change banknotes or bills-of-exchange at a discount.
7. The Stone Mill was extended over the next half century until in 1844, after Samuel's death, it was purchased by the Barlow family. It was replaced some years later by 'New Vale Mill' a five-storey building under the name Edgworth Spinning Co. All of these buildings have now been demolished.
8. From the earliest days the mills were known as 'Horrockses' and this spelling is used throughout the text of this book. The official title was 'Horrocks & Co.'
9. It appears that the Lancashire cotton masters were not perturbed that their raw material was produced by African slave labour. But Parliamentary records

show that John's brother Samuel, when he became a Member of Parliament, 'was a staunch supporter of the anti-slavery lobby'.

10. Preston had always produced good quality cloth so Horrocks was continuing that tradition. Kuerden's Guild Records in the fourteenth century record that cloth searchers were employed 'to diligently see that all such woollen cloth as is made within this borough shall be so rightly made, manufactured, pressed and dyed without putting thereto any deceitful thing or mixing the same with bad colours. All cloths with default in making etc ... shall be seized forthwith and the names of such offending persons be presented'.

11. The Derby supporters were the Shawe, Burgoyne, Hornby and Whitehead families. The Corporation group included the Pedders, Starkies and Gorsts.

12. In later years the house reverted to its original name 'Charnleys' and was sold to Richard Palmer, Solicitor, an old friend.

13. Thomas Miller, born 14 October 1767 was the son of Henry and Ann Miller of St James' parish in Whitehaven.

14. Published by Alan Sutton under the title 'A Lancashire Gentleman' edited by F & K Wood.

15. See Chapter 3 for a description of Preston Guild 1842

16. In 1637 John Horrocks of Edgworth married Hannah Crompton of Breightmet. Henry Horrocks of Mottram invented a loom which was left in his will to Hannah's family. Samuel Crompton used this model in his water-frame 'Mule'.

17. Richard Ainsworth (1763–1833) of Moss Bank, Halliwell, nr. Bolton, inherited his father's bleaching business and was considered to be one of the finest bleachers in the country. He was John Horrocks' closest and lifelong friend. Each called their first son Peter, and later children were named John Horrocks Ainsworth, and John Ainsworth Horrocks. The two families remained friends throughout the period of these chronicles. Peter Ainsworth Junior purchased Smithills Hall, Halliwell in 1801 and lived there until his death in 1870.

18. For 100 years from the 1860s they formed the core of St Augustine's Girls' School. The high hayloft was the staff room and headmistress's study. Lark Hill House is now at the centre of Cardinal Newman College. Most of the rooms are preserved with their original Georgian fittings and have been well adapted to their present use

19. 'hands' – this word was a shortening of the term 'handloom weavers' and was commonly used to describe any textile worker.

20. As Sam always used this diminutive of Samuel to distinguish himself from his father of the same name, that form is used throughout this book when referring to him. The name Samuel always refers to his father, the MP

21. Thirty years after this date this author's father, John Harrison, was one of these 'half-timers' at St Augustines.

22. The grave, with its flat engraved stone surrounded by iron railings, lay in the quiet churchyard in the centre of Preston for over 150 years. In 1999 the church was reordered and all the gravestones removed.

23. At the 1992 Guild the Principal of Cardinal Newman College, the late Mr

Peter Newsome (R. I. P.), arranged for a full-size copy of this portrait to be hung in Lark Hill House, now the nucleus of the College campus. The original oil painting, by Lonsdale, is in the Harris Art Gallery Preston.

24. See '1842 Samuel Horrocks (Junior)' for a description of Preston Guild celebrations.

25. Charles Macintosh F.R.S. who discovered the method of waterproofing fabric and gave his name to the raincoat, was one of the outstanding figures in the early development of the chemicals industry. A brilliant chemist with a genius for invention, his career covered every aspect of the science, yet he never became a very rich man whilst others benefitted hugely from his inventions. While he was in partnership with Charles Tennant and others producing liquid bleach for the textiles industry, Macintosh discovered the formula for producing dry bleach powder which should have made him a fortune. But the patent was registered by Tennant in his own name. In 1814 when the patent (no. 2312) lapsed, Macintosh was persuaded to retire from the company, which went on to become the largest chemical works in Europe. His son George felt that he had been squeezed out and only scantily remunerated for the sacrifices which he had made in the establishment of the business. Messrs. Musson and Robinson in their book 'Science and Technology in the Industrial Revolution' (1969) wrote, regarding Tennants Patent 2312, 'This was not his own invention but that of Charles Macintosh ... Tennant then proceeded by exploitation of this process to achieve world fame and a great fortune'.

26. Mary Macintosh was not the first of her clan to visit Preston. Just a century earlier in the 1715 Stuart uprising Brigadier Macintosh of Borlum, Rosshire was Commander of Lord Kenmure's men in the Pretenders' army which marched into the town on 9 November and proclaimed James Stuart as King in the Market Place. After the fierce battle which followed, MacIntosh and the Earl of Derwentwater were taken as hostages to London and found guilty of high treason. Derwentwater was beheaded. MacIntosh with fifteen other rebels escaped from Newgate prison to the continent where he took the pseudonym William Deark, and eventually returned to Scotland. In 1795 part of the Campsie estate confiscated from Viscount Kilsyth, when attainted for his part in the 1715 rebellion, came into the possession of Charles Macintosh of 'Dunchattan and Campsie'. He established lucrative alum works there.

27. Alum, the mordaunt use in dyeing, was manufactured from sulphate of alumina and potash aluminous shistus found in coal waste.

28. 'Morganatic'. The word comes from the German and in this context means a marriage between a high-class man and a lady of inferior rank. The wife did not partake of his rank or transmit any rights of inheritance to her children.

29. Mediatised.:This word was used in Germany to indicate small states annexed or placed in a mediate relation to the Emperor.

30. After Peter's dismissal the Millers and Samuel Horrocks continued to run Horrockses until Thomas Miller Senior died in January 1840 aged seventy-three. Two years later Samuel Horrocks died aged seventy-six. Young Sam was then

in control until his own untimely death in 1846 when Thomas Miller (Junior) became sole proprietor until his death twenty years later. In 1865 the business went out of the hands of the long-established Horrocks/Miller partnership.

31. An interesting entry in the 'Oxford Literary Guide to the British Isles, states that Charles Dickens visited Beomonds House in the next few years. Apparently he used the local inn 'The Black Swann' in his 1838 novel *Oliver Twist*, and modelled Mr Pecksniff in *Martin Chuzzlewit* (1843) on a local resident.

Sources

Chapter 1

Bibliography

Hodgkinson, Richard – *A Lancs Gentleman* 1763–1847 Letters and Journals, edited by Florence and Kenneth Wood, published by Alan Sutton 1992.

Gale, Pedrick – *The Story of Horrockses* published privately by the company, 1950.

Farington, Joseph R. A. – *The Farington Diary Vol. II,* published New York 1923.

Hunt, David – *History of Preston* 1992.

Abram, W. *Sketches in Local History.*

Corry – *History of Lancashire*

Dobson, Wm – *Parliamentary Representation of Preston*

Dickinson, T. C. – *Industrial Archaeology of the Preston Cotton Industry – Mill Engines* – 1980

Dobson, Wm. – *A History of Preston Guild* 1862

Abram, Wm. – *Memorials of the Preston Guilds,* 1882

Hardwick, Chas. – *History of the Borough of Preston* 1857

Hewitson, Anthony – *History of Preston*

Barton, B T – *Bolton and District Historical Gleanings* 1883

Lindlop, Roy – *Tales of Turton*

Dictionary of National Biography

Clegg, J – *Annals of Bolton*

Birtles, Sylvia – *The Development of a Cotton Enterprise,* Lancashire Records Office

Crewdson, H – *The Story of Cotton,* Lancashire Records Office

Newspapers

Preston Guardian: Local Sketches No. 745 – reprinted 21/9/1878

Article by E Beattie 14/9/1895

Research

J. J. Francis – Thos. Belasye 1717, Registration of Papist's Estates, Lecture on Birches Farm 19/4/1998. Land tax records, etc.

Rev. Joseph Gilbert and Mrs Joan Gilbert – Horrocks Family Tree, Stone Mill, etc.

Mary Boys-Adam – Horrocks genealogy etc. Photographs.

Letters

Horrocks' Collection, NZ – Letters from John Horrocks MP to Richard Ainsworth 4/11/1801 and 22/4/1802.

Documents

Lancashire Records Office:

Ref. DDHs Boxes 25, 68, 73, 76, 78

DDX 1008 / 1–18

DPPr 138 / 29

Maps. DDK 1549–1 (Lang 1774)

DP 189 (Buck 1728)

Will of Mary Horrocks WCW 1829

Chapter 2

Bibliography

Blake, Steven – *Pittville 1824 – 1860* – Cheltenham Art Gallery & Museums, 1988

Diaries of Rev. Francis Witts 1825, The diary of a Cotswold Parson, published D Verey 1978.

Letters

Whittaker papers, Lancashire Records Office (Ref. DDWh)

Horrocks' Collection, NZ

Wordsworth Museum, Grasmere – ref: Hut/Monk No. 88

Documents

Lancashire Records Office

LRO DDHs Box 73

LRO DDWh 3 and 4

Chapter 3

Bibliography

Abram, W – *History of Blackburn* (p. 1877)

Wood and Wilmore – *The Romance of the Cotton Industry in England*, OUP (1927)

French, J G – *Life and Times of Samuel Crompton* (1859)

Dobson, Wm. – *Parliamentary Representation of Preston*, Harris Reference Library

Thorne – *History of Parliamentary Trust Vol. VI*

Fishwick – *History of the Borough of Preston* (1822)

Abram, W – *Sketches in Local History, Vol. II, (No. 238)*

The Test of Time – privately published by Horrocks Miller & Co. 1888

Horrocks, Celia – *Memoirs of the family of John Ainsworth Horrocks* (private publication)

Hunt, David – *A History of Preston* (Carnegie Publishing, 1992)

Bryant, Arthur – *The Age of Elegance 1812–22* (Penguin, 1950)

Crosby, Alan – *The family records of Benjamin Shaw 1772–1884* (RSLC, 1991)

Crewdson, H – *The Story of Cotton*

The Trial of Andrew Ryding (pamphlet) – Harris Reference Library, Preston

De-Selincourt, E – *The Poetical Works of William Wordsworth, Vol. III Part 1* (OU Clarendon Press, 1946)

De-Selincourt, E – *Letters of William and Dorothy Wordsworth, The Middle Years (1812–1820), The Later Years (1821–28)*, revised by Alan Hill (OUP, 1978)

Dorothy Wordsworth, Journals of edited by W Knight (Macmillan, 1924)

Hunter Davies – *William Wordsworth* (Weidenfield, 1980)

Lady Shelley's Diary – Harris Reference Library

Newspapers

Preston Chronicle 24/2/1816

London Magazine 1823

Letters

Wordsworth Trust Library, Grasmere:

Ref: Hut / Monk MDF No. 44, 45, 46.

Ref: Hut / Monk HO-MC Nos. 42,43,780/14, 15.

Lancashire Records Office: Ref. DDWh 4 – 46 and 94

Documents

LRO DDHs Boxes 67, 70, 71, 73, 76

LRO DDHs IC P716 & P721

FCJ archives, Broadstairs Convent

Lark Hill House Deeds. Abstract of Title. Details from Wills of Samuel Horrocks 1842, Samuel Horrocks (Junior) and Mrs Eliza Horrocks (née Miller) – courtesy of Mark Belderbos of Oswald Goodier & Co. Solicitors, Chapel Street, Preston.

Acts of Parliament:

Incorporation of Preston Gas Light Co. 19/4/1839, Harris Ref. Library

Supply of Water to the Borough of Preston 3/4/1832

Chapter 4

Bibliography

Crathorne, Nancy – *Tennant's Stalk* (Macmillan, 1973)

Grant, Elizabeth – *Memoirs of a Highland Lady, Vol. II* (1817/18), (Canongate Press, 1992)

Macintosh, George – *Biographical Memoir of Charles Macintosh FRS* (private pub. 1857)

Musson, A E & Robinson, E – *Science and Technology in the Industrial Revolution* (Gordon & Breach, 1969)

Neill – *Records and Reminiscences of Bonhill Parish*

Irving, Joseph – *History of Dumbarton*

LRO Manchester Grammar School Register, Vol. II, CS LXXIII Alfred Hadfield

Research

Glasgow City Council:

Culture & Leisure Services, re Dunchattan House

Mitchell Library History & Topography Dept., re Tullichewan Castle.

Dumbarton District Libraries HQ, re Tullichewan Castle.

Documents

LRO DDHs Box 73 – February – April 1815

Chapter 5

Bibliography

Lehmann & Constable – *Vienna – A Traveller's Companion* (Constable, 1988)

Lander, J and Chapman, G – *Historic Chertsey* (Chertsey Museum 1992)

Horrocks, Celia – *Records of the family of John Ainsworth Horrocks,* Private publication 1890, LRO

Newspapers

Bolton Journal 6/12/1836

Research

Chertsey Museum and Bernard Pardoe re Beomond House

Documents

Australia – Horrocks family papers held by Pamela McTaggart of Mendinie, S. Australia. Autobiographies of Arthur and Ann Horrocks and John Ainsworth Horrocks.

N. Zealand – Extensive family papers. John Brownlow Horrocks of Auckland, John his son, of Wellington and Christopher, of Masterton.

LRO – Penwortham Lodge DDX1008/17

Harris Reference Library:

Catalogue of Library at Penwortham Lodge 1823

Penwortham Hall Sales Papers 1930 (Ref D41 Pen).

Death certificate of Peter Horrocks 1841 (No. 25) Chertsey

Will of Peter Horrocks 1840